Food Lovers' London

by Jenny Linford

Photography by Chris Windsor

Food Lovers' London

Written by Jenny Linford
Photography by Chris Windsor
Edited by Lydia Linford
Illustrations by Lesley Gilmour
Book design by Susi Koch and Lesley Gilmour

First published in Great Britain 1991 by Macmillan, updated editions published
in 1995, 1999, 2003, 2005 and 2010 by Metro Publications Ltd.

Published in 2013 by **Metro Publications, PO Box 6336, London, N1 6PY**

Printed and bound in India.
This book is produced using paper from registered sustainable and managed
sources. Suppliers have provided both LEI and MUTU certification.

ISBN 978 1 902910 47 5

for Mummy, Daddy, Chris and Ben and
in memory of Harry Greenwald who
believed in me

About the Author

Jenny Linford is a freelance food writer based in London and a member of the Guild of Food Writers. She is the author of several books including *The London Cookbook* (Metro Publications), a celebration of London's gastronomy past and present and *Great British Cheeses* (Dorling Kindersley), a reference book detailing over 300 British and Irish cheeses. Her work has ranged from research and writing for the British Library's Food Stories website to food writing for newspapers including The Financial Times.

An inveterate food shopper, Jenny founded the highly successful Gastro-Soho Tours in 1994. The personal guided tours offer a unique exploration of Soho's culinary treasures from bustling Chinese supermarkets to vintage Italian delis. www.jennylinford.co.uk   Twitter @jennylinford

Chris Windsor is a freelance, professional photographer, based in London. Chris's work has ranged from advertising campaigns and company reports to books including *Food Lovers' London* and *The London Cookbook*. www.chriswindsor.com

Contents

Algerian Coffee Stores

Introduction

As a keen home cook who enjoys cooking tasty food for family and friends, to my mind the starting point for being able to cook well is being able to food shop well. Being able to find good ingredients – fresh vegetables and fruit, a decent loaf of real bread, good quality meat – is key to cooking and eating well. Whether it's succumbing to the temptation to buy a bargain-priced box of voluptuous Alphonso mangoes from an Indian food shop in Tooting, the thoroughly enjoyable process of sampling farmhouse cheeses at Neal's Yard Dairy as I try and decide which ones to buy or discussing with a knowledgeable butcher which cut of meat would best suit the dish I have in mind, food shopping is for me the pleasurable beginning of a meal.

Food shopping in London does not have to be a soulless trudge with a trolley around a vast, fluorescent-lit supermarket. This book is a witness to that. We are blessed in this city with an extraordinary diversity of food shops, from venerable, specialist establishments, which can trace their histories back over a hundred years, to the latest, innovative expressions of food-selling springing up in the fertile ground which is London's food scene.

The way in which London's food markets are re-inventing themselves, showcasing British producers and offering great street food, is a case in point. Diversity, too, because London is home to many immigrant and ex-pat communities – some long-established, others recent additions – each of which brings their own food culture to add to the richness of what's on offer here. From the extraordinary range of ingredients which can be found just in a single Chinese supermarket in London's Chinatown or an Indian food store in Southall to the pleasure of buying finely sliced Parma ham, a chunk of salty-sweet Parmesan cheese or some decent olives from a vintage Italian deli in Soho, London's food scene is wonderfully cosmopolitan, offering a chance to explore cuisines from around the globe. In these recessionary times, I'd also like to point out that many of these shops offer excellent value for money, charging remarkably reasonable prices for good food.

I do feel that food shops are the unsung heroes of our food scene. The sheer amount of hard work that goes into running a shop – sourcing ingredients, maintaining stock range and quality, recruiting and maintaining staff, staying open for longer and longer hours, offering good, knowledgeable service

–deserves our respect. These are tough times for our high streets and for the shops on them. High rents and rates, the impact of parking restrictions, traffic wardens, the Congestion Charge and the rise of on-line shopping and out-of-town shopping are making it harder and harder for shops, especially independent ones, to get by. The food shops and markets in this book not only deserve our respect, they deserve – and need – our support. If we don't shop at them, they won't be able to survive. Shopping at these shops and markets is so often an enjoyable experience, involving a friendly conversation, the satisfaction of good, knowledgeable service and the pleasure of buying good ingredients, so supporting them is no hardship. Without these food shops London would be infinitely less enticing and considerably less appetising.

Jenny Linford

Eating Out Price Key
Prices are approximate, average prices per head for a meal without wine

£	£5-£15
££	£15-£30
£££	£30-£50
££££	£50-£70
£££££	£70 plus

Espresso
SINGLE DOUBLE
£1.00p

Cappuccino
£1.20p

NO SEATING
NO INFLATED PRICES
JUST A PURE
CAFFEINE SHOT !!!!!

Algerian Coffee Stores

Patel Brothers

Andreas

Earth Natural Foods

Lina Stores

Soho

OXFORD ST
Oxford Circus
Tottenham Court road
ST GILES HIGH ST
SOHO SQUARE
NOEL ST
D'ARBLAY ST
GREAT MARLBOROUGH ST
POLAND ST
ST ANNE'S CRT.
WARDOUR ST
DEAN ST
FRITH ST
GREEK ST
MANETTE ST
CHARING CROSS ROAD
SHAFTESBURY AV
MARSHALL ST
CARNABY ST
KINGLY ST
BROADWICK ST
BERWICK ST
MEARD ST
OLD COMPTON ST
PETER ST
ROMILLY ST
LEXINGTON ST
BRIDLE LANE
BEAK ST
GOLDEN SQUARE
REGENT ST
WARWICK ST
BREWER ST
ARCHER ST
SHAFTESBURY AVENUE
GERRARD ST
LISLE ST
RUPERT ST
WHITCOMB ST
LEICESTER SQUARE
Leicester Square
GLASSHOUSE ST
Piccadilly Circus
SWALLOW ST
PICCADILLY

Shops

Eateries

Marylebone

Shops

Eateries

Notting Hill

● Shops

1) **American Food Store** p.325
2) **Artisan du Chocolat** (Chocolate) p.43
3) **Athenian Grocery** (Greek) p.200
4) **Books for Cooks** (Bookshop) p.347
5) **Costcutter Oriental Supermarket** (Asian) p.170
6) **Daylesford Organic** (Health Food) p.83
7) **Garcia R. & Sons** (Spanish) p.316
8) **Golborne Fisheries** (Fishmongers) p.68
9) **Hummingbird Bakery** p.345
10) **Kalinka** (Russian) p.334
11) **La Plaza Deli** (Spanish) p.316
12) **Le Marrakech** (Morrocan) p.268
13) **C. Lidgate** (Butchers) p.28
14) **Lisboa Delicatessen** (Portuguese) p.316
15) **Maison Blanc** (French) p.188
16) **Melograno Alimentari** (Italian) p.215
17) **Michanicou Brothers** (Grocers) p.78
18) **Melt** (Chocolate) p.47
19) **Mr Christians** (Deli) p.55
20) **Negozio Classica** (Italian) p.215
21) **Ottolenghi** (Mediterranean Deli) p.52
22) **Planet Organic** (Health Food) p.83
23) **Portobello Market** p.93
24) **Notting Hill Farmers' Market** p.96
25) **Recipease** (Cookery School/ Deli/Café) p.120
26) **Sara Super Market** (Iranian) p.268
27) **Speck** (Italian Deli) p.216
28) **Spice Shop** p.101
29) **Tavola** (Italian Deli) p.216
30) **Tawana** (Thai) p.299
31) **The Grocer on Elgin** (Deli) p.54
32) **Valentina** (Italian Deli) p.216

● Eateries

33) **Alounak** (Middle Eastern) p.275
34) **Assaggi** (Italian) p.222
35) **Café Garcia** (Spanish) p.321
36) **Café Oporto** (Portuguese) p.321
37) **Café Samovar** (Russian) p.334
38) **Four Seasons** (Chinese) p.176
39) **Fresco** (Lebanese) p.275
40) **Galicia** (Spanish) p.321
41) **Hafez** (Iranian) p.275
42) **Lisboa Patisserie** (Portuguese) p.317
21) **Ottolenghi** (Mediterranean Deli) p.52
25) **Recipease** (Cookery School/ Deli/Café) p.120
43) **Royal China** (Chinese) p.176
44) **Spinach and Agushi** (Ghanaian) p.134
45) **Taqueria** (Mexican) p.333
46) **Tawana** (Thai) p.305
32) **Valentina** (Italian) p.216

Brixton

Brixton Market is a much-loved local institution extending over the streets and shopping arcades that surround Brixton station. The arcades have seen a recent revival making this a great place to shop and eat.

● Shops

1) **A & C Continental Grocers** (Spanish & Portuguese Deli) p.317
2) **Brixton Cornercopia** (Deli) p.56
3) **Brixton Farmers' Market** p.132
4) **Brixton Wholefoods Transatlantic** (Health Food) p.83
5) **Cannon & Cannon** (Deli) p.57
6) **Indulgence Chocolate Artistry** (Chocolate) p.46
7) **Market Row Wines** p.116
8) **Nour Cash & Carry** (Iranian) p.271
9) **Rosie's Deli Café** p.58
10) **Wild Caper** (Deli) p.58
11) **Wing Tai Supermarket** (Chinese) p.170

Eateries

12) **Asmara** (Eritrean) p.135
2) **Brixton Cornercopia** p.56
5) **Cannon & Cannon** (Deli) p.57
13) **Casa Morito** (Mexican) p.332
14) **Franco Manca** (Italian) p.222
15) **KaoSarn** (Thai) p.305
9) **Rosie's Deli Café** p.58
10) **Wild Caper** (Deli) p.58
16) **Yum-D** (Thai) p.306

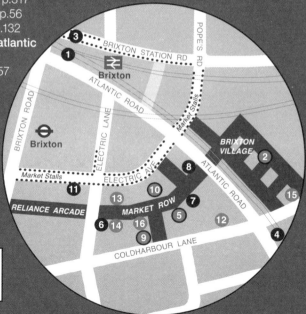

KEY
····· Brixton Street Market
▬ Shopping Arcades

Hackney

● Shops

1) **Bottle Apostle** (Wine Shops) p.116
2) **Broadway Market** p.91
3) **Climpson & Sons Café** p.107
4) **Deli Downstairs** p.62
5) **E5 Bakehouse** (Bakery) p.22
6) **Fin & Flounder** (Fishmonger) p.70
7) **The Ginger Pig** (Butcher) p.35
8) **Hoang-Nam** (Vietnamese) p.301
9) **Jonathan Norris** (Fishmonger) p.70
10) **L'Eau à la Bouche** (Deli Café) p.62
11) **Noble Fine Liquor** p.116
12) **Unpackaged at Arthaus**
    (Health Food Shop) p.85
13) **Violet Cakes** (Bakery) p.326

● Eateries

14) **Buen Ayre** (Argentinian) p.302
3) **Climpson & Sons Café** p.107
10) **L'Eau à la Bouche** (Deli Café) p.62
15) **Saigon Street Café**
    (Vietnamese) p.306
16) **Spinach and Agushi** (Ghanian) p.134
12) **Unpackaged at Arthaus** p.85
13) **Violet Cakes** (Bakery) p.326

RICHMOND RD
GAYHURST ROAD
Lido
LONDON LANE
WILMAN GROVE
LONDON FIELDS
London Fields
MENTMORE TERRACE
LAMB LANE
LONDON FIELDS EAST SIDE
MARE ST
WELL ST
LANSDOWNE DRIVE
WARBURTON RD
TREDERWEN RD
LAURISTON ROUNDABOUT
VICTORIA PARK RD
LAURISTON RD
BROADWAY MARKET
DUNCAN
RUTLAND RD
WETHERELL RD
ADA ST
MORPETH RD
VICTORIA PARK
Regent's Canal

General Foodshops

Bakers & Patisseries

E5 Bakehouse

During the 1990s pioneering bakeries such as Clarke's and De Gustibus showed just how delicious real bread could be. Nowadays, London is home to a thriving baking scene, with several new craft bakers setting up business, selling through stalls at farmers' markets round the capital and opening shops offering artisan breads such as focaccia, sourdough and rye breads alongside tempting cakes and pastries.

Central

Baker & Spice
🖂 *54-56 Elizabeth Street, SW1W 9PB*
☎ *020 7730 3033*
🖱 *www.bakerandspice.uk.com*
🚌 *Sloane Square LU, Victoria LU/Rail*
🕐 *Mon-Sat 7am-7pm, Sun 8am-5pm*

An attractive café-cum-shop, one of a small chain, offering Baker & Spice's trademark range of own-baked cakes, pastries and breads.

Cocomaya
🖂 *12 Connaught Street, W2 2AF*
☎ *020 7706 2770*
🖱 *www.cocomaya.co.uk*
🚌 *Marble Arch*
🕐 *Mon-Fri 7am-7pm, Sat 8am-7pm, Sun 8am-6pm*

This dainty bakery and tea-room (linked to the delectable chocolate shop and part of a small chain) offers tempting, freshly-baked cakes and patisserie – from light blueberry muffins and to luxurious cakes and flans. *Branches: 235 Brompton Road, SW3 2EP Unit 10, 186 Pavilion Road, SW1X 0BJ*

Maison Bertaux
🖂 *28 Greek Street, W1D 5DQ*
☎ *020 7437 6007*
🖱 *www.maisonbertaux.com*
🚌 *Leicester Square LU*
🕐 *Mon-Sat 8.30am-11pm, Sun 8.30am-9pm*

Founded in 1871, this characterful French patisserie has a loyal clientele who enjoy the pastries, such as their trademark almond croisssants, good coffee and Bohemian atmosphere, lovingly sustained by Michelle, the manager (see also French London).

Le Pain Quotidien
🖂 *72-75 Marylebone High Street, W1U 5JW*
☎ *020 7486 6154*
🖱 *www.lepainquotidien.com*
🚌 *Baker Street LU*
🕐 Mon-Fri 7am-7pm, Sat 8am-6pm, Sun 9am-6pm

London's first branch of this bakery-cum-café chain, is a roomy, rustically-styled affair. There is a range of sourdough breads available and a café to taste their wares.

Paul

🏠 *29 Bedford Street, WC2E 9PD*
☎ *020 7836 3304*
🌐 *www.paul-uk.com*
🚇 *Covent Garden LU*
🕐 *Mon-Fri 7am-9pm, Sat & Sun 8am-9pm*

This branch of Paul's was the first London branch of the French chain, now well-established here with numerous branches. It offers an attractive range of pastries and cakes and French-style breads, all baked on the premises. This Gallic enterprise attracts patient queues both for the bakery and the back-room salon du thé (see also French London).

Peyton and Byrne

🏠 *196 Tottenham Court Road, W1T 7LQ*
☎ *020 7580 3451*
🌐 *www.peytonandbyrne.com*
🚇 *Goodge Street LU*
🕐 *Mon-Wed, Fri 10am-6.30pm,*
Thurs 10am-8pm,
Sat 9.30am-6.30pm, Sun 12noon-6pm

The first bakery shop in what is now a chain of bakeries-cum-cafés from restaurateur Oliver Peyton, offering British sweet and savoury treats, from fairy cakes to pies.

Pierre Hermé

🏠 *13 Lowndes Street, SW1X 9EX*
☎ *020 7245 0317*
🌐 *www.pierreherme.com*
🚇 *Sloane Square LU*
🕐 *Mon-Sat 10am-6.30pm*
Sun 12noon-5pm

As elegant as its neighbouring haute couture shops, Pierre Herme's chic boutique showcases Herme's acclaimed macarons, cakes, pastries and chocolates, all of which are hand-made in France. The subtly colourful macaroons – with their thin, crisp shells and soft interiors are the perfect image of daintiness. Flavours range from perennial favourites, such as salted butter caramel to new seasonal creations.

Poilâne

🏠 *46 Elizabeth Street, SW1W 9PA*
☎ *020 7808 4910*
🌐 *www.poilane.fr*
🚇 *Sloane Square LU, Victoria LU/Rail*
🕐 *Mon-Fri 7am-7pm, Sat 7am-6pm*

This elegant shop is a London outpost of Poilâne's famous Parisian bakery, complete with a wood-fired oven in the basement. Regulars return for Poilâne's huge, round sourdough loaves, with their distinctive tang, and addictive punitons. The loaves are sold whole, halved, quartered or simply by the slice (see also French London).

Princi

- 135 Wardour Street, W1F 0UT
- 020 7478 8888
- www.princi.co.uk
- Leicester Square LU
  Oxford Circus LU, Piccadilly Circus LU
- Mon-Sat 8am-12midnight,
  Sun 8.30am-10pm

This stylish addition to London's baking scene combines a pasticceria, bakery, café and pizzeria. It serves up its own-made Italian breads, cakes and pastries, displayed in a long glass counter. Highlights include pizza and focaccia – freshly baked in a wood-fired oven – and brought warm to the counter. The food here tastes as good as it looks (see also Italian London).

St John Bakery

- Arch 72, SE1 2DU
- 020 7237 5999
- www.stjohnbakerycompany.com
- London Bridge LU/Rail
- Sat 9am-2pm

Such was the demand for the sourdough bread baked at Fergus Henderson's acclaimed Clerkenwell restaurant St John that the St John Bakery was established, showcasing the considerable talents of Head Baker Justin Gellatly. The bakery supplies the St John restaurants and various retail outlets, including Selfridges. Saturday mornings offer a chance to buy direct from the bakery, with the ethereal custard doughnuts acquiring a cult following.

William Curley

- 198 Ebury Street, SW1W 8UN
- 020 7730 5522
- www.williamcurley.co.uk
- Sloane Square LU
- Mon-Thurs 10am-7pm, Fri 10am-8pm,
  Sat 9-8pm, Sun 10am-6pm

This distinctly chic establishment offers a selection of William Curley's acclaimed patisserie, which can be enjoyed in the café area or bought to take away.
Branch at: 10 Paved Court, Richmond, Surrey, TW9 1LZ

North

Dunn's

- 6 The Broadway, N8 9SN
- 020 8340 1614
- www.dunns-bakery.co.uk
- Mon-Sat 6am-6pm, Sun 9am-5pm
- Finsbury Park LU/Rail, then bus W7

This family-run bakery, established in 1820 and a Crouch End institution, has a loyal local following and sells an extensive range of freshly-baked breads, cakes and pastries.

Euphorium

- 202 Upper Street, N1 1RQ
- 020 7704 6705
- www.euphoriumbakery.com
- Angel, Highbury and Islington
- Mon-Fri 7am-10pm, Sat-Sun 8am-10pm

The first Islington branch of what is now a chain of popular bakery-cum-cafés offering breads, pastries and cakes.

Gail's

- 64 Hampstead High St, NW3 1QH
- 020 7794 5700
- www.gailsbread.co.uk
- Hampstead LU
- Mon-Fri 7am-8pm, Sat-Sun 7.30am-8pm

This small, bustling café-cum-shop, the first in what is now a chain, offers Gail's trademark range of high-quality, internationally-inspired breads, cakes and pastries.

Lanka

- 71 Regents Park Road, NW1 8UY
- 020 7483 2544
- www.lanka-uk.com
- Chalk Farm LU
- Tues-Sat 9am-6.30pm,
  Sun 9am-5.30pm

Coolly elegant, this cake shop-cum-café sells a seasonal range of chef Masayuki Hara's exquisite, upmarket patisserie, from green tea chocolate gateau to classic Paris Brest.

Primrose Bakery

- 69 Gloucester Avenue, NW1 8LD
- 020 7483 4222
- www.primrosebakery.org.uk
- Chalk Farm LU
- Mon-Sat 8.30am-6pm,
  Sun 9.30am-5.30pm

A key player in the cupcake boom which has gripped the capital, Martha Swift and Lisa Thomas's pretty Primrose Hill cake shop-cum-café offers its trademark iced concoctions.
Branch: 42 Tavistock Street, WC2E 7PB

The Spence Bakery

- 161 Stoke Newington Church St. N16 0JL
- 020 7249 4927
- www.thespence.co.uk
- Stoke Newington Rail
- Mon-Sat 8am-6pm. Sun 9am-6pm

This small, friendly bakery-cum-café, with a loyal local following, sells its own hand-made breads, freshly baked on the premises.

Victoria Bakery

- 83 High Street, Barnet, EN5 5UR
- 020 8449 0790
- www.victoriabakery.co.uk
- High Barnet LU
- Mon-Sat 7.30am-5pm

This small, traditional English bakery, a family business established in 1827, offers a range of freshly baked white, brown and soda breads. The cheese straws and iced ring doughnuts go down a storm with local schoolchildren.

West

& Clarke's

- 122 Kensington Church Street, W8 4BH
- 020 7229 2190
- www.sallyclarke.com
- High Street Kensington LU, Notting Hill LU
- Mon-Sat 8am-5pm, Sun 10am-4pm

Chef Sally Clarke was a pioneer of the artisanal loaf movement in London, establishing her bakery in 1990. This elegantly rustic shop, next door to her famous restaurant, sells a range of Clarke's breads and other own-baked treats from savoury pizzas and flans to sweet tarts and pastries.

Exeter Street Bakery

- 18 Argyll Road, W8
- 020 7937 8484
- www.exeterstreetbakery.co.uk
- High Street Kensington LU
- Mon-Sat 8am-7pm, Sun 9am-6pm

This small shop sells traditionally-made Italian breads, such as ciabatta or pane Pugliese.

Outsider Tart

- 83 Chiswick High Road, W4 2EF
- 020 7096 1609
- www.outsidertart.com
- Turnham Green LU/Rail
- Mon-Wed, Fri-Sun 8am-6pm, Thurs 9am-10pm

An exuberant offering from American duo David Lesniak and David Muniz, this relaxed bakery-cum-café showcases a wonderful and extensive array of creative, American-inspired baked goods. Friendly staff are happy to talk you through what's on offer that day, from assorted brownies (chocolate peanut butter, cappuccino, blondie), whoopie pies, tray cakes, sheet cookies and breakfast puffs.

Pitshanger Village Bakery

- 117 Pitshanger Lane, W5 1RH
- 020 8991 5735
- Hanger Lane LU
- Mon-Sat 8.30am-4pm

This small, attractive bakery offers a range of breads and baked goods including decent sourdough and pretty, French-style dainty fruit tarts.

William Curley

- 10 Paved Court, Richmond, TW9 1LZ
- 020 8332 3002
- www.williamcurley.com
- Richmond LU/Rail
- Mon-Sat 9.30am-6.30pm,
  Sun 10.30am-6pm

William Curley's minimalist shop, discreetly located on a historic Richmond side-street, showcases William's exquisite patisserie and his acclaimed chocolates.

South

De Gustibus

- 4 Southwark Street, SE1 1TQ
- 020 7407 3625
- www.degustibus.co.uk
- London Bridge LU/Rail
- Mon-Fri 7am-5pm, Sat 7am-4pm

A veteran presence in Borough Market, this is a London outlet for pioneering artisanal baker Dan Schickentanz. It offers a range of his breads such as Six Day Sour (made with a sourdough starter) and Polish Rye. The lunchtime trade is catered for with superior sandwiches, including salt beef.
Branch: 53-55 Carter Lane, EC4V 5AE

Konditor & Cook

- 22 Cornwall Road, SE1 8TW
- 020 7261 0456
- www.konditorandcook.com
- Waterloo LU/Rail
- Mon-Fri 7.30am-6.30pm, 8.30am-3pm

Gerhard Jenne's bakery (which has a number of branches) is noted for its creative hand-made cakes and pastries, from wildly colourful 'magic cakes' to imaginatively personalised birthday cakes (much in demand with celebrity clients). One reason for Gerhard's success is that he firmly believes everything should taste as good as it looks.

South-West

Breadstall

- Outside 56-60 Northcote Rd, SW11 1PA
- www.breadstall.com
- Clapham Junction Rail
- Mon-Sun 7am-6pm

A bread stall – but not as you know it. Housed in a huge, smart trailer, this is street bread selling on a major scale. The wide-ranging stock, sensibly divided into bread and cakes and savoury, is sourced from the best bakeries by owner Sebastian Vince. It's always busy, with customers queuing for the huge sausage rolls and artisanal bread.

CakeBoy

Unit 2 Kingfisher House, Battersea
Reach, Juniper Drive, SW18 1TX

020 7978 5555

www.cake-boy.co.uk

Wandsworth Town Rail

Mon-Fri 8am-6pm, Sat 9am-6pm

A glamorous 'cake boutique' café showcasing the talents of acclaimed patissier Eric Lanlard aka 'Cake Boy'. On offer are skilfully-made, beautiful cake and pastry creations – such as Fraisier or Diva – which taste as good as they look.

Newens: the Original Maids of Honour

288 Kew Road, TW9

020 8940 2752

www.theoriginalmaidsofhonour.co.uk

Kew Gardens LU

Mon-Sun 8.30am-6pm

A wonderfully retro bakery-cum-tea rooms, housed in a Tudor-style building just by Kew Gardens. On offer are freshly baked British treats, including Maids of Honour (traditional almond tarts associated with Richmond since the eighteenth century, made to a secret Newens family recipe), splendid steak and salmon pies and custard tarts.

Old Post Office Bakery

76 Landor Road, SW9 9PH

020 7326 4408

www.oldpostofficebakery.co.uk

Clapham North LU

Mon, Wed, Thurs 7am-7pm,
Tues 7am-5.30pm, Fri 7am-6pm,
Sat 7am-5.30pm, Sun 9am-2pm

Founded in 1982, London's first organic bakery is still going strong, though no longer housed in the 'old post office' which was its first home. Loyal customers return for the handmade breads (including sourdough rye and three seed wholewheat) and the excellent pastries. All the goods here are freshly baked on the premises by Richard Scroggs and John Dungevel and the prices are very reasonable.

South-East

Blackbird Bakery

208 Railton Road, SE24 0JT

020 7095 8800

www.blackbirdbakerylondon.co.uk

Herne Hill Rail

Mon-Fri 7am-7pm, Sat 8am-5pm

This south-east London bakery (now one of a small chain) has built up an appreciative customer base for its freshly baked breads, from bloomers to sourdough, cakes and pastries.

Little Bread Pedlar

105 Abbey Street, SE1 3NP

www.lbpedlar.com

C10 bus

*Tues-Fri 8.30am-2.30pm,
Sat-Sun 10am-2.30pm*

Tucked away in a down-to-earth parade of shops in Bermondsey, this small shop-cum-café showcases the baking talents of the Little Bread Pedlar, whose bakery is based at nearby Spa Terminus. The setting is relaxed and informal, while the baking is seriously good. Sit at a formica table and enjoy delights such as a savoury Parma rose, croissant or Eccles cake with Kirkham's Lancashire cheese with a cup of tea or coffee or buy a loaf of their sourdough.

East

E5 Bakehouse

*395 Railway Arches,
Mentmore Terrace, E8 3PH*

020 8525 2890

www.e5bakehouse.com

London Fields Rail

Daily 7am-7pm

Housed under a railway arch, Ben Mackinnon's down-to-earth, informal, open-plan bakery-cum-café does a roaring business and has a loyal community following. On offer here is a range of flavourful sourdough breads, including Ben's signature Hackney Wild and Route 66, a 66% rye bread, made by the team of bakers working away industriously in the baking area behind the counter. Customers drop in to pick up one of the freshly baked loaves and enjoy a cup of coffee in the small seating area, while baking courses are another popular attraction.

Violet Cakes

47 Wilton Way, E8 3ED

020 7275 8360

www.violetcakes.com

Hackney Central Rail

*Tues-Fri 8am-6pm, Sat 9.30am-6pm,
Sun 9.30am-5pm*

Founded by baker Claire Ptak, formerly a pastry chef at California's famous Chez Panisse restaurant, this small, appealing cake shop-cum-café has achieved a cult following for its seasonal, high-quality baked goods, including her delectable, signature cup cakes

Butchers

Allens of Mayfair

High-street butchers have had a tough time, but the recent food crises of BSE and more recently the horsemeat scandal has increased the demand for quality meat from a trustworthy source. Encouragingly, recent years have seen more quality butchers opening in London offering their customers plant-fed, free-range or organic meat as well as great service.

Central

Allens of Mayfair

117 Mount Street, W1K 3LA
020 7499 5831
www.allensofmayfair.co.uk
Bond Street LU
Mon-Fri 7am-7pm,
Sat 7am-5pm, Sun 10am-2pm

With its beautiful tiles and huge wooden chopping block , this venerable butchers (the oldest in London) is a Mayfair institution, with its customers ranging from film stars to famous chefs. Game is a particular forte of Allens, which is noted both for the quality and the range of game it carries; during the game season the shop has a spectacular display of feathered and furred game. Another speciality for which Allens is especially noted is its ma-tured, prime Scotch beef. Butchery classes are booked out months ahead.

Biggles

66 Marylebone Lane, W1U 2PF
020 7224 5937
www.ebiggles.co.uk
Bond Street LU
Mon-Sat 10am-4.30pm,
Tues-Fri 10am-6pm

Biggles is a sausage specialist, established in 1989. The assorted, gluten-free sausages, ranging from Marylebone Pork and Beef & Guinness to Toulouse and merguez, are freshly made-on-the-premises.

The Ginger Pig

8-10 Moxon Street, W1U 4EW
020 7935 7788
www.thegingerpig.co.uk
Bond Street LU
Mon-Thurs 9am-6pm
Fri-Sat 9am-6.30pm, Sun 10am-3pm

This handsome shop showcases Tim Wilson's own-reared meat from the Yorkshire Dales. Here can be found flavourful, well-hung beef from long-horn cattle, prime pork from rare breed pigs, and lamb and mutton from Swaledale sheep, plus a range of French poultry, such as poulet noir, brought back weekly from Rungis Market near Paris. There is also a splendid charcuterie counter laden with their own-made (huge) sausage rolls, pies, terrines and pâtés. The butchery classes are proving to be a big hit.

Jack O'Shea's

11 Montpelier Street, SW7 1EX

020 7581 7771

www.jackoshea.com

Knightsbridge LU

Mon-Fri 8am-6.30pm, Sat 8am-5pm

As befits its Knightsbridge location, this is a smart-looking shop, a London outlet for an Irish family butchers established in 1790. Free-range and organic meat is on offer including grass-fed Irish veal and Shetland Island, seaweed-fed lamb.

Jago's of Chelsea

5 Elystan Street, SW3 3NT

020 7589 5531

www.jagobutchersofchelsea.co.uk

South Kensington LU

Mon-Fri 8.30am-5pm, Sat 8.30am-1pm

Established in 1973, this small, neat Chelsea butchers offers an up-market range of quality meat and free-range poultry, with its seasonal game, from grouse to venison, a particular speciality. Own-made sausages are another popular draw as are the experienced, genially helpful staff.

McKenna

21 Theobald's Road, WC1

020 7242 7740

Holborn LU

Mon-Fri 6am-5.30pm, Sat 6am-2.30pm

This small, down-to-earth Bloomsbury butchers shop is well known for both the range and quality of its meat and the competitiveness of its pricing. It consequently has a loyal local following – expect to queue! Game is a particular forte here and the staff very helpful.

North

Harry's Fine Food

258 Kentish Town Road, NW5 2AA

020 7485 0346

Kentish Town LU/Rail

Mon-Sat 7.30am-5.30pm

This friendly, down-to-earth shop offers an excellent range of organic meat and poultry, carefully sourced from organic suppliers. As well as a fresh fish counter.

Baldwins

469 Green Lanes, N4 1AJ

020 8340 5934

www.baldwinsfoods.com

Manor House LU, then bus 29, 141, 341

Mon-Sat 8am-6.30pm, Sun 8am-4pm

Attractively spick and span, this smart corner shop with friendly staff, offers an excellent selection of meat and poultry. Their produce includes more unusual meats such as rabbit and venison.

Barrett's of Belsize

- 40 England's Lane, NW3 4UE
- 020 7720 1131
- www.barrettsbutchers.co.uk
- Belsize Park LU
- 8.30am-5.30pm

A well-established butcher's shop, with a loyal local following, known especially for Scotch beef.

James Elliott

- 96 Essex Road, N1 8LU
- 020 7226 3658
- Angel LU
- Mon-Thurs 8am-5pm, Fri 8am-6pm, Sat 8am-5pm

A well-established shop that sells excellent, well-hung, free-range meat and poultry, plus a selection of cheeses. Elliot's is particularly known for its prime Scotch beef and its own-cooked hams. It attracts a steady stream of regulars, who enjoy the butcher's banter as he expertly cuts their meat to order.

Frank Godfrey Ltd

- 7 Highbury Park, N5 1QJ
- 020 7226 2425
- www.godfreys.co.uk
- Arsenal LU
- Mon-Fri 8am-6pm, Sat 8am-5pm

This smart family butchers – now run by fourth generation brothers Chris and Jeremy

Godfrey – has a devoted following. All the meat sold here is free-range and very good quality, from the English corn-fed chickens to the plant-fed pork and Orkney Island beef. The brothers work closely with their suppliers to ensure high welfare standards and this is reflected in the quality of the meat.

Hampstead Butcher & Providore

- 56 Rosslyn Hill, NW3 1ND
- 020 7794 9210
- www.hampsteadbutcher.com
- Hampstead LU
- Mon-Sat 9am-7pm. Sun 9am-6pm

This handsome, spacious shop (on the site of the former Rosslyn Deli) combines an impressive butchers counter, showcasing traditional-breed, free-range and ethically reared British meats, with a delicatessen and wine shop.

Highland Organics

- 14 Bittacy Hill, NW7 1LB
- 020 8346 1055
- www.organicbutcher.net
- Mill Hill LU
- Mon-Sat 8am-6pm

As the name suggests, organic meat is on offer here, from Welsh Black beef steaks to huge plump home-made sausages. Customers can also stock up on basic organic groceries such as fresh bread.

Meat Naturally

🏠 *78 Hampstead High Street, NW3 1RE*
☎ *07596 454 538 / 07832 289015*
🚇 *Hampstead LU*
🕐 *Mon-Sat 9am-5pm*

Located in Hampstead Community Market, this small, friendly butchers stall specialises in organic and free-range meat and poultry.

Meat N16

🏠 *104 Stoke Newington Church Street, N16 0LA*
☎ *020 7254 0724*
🌐 *www.meatlondon.co.uk*
🚌 *Bus 149, 243*
🕐 *Tues-Fri 9.30am-7pm, Sat 9am-5pm, Sun 9.30am-4pm*

A smart butchers shop, offering a carefully-sourced selection of meat and free-range poultry including Packington chickens, Blythburgh pork and Colne Valley Lambs with own-made sausages proving popular. In addition, the shop offers some deli items and a wine room at the back.

Midhurst

🏠 *2 Midhurst Parade, N10 3EJ*
☎ *020 8883 5303*
🚇 *East Finchley LU, then 102 bus*
🕐 *Mon-Thurs 8am-4.45pm, Fri 7am-4.45pm, Sat 7am-4pm*

Tucked away in a little parade of shops between Muswell Hill and East Finchley, this small shop offers decent meat (some organic) with fresh fruit and veg outside.

Moore & Sons

🏠 *25 Greenhill Parade, Great North Rd, EN5*
☎ *020 8449 9649*
🌐 *www.mooreandsonsbutchers.co.uk*
🚇 *High Barnet LU*
🕐 *Mon-Fri 8am-530pm, Sat 8am-4pm*

A small, traditional, well-established butchers with friendly staff. Specialities include Scotch beef, own-made sausages and a fine display of game.

Morley Butchers

🏠 *23 Broadway Parade, N8 9DE*
☎ *020 8340 2436*
🚇 *Finsbury Park LU/Rail, then bus W3 or W7*
🕐 *Mon-Fri 8.30am-5pm, Sat 8.30am-4pm*

This small, friendly Crouch End butchers has a loyal local following. Customers return for the Scotch beef, English lamb, pork and poultry and a good range of furred and feathered game during the season.

West

The Ginger Pig

137-139 Askew Road, W12 9AU

020 8740 4297

www.thegingerpig.co.uk

Mon, Tues, Sat 9am-5.30pm,
Wed-Fri 9am-6.30pm

This roomy branch of noted butchers Ginger Pig has quickly built up a keen local following. In addition to the prime quality meat and poultry, including superb matured beef and excellent pork, there's a deli counter section, traiteur counter and fresh produce section, making it a very useful shop.

Hook and Cleaver

133 Pitshanger Lane, W5 1RH

020 8997 6988

www.hookandcleaver.co.uk

Hanger Lane LU

Mon-Fri 8am-6pm, Sat 8am-5.30pm

Spic and span, with white and black tiles, Paul Dzido's shop, warmly recommended by food writer Catherine Phipps, is a welcome addition to this West London high street. Stock includes grass-fed, dry-aged beef, Plantation Pigs pork, free-range chickens and lamb and service is knowledgeable and friendly.

C. Lidgate

110 Holland Park Avenue, W11 4UA

020 7727 8243

www.lidgates.com

Holland Park LU

Mon-Fri 7.30am-7pm,
Sat 6.30am-6.30pm

A grand old butchers established in 1850, which specialises in high-quality, naturally-grown and fed meat and poultry. Run with great expertise and commitment by David Lidgate, the shop's stock includes organic meat from Highgrove (The Prince of Wales's estate), free-range bronze turkeys and geese. In addition, this family-run business sells award-winning home-made pies and own-cooked hams.

Macken Bros

44 Turnham Green Terrace, W4 1QP

020 8994 2646

www.mackenbros.co.uk

Turnham Green LU

Mon-Fri 7am-6pm, Sat 7am-5.30pm

A seemingly perpetual queue testifies to this well-established shop's popularity. Staff are helpful and friendly and the range of meat and poultry is extensive while the quality remains very high. In fact, such is Macken's reputation, that it's now also opened in the Selfridges Food Hall.

Meat Like It Used To Be

🏠 *50 Cannon Lane, HA5 1AW*
☎ *020 8866 4611*
🚇 *Pinner LU*
🕐 *Mon- Fri 7.30am-6pm,
Sat 7.30am-5pm Sun 9am-1pm*

The name says it all. This friendly, well-run butchers stocks an impressive range of fully-traceable free-range meat and poultry. Stock includes certified Aberdeen Angus beef, Kelly Bronze turkeys and a good selection of game.

Richardsons

🏠 *88 Northfield Avenue, W13 9RR*
☎ *020 8567 1064*
🚇 *Northfield LU*
🕐 *Mon-Fri 8am-5.30pm, Sat 8am-4.30pm*

This down-to-earth, busy butcher's attracts a loyal local clientele.

Sheepdrove Organic Farm Family Butcher

🏠 *5 Clifton Road, W9 1SZ*
☎ *020 7266 3838*
🌐 *www.sheepdrove.com*
🚇 *Maida Vale LU*
🕐 *Mon-Fri 9am-7pm,
Sat 9am-5pm, Sun 10am-4pm*

This small butchers has impeccable organic credentials with all meat coming from Sheepdrove Organic Farm. The counter is filled with good-looking meat and poultry.

H. G. Walter

🏠 *51 Palliser Road, W14 9EB*
☎ *020 7385 6466*
🌐 *www.hgwalter.com*
🚇 *Baron's Court LU*
🕐 *Mon-Fri 8am-7pm, Sat 8am-5pm*

This small, immaculate blue-and-white tiled butchers shop has a notable reputation. They proudly display their award as 'Best Small Butchers' Shop in Great Britain' on the window. It is run with friendly efficiency and an eye for detail by brother-and-sister team Adam and Clare Heanen. All the meat is free-range or organic and their Scotch beef, dry-aged for 28 days in a purpose-built cool room, is a source of particular pride. Also on offer is a range of seasonal game (including rarities such as grey partridge), Plantation Pig pork, luxuriously expensive Wagyu beef and home-made burgers and sausages. .

Wyndham House

🏠 *229 Chiswick High Road, W4 2DW*
☎ *020-89941414*
🌐 *www.wyndham-house.com*
🚇 *Turnham Green LU*
🕐 *Mon-Sat 8am-6pm, Sun 10am-5pm*

A small, smart shop, with an excellent range of meat and poultry, including free-range chickens, 30-day-aged steaks, venison burgers and sausages. Staff are knowledgeable and helpful.

South-West

The Butcher & Grill

- 39-41 Parkgate Road, SW11 4NP
- 020 7924 3999
- www.thebutcherandgrill.com
- Clapham Junction Rail
- Mon-Sat 9am-7pm, Sun 8.30am-4pm

A contemporary outfit, combining an upmarket butchers with a spacious restaurant. The shop also offers fresh fruit and veg and some delicatessen items too.

Chadwicks

- 109 Balham High Street, SW12 9AP
- 020 8772 1895
- www.chadwicksbutchers.co.uk
- Balham LU
- Mon-Fri 9am-6pm, Sat 9am-5.30pm, Sun 10am-3pm

Master butcher Gary Chadwick's shop is run with warmth and charm. The meat and poultry sold here is carefully sourced from respected suppliers such as Plantation Pigs and Orkney Meat.

Cleavers

- 537 Old York Road, SW18 1TG
- 020 8871 9775
- www.cleaversbutchers.com
- Wandsworth Town Rail
- Mon-Fri 8am-8pm, Sat-Sun 8am-7pm

This attractive butchers shop offers an excellent range of high-quality meat and poultry, including Galloway beef and rare breed pork, as well as own-made sausages and Scotch eggs. There is also a range of deli items, making this a very useful shop.

Cleavers

- 4/6 Battersea Rise, SW11 1ED
- 020 7924 2192
- www.cleaversbutchers.com
- Wandsworth Town Rail
- Mon-Thurs 10am-6pm, Fri 8am-6pm, Sat 8am-7pm, Sun 8am-5pm

This small, neat butchers shop offers a range of carefully-sourced high-quality meat and poultry, such as Packington's free-range chickens, with a range of useful deli items and traiteur dishes as well.

A. Dove & Son

- 71 Northcote Road, SW11 6PJ
- 020 7223 5191
- www.doveandson.co.uk
- Clapham Junction Rail
- Mon 8am-4pm, Tues-Sat 8am-5.30pm

This family butchers shop was established in 1889 and has a loyal clientele. Highlights include the well-hung beef, popular meat pies and excellent bronze turkeys.

Hennessy's

80 Northcote Road, SW11 6QN

020 7228 0894

Clapham Junction Rail

Tues-Sat 9.30am-6pm,
Sun 9.30am-1pm

This down-to-earth, established butcher's shop offers organic and free-range meats and home-made sausages.

Laverstoke Park Farm Butchers Shop

35 King Street Parade, TW1 3SD

020 8744 1112

www.laverstokepark.co.uk

Mon-Wed 9am-6pm, Thurs-Fri 9am-7pm,
Sat 9am-6.30pm, Sun 9am-5pm

An eye-catching display of meat from Laverstoke Park Farm is on offer here, with carcasses hanging in a glass-walled maturing room at the back. All the meat here is reared to high welfare standards, following Laverstoke's organic and biodynamic principles. The range is impressive, from bargain offal such as ox hearts to tender buffalo steaks. In addition, the shop sells Laverstoke Park Farm products including its own-made pies and ice creams.

M. Moen & Sons

24 The Pavement, SW4 0JA

020 7622 1624

www.moen.co.uk

Clapham Common LU

Mon-Fri 8.30am-6pm, Sat 8am-5pm

This well-established butchers offers a distinctly upmarket stock. The meat is good quality – from home-made sausages to a range of in-season game. Additional delights include wild mushrooms and seasonal produce like sea-kale.

The Parsons Nose

753 Fulham Road, SW6 5UU

020 7736 4492

www.parsonsnose.co.uk

Parsons Green LU

Mon-Fri 9am-7pm, Sat 9am-6pm,
Sun 10am-4pm

One of the new breed of up-market butchers shops, this smart, friendly establishment offers an excellent selection of carefully sourced meats, including rare breed meats and Childhay Manor free-range and organic meats. Goat and game are among the more unusual items stocked and staff are knowledgeable and helpful. *Branch: 88 Lower Richmond Road, SW15 1LL (020 8788 6160)*

Pethers of Kew

- 16 Station Parade,
  Kew Gardens, TW9 3PZ
- 020 8940 0163
- Kew Gardens LU
- Mon-Fri 7.30am-6pm, Sat 7.30am-5pm

An appetising smell of spit-roasted chicken wafts out from this old-fashioned butchers. All the meat here is free-range and the shop does a roaring trade in home-made pies.

Randalls

- 113 Wandsworth Bridge Road, SW6 2TE
- 020 7736 3426
- Fulham Broadway LU
- Mon-Fri 8.30am-5.30pm, Sat 8am-4pm

This fine butchers offers top-notch, free-range and organic meat all beautifully displayed. The marinated meats and own-made sausages are particularly popular.

Robert and Edwards

- 19 Leopold Road, SW19 7BB
- 020 8946 5834
- www.robertandedwards.co.uk
- Wimbledon Rail
- Mon-Fri 6.30am-5.30pm, Sat 6.30am-5pm

Down the road from Wimbledon Village, this smart butchers shop offers a carefully-selected range of good quality meat and free-range poultry as well as dry-cured bacon and Wimbledon Royal sausages.

Wyndham House

- 339 Fulham Road, SW10 9TW
- 020 7352 7888
- www.wyndham-house.com
- Fulham Broadway LU
- Mon-Sat 7.30am-6pm

This small, smart shop offers a cracking range of attractively presented, free-range meat and poultry. Stock includes Label Anglaise chickens, lamb, pork and Welsh Black beef. This is also a very good place to source game during the season.

South-East

The Butchery SE23

- 49 London Road, SE23 3TY
- www.thebutcheryltd.com
- Forest Hill Rail
- Wed-Sun 10am-6pm

Nathan Mills and his partner Ruth Siwinski have a reputation for providing discriminatingly sourced, rare-breed meat ('much the tastiest') to the restaurant trade. They have now opened their first butchers shop in Forest Hill, offering the same carefully sourced meat to grateful locals. On Saturdays between 9am-2pm they also sell from their wholesale premises, The Butchery at Arch 13, Dockley Rd, SE1 2HQ.

Flock and Herd

⌗ *167 Bellenden Road, SE15 4DH*
☎ *020 7635 7733*
🖰 *www.flockandherd.com*
🚃 *Peckham Rye Rail*
🕓 *Tues-Fri 9am-6pm, Sat 8am-6pm*

Charlie Shaw's new butchers shop in Peckham has struck a chord with locals enjoying the opportunity to buy traditional cuts such as skirt steak and ox cheek, alongside Charlie's own-made sausages and faggots, pork pies and sliced meats.

Heaps Sausages

⌗ *8 Nevada Street, SE10 9JL*
☎ *020 8293 9199*
🖰 *www.heapssausages.com*
🚃 *Greenwich DLR and Rail*
🕓 *Daily 9am-6pm*

This buzzing shop and café offers a chance to sample specialist sausage-maker Martin Heap's creations, hand-made on the site using natural casings and in a host of flavours including lamb and mint.

K. Libretto

⌗ *112 Wood Vale, SE23 3EB*
☎ *020 8693 3175*
🚃 *Forest Hill Rail*
🕓 *Tues & Thurs 10am-5pm,*
Wed 10am-1pm,
Fri 10am-6pm, Sat 8.30am-2pm

This traditional butchers shop is run with amiable friendliness by Kim Libretto. Customers range from regulars who have shopped here for years to new arrivals to the area. Kim is happy to offer advice on which cuts of meat to buy and has lots of great cooking tips.

O'Shea's Butchers

⌗ *120 Druid Street, SE1 2HH*
☎ *020 7064 1712*
🚃 *Bermondsey LU*
🖰 *www.osheasbutchers.com*
🕓 *Sat 9am-2pm*

Saturday mornings offers the public a chance to buy prime meat from acclaimed Irish butcher Darragh O'Shea. This family business has built its reputation on supplying leading restaurants and chefs.

William Rose

⌗ *126 Lordship Lane, SE22 8HD*
☎ *020 8693 9191*
🖰 *www.williamrosebutchers.com*
🚃 *East Dulwich Rail*
🕓 *Tues-Sat 8am-5pm*

Established in 1862, this upmarket, family butchers moved from Vauxhall to Dulwich in 2005 and has been greeted with enthusiasm by the local community. On offer is a fine range of carefully-sourced, quality, rare breed, free-range and organic meat and poultry and game, from matured beef from longhorn or red poll cattle to excellent sausages. Customers return, too, for the genial, knowledgeable and helpful service, with Saturdays doing brisk business with locals stocking up on joints or poultry for the Sunday roast..

East

Barbecoa Butcher Shop

🏠 *82 Watling Street, EC4M 9BX*
☎ *020 3375 5553*
🌐 *www.barbecoa.com*
🚇 *St Paul's LU*
🕐 *Mon-Fri 7am-7pm, Sat 9am-5pm. Sun 12noon-4pm*

Run with friendly, knowledgeable enthusiasm by a team of young butchers, the butchers shop attached to Barbecoa, Jamie Oliver's and Adam Perry Lang's barbecue steakhouse, is a striking affair, dominated by its glass room of maturing carcasses. The British beef, matured for around one-and-a-half months, is a particular highlight with the butchers taking pride in offering less familiar cuts, such as picanha steaks. Also on offer are Gower salt marsh lamb, game and, at Christmas, turkeys, geese and difficult to find apple-fed cockrels.

Butcher at Leadenhall

🏠 *6-7 Leadenhall Market, EC3V 1LR*
☎ *020 7283 1661*
🌐 *www.butcheratleadenhall.com*
🚇 *Bank or Monument LU*
🕐 *Mon-Fri 7am-10pm*

A combined 'shop and grill', the butchers counter here, alongside the popular 'grill' restaurant area, sells grass-fed, outdoor-reared, matured beef, lamb and pork, all sourced from Staffordshire farms, plus free-range poultry including Packington chickens, Norfolk bronze turkeys and game.

The Ginger Pig

🏠 *99 Lauriston Road, E9 7HJ*
☎ *020 8986 6911*
🌐 *www.thegingerpig.co.uk*
🚇 *London Fields Rail*
🕐 *Tues 9am-5.30pm, Wed-Fri 9am-6.30pm, Sat 9am-6pm, Sun 9am-3pm*

A smart Hackney branch of this excellent butchers, a much-appreciated addition to the area, helped by the growing popularity of Lauriston as a foodie enclave with shops such as Bottle Apostle, Loafing and Jonathan Norris fishmongers.

Cheese Shops

GOAT · SHEEP CHEESE · SEMI-SOFT CHEESES · ENGLISH REGIONAL

OCAMADOUR RACHEL SAINT MAURE
BERKSWELL YARG

SWEET
GRASSY

Androuet

I f you enjoy eating cheese, then it is well worth finding a good cheesemonger to shop at. Looking after artisanally-made cheese so that it can be eaten and enjoyed at its best, requires skill, care and attention. The best cheesemongers not only pride themselves on the quality of the cheeses that they stock, but also enjoy sharing their knowledge and enthusiasm for cheese, recommending new cheeses to try and advising on what's at its peak that day. Visiting such stores is a great experience.

Central

Cheese at Leadenhall

4-5 Leadenhall Market, EC3V 1LR

020 7929 1697

www.cheeseatleadenhall.co.uk

Liverpool Street LU/Rail

Mon-Wed 9am-5pm, Thurs-Fri 9am-8pm

Housed in a long narrow space, formerly a butchers shop, Cheese at Leadenhall is run with knowledgeable panache by Sue Cloke. On offer is a range of around 150 British, Irish and European cheeses, many sourced directly from producers, ranging from classics such as 22-months-old Comte to lesser-known gems like Barkham Blue. Sue also stocks a range of wines and ports, chosen to complement cheese, while a cheese bar offers a chance to try before you buy.

La Cave du Fromage

24-25 Cromwell Place SW7 2LD

0845 1088 222

www.la-cave.co.uk

South Kensington LU

Mon-Thurs 10am-7pm
Fri-Sat 10am-9pm, Sun 11am-6pm

This smart cheese shop comes with impressive credentials – set up by Eric Charriaux and Amnon Paldi who run a company supplying farmhouse cheeses to top restaurants. On offer in the shop is an extensive range of 160 cheeses from Britain, France, Italy and Spain, matured in-house and varying seasonally. Bestsellers include Fourme au Maury, Tartufette and Epoisse. The cave also contains a select range of charcuterie, freshly baked bread and wines.

La Fromagerie

2-4 Moxon Street, W1U 4EW

020 7935 0341

www.lafromagerie.co.uk

Baker Street LU

Mon-Fri 8am-7.30pm,
Sat 9am-7pm, Sun 10am-6pm

Just off Marylebone High Street, this spacious, attractive shop is an alluring destination for cheese-lovers, with its temperature-controlled cheese room very much at the heart of the shop. Owner Patricia Michelson, whose passionate enthusiasm for cheese is genuine

LA FROMAGERIE

Stylish and unconventional LA FROMAGERIE is recognised as being one of the best cheese shops in England. Both shops & Tasting Cafés are open everyday serving **Breakfast, Lunch & Afternoon Tea**

www.lafromagerie.co.uk
www.twitter.com/LaFromagerieUK

LA FROMAGERIE
2-6 Moxon St, Marylebone,
London, W1U 4EW
Tel: 020 7935 0341
moxon@lafromagerie.co.uk

LA FROMAGERIE
No 30 Highbury Park,
London, N5 2AA
Tel: 020 7359 7440
highbury@lafromagerie.co.uk

- ON SITE MATURING ROOMS
- WALK IN CHEESE ROOM
- TASTING CAFÉ
- TUTORED CHEESE & WINE TASTINGS
- REGIONAL TASTING SUPPERS
- AVAILABLE FOR PRIVATE HIRE
- BESPOKE WHOLESALE SUPPLYING SOME OF THE BEST RESTAURANTS IN AND AROUND LONDON

and infectious, carefully sources her artisanal cheeses direct from the producers and also matures them. The shop stocks between 150-200 seasonal farmhouse cheeses, featuring both classics such as Beaufort Chalet d'Alpage or burrata and less well-known cheeses such as Spanish garrotxa and Italian scimudin.

Neal's Yard Dairy

17 Shorts Gardens, WC2H 9AT
020 7240 5700
www.nealsyarddairy.co.uk
Covent Garden LU
Mon-Sat 10am-7pm

A pioneering champion of British farmhouse cheeses, this small shop has an impressive range of traditionally-made farmhouse cheeses including classics such as Appleby's Cheshire and Kirkham's Lancashire and a wide range of new cheeses, from Stichelton to Stinking Bishop. Other produce includes good-quality breads, pickles and chutneys and butter.

Paxton & Whitfield

93 Jermyn Street, SW1Y 6JE
020 7930 0259
www.paxtonandwhitfield.co.uk
Piccadilly Circus LU
Mon-Sat 9.30am-6pm, Sun 11am-5pm

This picturesque, vintage shop, established in 1797, is a grand old name in cheese-selling and prides itself on the quality and range of British and continental cheeses stocked. While bestsellers include Cheddar and Cropwell Bishop Stilton, they also sell own-imported mozzarella within 24 hours of making. A partnership with Androuet in Paris means that there's an impressive range of French cheese. There are also biscuits, chutneys and relishes.

Rippon Cheese Stores

26 Upper Tachbrook Street, SW1V 1SW
020 7931 0628
www.ripponcheese.com
Pimlico LU, Victoria LU/Rail
Mon-Fri 8am-5.30pm, Sat 8.30am-5pm

Well-known for their wholesale cheese business, Karen and Philip Rippon stock an astonishing assortment of around 550 European cheeses in this cool, neat shop. Karen, Philip and their helpful staff are very happy to offer advice and guidance to their extensive range of cheeses.

North

Cheeses

11 Fortis Green Road, N10 3HP
020 8444 9141
www.cheesesonline.co.uk
East Finchley LU, Bus 134
Tues-Sat 9.30am-5.30pm

Tucked away in an old-fashioned parade of shops just off Muswell Hill Broadway, this tiny shop offers a carefully sourced range of British and European cheeses and has a loyal, local following.

La Fromagerie

30 Highbury Park, N5 2AA
020 7937 8004
www.lafromagerie.co.uk
Highbury & Islington LU/Rail
Mon 10.30am-7pm, Tues-Sat 9am-7pm, Sun 10am-5pm

Patricia Michelson's Islington shop features a cool backroom, filled with a carefully sourced range of between 200-250 seasonal farmhouse cheeses. Complementing the cheeses is a delicious range of breads and patisserie.

West

Jeroboams

- 96 Holland Park, W11 3rb
- 020 7727 9359
- www.jeroboams.co.uk
- Holland Park LU
- Mon-Fri 8am-8pm, Sat 8.30am-7pm, Sun 10am-6pm

This branch of the noted wine merchant also offers an carefully selected range of high-quality, artisanal British and European cheeses, with a particular highlight being the French cheeses such as 22-months-old Mimolette or carefully matured chèvre.

The Real Cheese Shop

- 62 Barnes High Street, SW13 9LF
- 020 8878 6676
- Barnes Bridge Rail
- Tues-Sat 9.30am-5pm

This small, neat shop offers a range of over 100 British and continental cheeses and has an appreciative local following.

Teddington Cheeses

- 42 Station Road, Teddington, TW11 9AA
- 020 8977 6868
- www.teddingtoncheese.co.uk
- Teddington Rail
- Tues-Wed 10am-5pm, Thurs-Sat 9.30am-5.30pm

This store offers an excellent, wide-ranging selection of British and European cheeses. The staff offer knowledgeable and helpful service which has acquired a loyal local following.
Branch: 74 Hill Rise, Richmond, TW10 6UB (020 8948 57)

South

Neal's Yard Dairy

- 6 Park Street, SE1 9AB
- 020 7367 0799
- www.nealsyarddairy.co.uk
- London Bridge LU/Rail
- Mon-Sat 9am-6pm

With its eye-catching display of cloth-wrapped Somerset Cheddar cheeses and impressive long counter display of artisanal British and Irish cheeses, this spacious shop is a real treat for cheese-lovers. On offer here is a carefully-chosen selection, ranging from traditional cheeses such as Cheddar, Stilton and Wensleydale to contemporary cheeses such as Stichelton (a blue-veined cheese made from unpasteurised organic cow's milk), delicate Perroche (a soft goat's cheese) and Gubbeen (a rich, Irish, washed-rind cheese). Tastings are offered by the staff, who are happy to offer advice and suggestions. Additional stock ranges from dairy produce to St John Bakery's Eccles cakes. The autumn months see boxes of rare apples and pears from Brogdale Trust.

Hamish Johnston

- 48 Northcote Road, SW11 1PA
- 020 7738 0741
- www.hamishjohnston.com
- Clapham Junction Rail
- Mon-Sat 9am-6pm, Sun 11am-4pm

This dapper shop has a loyal following, drawn by the great selection of cheeses, numbering around 150, depending on the time of year and the polite, friendly and helpful service. Preference is given to small-scale cheese producers, with delights on offer ranging from Golden Cross to Picos de Europa. The shop also sells an excellent range of deli items, from olive oils and vinegars to top quality ham and smoked wild sea trout from Wales.

South-East

The Cheese Block

- 69 Lordship Lane, SE22 8EP
- 020 8299 3636
- East Dulwich Rail
- Mon-Fri 9.30am-6.30pm, Sat 9am-6pm

This small, down-to-earth shop has an impressive range of over 260 cheeses from Britain and Europe.

The Cheeseboard

- 26 Royal Hill, SE10 8RT
- 020 8305 0401
- www.cheese-board.co.uk
- Greenwich DLR/Rail
- Mon-Wed & Fri 9am-5pm,
  Thurs 9am-1pm, Sat 8.30am-4.30pm

This small, friendly cheesemongers stocks around 100 British and continental cheeses. Stock ranges from classics such as Italian Parmesan or buffalo mozzarella to Spanish Payoyo and French Boulette d'Avesnes.

Androuet

- Old Spitalfields Market,
  107b Commercial Street, E1 6BG
- 020 7375 3168
- www.androuet.co.uk
- Liverpool Street LU/Rail
- Mon-Sun 10am-7pm

Run with knowledgeable enthusiasm by Alexandre Guarneri, this elegant London branch of the famous Parisian cheesemongers sells a varied, discerningly selected range of high-quality French and British cheeses. Cheeses on offer range from classics such as Roquefort to flavourful Couronne Lochoise. Alexandre takes immense pride in his shop, shown both in the quality of his cheeses and the care he takes when advising customers. Cheese-lovers can also enjoy Androuet's cheeses in the intimate restaurant next door.

Chocolate & Sweets

William Curley

These are exciting times for chocolate-lovers in London. Whereas once good quality chocolate was distinctly thin on the ground in the city, nowadays London is home to a number of talented chocolatiers, many of whom have set up their own shops. The emphasis in these establishments is on artisanal, hand-made chocolates using quality ingredients and imaginative flavourings. Look out, too, for annual events, such as The Chocolate Festival and Chocolate Unwrapped which bring in chocolatiers from around the country and abroad.

Central

Artisan du Chocolat

- 89 Lower Sloane Street, SW1W 8DA
- 020 7824 8365
- www.artisanduchocolat.com
- Sloane Square LU
- Mon-Sat 10am-7pm, Sun 12noon-5pm

This austerely chic shop showcases the considerable talents of chocolatier Gerard Coleman and his partner Anne Weyns. Here one can buy Gerard's elegant chocolates, including ganache-filled creations, lustrous 'pearls' and his famous sea-salted caramels.

Bateel

- 76 New Bond Street, W1S 1RX
- 020 7493 3199
- www.bateel.co.uk
- Bond Street LU
- Mon-Fri 8.30am-8pm,
  Sat 10am-8pm, Sun 11am-6.30pm

This elegant shop-cum-café, with cool marble floors and dark wood counters and courteous staff, offers a 'gourmet date experience'. In addition to offering 22 varieties of high-quality natural dates, there is a tempting range of stuffed dates, chocolate-coated dates and chocolates.

Charbonnel et Walker

- 1 The Royal Arcade,
  28 Old Bond St, W1S 4BT
- 020 7491 0939
- www.charbonnel.co.uk
- Piccadilly Circus LU
- Mon-Sat 10am-6pm, Sun 12noon-5pm

A vintage chocolatiers, established in 1875, offering smartly-packaged chocolate gifts.

Choccywoccydoodah

- 30-32 Foubert Place, W1F 7PS
- 020 7734 9713
- www.choccywoccydoodah.com
- Oxford Circus LU
- Mon-Wed, Fri-Sat 10am-7pm,
  Thurs 10am-8pm, Sun 12noon-6pm

As exuberant as its name suggests, this over-the-top shop and café features a spectacular display of chocolate creations and offers a range of in-house chocolate treats.

Cocomaya

- 3 Porchester Place, W2 2BS
- 020 7706 2770
- www.cocomaya.co.uk
- Marble Arch LU
- Mon-Sat 10am-7pm, Sun 11am-6pm

Positioned in a peaceful side-street, this delightfully decorative chocolate shop, founded by two leading lights in the fashion industry, offers a range of gloriously-displayed delectable chocolates. A long table displays a range of beautiful dishes, each enticingly filled with gorgeously colourful, jewel-like chocolates, with flavours changing seasonally.

Hope and Greenwood

- 1 Russell Street, WC2B 5JD
- 020 7240 3314
- www.hopeandgreenwood.co.uk
- Covent Garden or Holborn LU
- Mon-Fri 11am-7pm, Sat 10.30am-7.30pm, Sun 12noon-6pm

An old-fashioned sweetshop from the trend-setting purveyors of nostalgic confectionary, filled with jars and pretty packets of sweets from sherbet lemons to strawberry bonbons

La Maison du Chocolat

- 46 Piccadilly, W1J 0DS
- 020 7287 8500
- www.lamaisonduchocolat.co.uk
- Piccadilly LU
- Mon-Sat 10am-7pm, Sun 12noon-6pm

Seriously elegant, La Maison du Chocolat, with its marble and wood fittings and phalanx of suited staff, brings chocolate-shopping à la Parisienne to London. La Maison du Chocolat, founded in Paris In 1977 by legendary chocolatier Robert Linxe, is noted for its elegant, sophisticated high quality chocolates.

Liberty

- Regent Street, W1B 5AH
- 020 7734 1234
- www.liberty.co.uk
- Oxford Circus LU
- Mon-Sat 10am-9pm, Sun 12noon-8pm

This elegant, fashionable department store now boasts a 'chocolate shop' complete with its own Carnaby Street entrance. Stock includes many of the leading lights in the world of British chocolate, such as Rococo, Damian Allsop, William Curley and Amelia Rope.

Paul A Young

143 Wardour Street, W1F 8WA
020 7437 0011
www.paulayoung.co.uk
Leicester Square or
Tottenham Court Road LU
Mon-Wed, Fri-Sat 10am-8pm,
Thurs 10am-9pm, Sun 12noon-7pm

A flagship store for the talented British chocolatier, décorated in rich purple and gold and selling an assortment of Paul's trademark artisanal confections, from boldly imaginative flavoured truffles to his best-selling, seriously rich brownies, all made on the premises in the downstairs kitchen. A popular series of chocolate-making and tasting classes are also on offer here.

Prestat

14 Princes Arcade, SW1Y 6DS
0800 0213 023
www.prestat.co.uk
Green Park/Piccadilly Circus LU
Mon-Fri 9.30am-6pm, Sat 10am-5pm

Proud holders of a Royal Warrant, Prestat's shop is a small, brightly colourful affair, selling Prestat's chocolates from bars to artisan truffles. All the chocolates are packaged in Prestat's trademark vibrant colours.

Rococo

3 Moxon Street, W1U 4EP
020 7935 7780
www.rococochocolates.com
Baker Street LU
Mon-Sat 10am-6.30pm,
Sun-Mon 11am-6pm

Chantal Coady's elegant Marylebone shop, now just off Marylebone High Street opposite La Fromagerie, offers Rococo's delicious blend of beautifully packaged, high quality chocolate treats. Stock includes Rococo's trademark, flavoured chocolate bars and chocolate wafers, indulgences such as salted caramel ravioli and own-made marshmallows and a seasonally changing range of dainty, hand-made, ganache-filled chocolates.

Rococo

5 Motcomb Street, SW1
020 7245 0993
www.rococochocolates.com
Sloane Square/South Kensington LU
Mon-Sat 10am-6.30pm,
Sun 12noon-5pm

Tucked away down a peaceful Belgravia side-street, this stylish shop-cum-café showcases Rococo's range of elegant chocolates, from hand-painted, playful chocolate figurines to flavoured wafers and bars. It comes complete with a tiny, Moroccan 'secret garden' in which to sit and sip Rococo's rich hot chocolate.

William Curley

198 Ebury Street SW1W 8UN

020 7730 5522

www.williamcurley.com

Sloane Square LU

Mon-Thurs 10am-7pm, Fri 10am-8pm, Sat 9-8pm, Sun 10am-6pm

This immaculate chocolate boutique celebrates the considerable, award-winning talents of noted chocolatier and patissier William Curley. William is noted for the quality of his chocolates and his sophisticated use of flavours such as Japanese black vinegar or rosemary and olive oil. Customers can sit in comfort and sample William's exquisite creations or buy and take away.

North

Paul A Young

33 Camden Passage, N1 8EA

020 7424 5750

www.paulayoung.co.uk

Angel LU

Tues-Thurs 10am-7pm, Fri 10am-7.30pm, Sat 10am-7pm, Sun 11am-6pm

This dapper shop, the first opened by creative chocolatier Paul A Young, showcases his creations from signature marmite truffles to seriously rich brownies, all freshly hand-made on the premises. As well as offering beloved favourites, there are witty seasonal creations.

South

Indulgence Chocolate Artistry

2b Market Row, Brixton, SW9 8LD

www.paulwaynegregory.com

Brixton LU/Rail

Tues-Sat 11am-10pm, Sun 12noon-6pm

This tiny shop, which began life as a pop-up but has now taken on a lease, showcases the considerable talents of chocolatier Paul Wayne Gregory. On offer are his handmade chocolates, with pride of place going to his Pure Indulgence collection, in which every chocolate, such as passion fruit or rum, has won an individual award.

West

Alexeeva & Jones

297 Westbourne Grove, W11 2QA

020 7229 1199

www.alexeevajones.com

Bayswater/Notting Hill/Queensway LU

Mon-Wed 10am-6pm, Thurs-Sat 10am-7pm, Sun 11am-4pm

This elegant shop showcases fine, fresh chocolates from a host of leading British and European chocolatiers including Iain Burnett, Damian Allsop, Paul Wayne Gregory and Franck Daubos.

Artisan du Chocolat

81 Westbourne Grove, W2 4UL
0845 2706 996
www.artisanduchocolat.com
Notting Hill/Queensway LU
Mon-Sat 10am-7pm, Sun 12noon-5pm

This funky-looking shop and 'chocolateria' not only offers Artisan's distinctive chocolates but also has a café area with indulgent treats such as salted caramel tart, chocolate ice cream and hot chocolate.

Melt

59 Ledbury Road, W11 2AA
020 7727 5030
www.meltchocolates.com
Notting Hill LU
Mon-Sat 10am-6.30pm, Sun 11am-4pm

This distinctly chic chocolate boutique, with its cool, white interior and minimal styling, sells a witty and playful range of hand-made chocolate, created by Head Chocolatier Chika Watanabe. Creations range from appealing bars to chocolate caramels.

William Curley

10 Paved Court, Richmond, TW9 1LZ
020 8332 3002
www.williamcurley.com
Richmond LU/Rail
Mon-Sat 9.30am-6.30pm,
Sun 10.30am-6pm

This small, dainty 'boutique' (acclaimed chocolatier and patissier William Curley's first shop) showcases not only William's beautiful patisserie, freshly prepared upstairs, but his own elegant, hand-made chocolates.

South-West

The Hive Honey Shop

93 Northcote Road, SW11 6PL
020 7924 6233
www.thehivehoneyshop.co.uk
Clapham Junction Rail
Mon-Sat 10am-5pm

James Hamill has been promoting the culinary and medicinal virtues of honey from his idiosyncratic Battersea shop for many years. The store comes complete with a five-foot-high, glass-walled bee hive in addition to a huge, ever-changing selection of raw honeys, plus honey-flavoured confectionary.

Rococo

321 King's Road, SW3 5EP
020 7352 5857
www.rococochocolates.com
Sloane Square LU,
then the 11, 19 or 22 bus
Mon 12noon-5pm,
Tues-Sat 10am-6.30pm, Sun 11am-6pm

Quality chocolate pioneer Chantal Coady set up this pretty shop in 1983. On offer here are Rococo's appealingly packaged, stylish in-house chocolates, from hand-made truffles to flavoured bars.

South-East

The London Honey Co.

Unit 6, Dockley Road

www.thelondonhoneycompany.co.uk

Sat 9am-2pm

A pioneer of London's thriving urban honey scene, beekeeper Steve Benbow sells his own delicious urban honeys, both jarred and in honeycomb form.

The Melange

184 Bellenden Road, SE15 4BW

007722 650711

www.themelange.com

Peckham Rye Rail

Wed-Fri 12noon-7pm,
Sat-Sun 10am-6pm

Isabel Alaya's pretty chocolate shop and café offers a range of Isabel's own hand-made chocolate bars and truffles, made using her trademark combinations of flavours.

Rabot Estate

2 Stoney Street, SE1 9AA

020 7403 9852

www.rabotestate.com

London Bridge LU/Rail

Mon-Wed 8am-6pm, Thurs 7.30am-6pm,
Fri 7.30am-6.30pm, Sat 9am-6.30pm

With its mellow 'rum shack' décor, this relaxed shop and café showcases an extensive range of chocolate from St Lucia's Rabot Estate.

East

Montezuma

51 Brushfield Street, E1 6AA

020 7539 9208

www.montezumas.co.uk

Liverpool Street LU/Rail

Mon-11am-4pm, Tues- Sun 10am-6pm

A London outlet for the West Sussex-based chocolate company.

Paul A Young

20 Royal Exchange, EC3V 3LP

020 7929 7007

www.paulayoung.co.uk

Bank LU

Mon-Wed, Fri 9am-6.30pm,
Thurs 9am-7pm

A petite branch of the eponymous chocolatier's business.

Mail Order

Amelia Rope

www.ameliarope.com

Amelia Rope has gained a cult following for her signature, discreetly-packaged, hand-made chocolate bars, subtly flavoured with flavours such as lime and sea salt, rose or spearmint.

Damian Allsop

www.damianallsop.com

Acclaimed patissier and chocolatier Damian Allsop is noted for his innovative and creative chocolates, from his signature water ganache to his Eat London series of flavour-changing bars, reflecting London's cosmopolitan nature through bars such as Chinatown, flavoured with roasted peanut, soy sauce and fresh ginger.

Demarquette Fine Chocolates

www.demarquette.com

Award-winning chocolatier Marc Demarquette is known for his elegant creations, from subtle-flavoured caramels to dainty ganache.

Paul Wayne Gregory

www.paulwaynegregory.com

Talented chocolatier Paul Wayne Gregory is known for his elegant chocolates, among them his award-winning Pure Indulgence range in flavours such as passion fruit and fresh mint.

Sir Hans Sloane

www.sirhanssloane.com

Chocolatier Bill McCarrick, founder of Sir Hans Sloane chocolate company, is a pioneer of the 'bean to bar' approach to chocolate-making, lovingly conching his own chocolate in a conching machine. His chocolate creations range from classic pralines to creative novelties such as his more-ish Sloane Marbles, flavoured, chocolate-coated biscuit balls, which resemble posh Maltesers.

Delicatessens

Owen's Food Store

L ondon's delicatessens range from
small, cosy, family-run shops
which have carved out a loyal, local
following in their neighbourhoods to larger-
scale, distinctly smart establishments
aimed at the affluent. With rents and rates
so high, many of London's delicatessens
increasingly offer a café in addition to a
food shopping experience.

Central

East India Company

🖾 *7-8 Conduit Street, W1S 2XF*
☎ *020 3205 3395*
🖱 *www.theeastindiacompany.com*
🚇 *Oxford Circus LU*
🕐 *Mon-Sat 10am-7pm, Sun 12noon-6pm*

This smart, spacious shop, with its striking
scarlet and black décor takes its inspiration
from the historic East India Company and its
trading activities around the globe. On offer,
therefore, are a handsomely packaged range
of in-house products including an extensive
range of over 100 teas, coffees (freshly
roasted to order), sweet and savoury biscuits,
condiments, high-end jams and marmalades
(including one containing gold leaf), cordials,
sugars and chocolates.

Natural Kitchen

🖾 *77-78 Marylebone High Street, W1U 5JX*
☎ *020 7486 8065*
🖱 *www.thenaturalkitchen.com*
🚇 *Baker Street, Bond Street LU*
🕐 *Mon-Fri 8am-8pm, Sat 9am-7pm,*
   Sun 10am-6pm

Smart and spacious, this store-cum-restaurant
offers an upmarket range of organic and
artisanal foods. The butchers' counter, offering
free-range and organic meat and poultry, is
particularly popular.
Branch: 15-17 New Street, Fetter Lane, EC4

Paul Rothe & Son

🖾 *35 Marylebone Lane, W1U 2NN*
☎ *020 7935 6783*
🚇 *Bond Street LU*
🕐 *Mon-Fri 8am-6pm,*
   Sat 11.30am-5.30pm

This charming, old-fashioned deli-cum-
sandwich bar was established by Paul Rothe in
1900. It remains a family business to this day,
run with affable courtesy by his grandson Paul
Rothe. The shelves are neatly lined with a huge
range of jams and jellies – such as medlar
and mulberry – chutneys and pickles. The
sandwich bar does a roaring lunch-time trade
with fillings such as home-made liptauer or
kummel and Paul's home-made soup.

North

The Hampstead Butcher & Providore

- 56 Rosslyn Hill, NW3 1ND
- 020 7794 9210
- www.hampsteadbutcher.com
- Hampstead LU
- Daily 8.30am-8.30pm

As well as its butchers counter, chef Guy Bossom's smart, spacious delicatessen offers an extensive range of upmarket foodstuffs, from charcuterie to larder items and fine wines, with an impressive range of cheeses stocked in the backroom. Hampstead Heath picnickers are catered for with a smart range of hampers and picnic lunches.

Melrose & Morgan

- 42 Gloucester Avenue, NW1 8JD
- 020 7722 0011
- www.melroseandmorgan.com
- Chalk Farm LU
- Mon-Fri 8am-7pm, Sat 8am -6pm, Sun 9am-5pm

Strikingly housed in a large, high-ceilinged modern space, Ian James's and Nick Selby's contemporary grocers showcases British fare, including a range of own-made traiteur dishes such as savoury tarts, comfort food such as fish pie or shepherds pie and cakes and pastries. In addition, there is a carefully selected range of both fresh and store-cupboard, fine quality foodstuffs, from artisanal breads and seasonal produce to British cheeses and charcuterie

Melrose & Morgan

- Oriel Hall, Oriel Place, NW3 1QN
- 020 7794 6727
- www.melroseandmorgan.com
- Chalk Farm LU
- Mon-Fri 8am-7pm, Sat 8am -6pm, Sun 9am-5pm

This jaunty, smart addition to Hampstead's food scene comes complete with a mezzanine café, in which to sample Melrose and Morgan's high-quality, seasonal own-made dishes. The spacious food shop area is temptingly filled with good things to eat, including artisanal cheeses, own-made salads, traiteur dishes to take home and Emmett's ham.

Ottolenghi

- 287 Upper Street, N1 2TZ
- 020 7288 1454
- www.ottolenghi.co.uk
- Angel, Highbury & Islington LU
- Mon-Sat 8am-11pm, Sun 9am-7pm

An alluring display of beautiful sweet and savoury food attracts a steady stream of customers to this elegant, flagship branch of Ottolenghi's. The shop offers both food-to-go and an airy restaurant in which to sit and eat.

Since opening their first branch, chefs Yotam Ottolenghi and Sami Tamimi have built up a dedicated clientele for their delicious seasonal salads and scrumptious cakes. *Branches: Branches: 63 Ledbury Road, W11; 1 Holland St, W8; 13 Motcomb St, SW1X*

Owen's Food Store

🏠 *92 Alexandria Park Road, N10 2AE*
☎ *020 8374 4444*
🖥 *www.owensfoodstore.co.uk*
🚎 *Muswell Hill Broadway, then bus 109 or 299*
🕐 *Mon-Fri 8am-7.30pm,*
   Sat 8am-6.30pm, Sun 9.30am-4pm

Opened by chef Simon Owen in 2010 on a peaceful Muswell Hill backstreet, this attractive food shop has struck a chord with local residents. Simon sources carefully and discriminatingly, with the fresh meat counter offering organic meat and poultry from Longward Farm and Sutton Hoo a particular source of pride. Farmhouse cheeses, fine charcuterie, Flourish breads, fresh fruit and veg, quality chocolate and 'Staples Corner' with larder basics make it possible to do a one-stop weekly shop here. This is very much a family business, with Simon cooking a popular range of traiteur dishes on the site, his wife Sarah using her creative skills to create the shop's attractive look (look out for her crocheted vegetables adorning the shop!) and a couple of their five sons also working there.

Pomona

🏠 *179 Haverstock Hill, NW3 4QS*
☎ *020 7916 2676*
🖥 *www.pomonafoods.co.uk*
🚎 *Belsize Park LU*
🕐 *Mon-Fri 6am-9pm, Sat-Sun 7am-7pm*

Martin Callaghan's genuinely useful food shop offers an impressive range of stock, from the attractively displayed array of seasonal fruit and veg outside to an array of fresh breads, delivered daily from notable craft bakeries, as well as fresh meat, fresh fish, ready-meals, groceries and organic wines. 'Natural, organic and local' is Martin's sourcing policy and he goes to a lot of trouble to pick food and drink he's proud to sell.

Sourced Market

🏠 *St Pancras International*
   Pancras Road, N1C 4QP
☎ *020 7833 9352*
🖥 *www.sourcedmarket.com*
🕐 *Mon-Fri 7am-9pm*
   Sat 8am-8pm, Sun 9am-8pm

Part of St Pancras International's handsome redevelopment is this smart food shop offering a range of fine quality foodstuffs and tipples. Stock includes Neal's Yard Dairy cheeses, Flour Power City breads, Monmouth Coffee, Brindisa charcuterie, and craft ales from the likes of London Fields Brewery.

West

Chegworth Farm Shop

221 Kensington Church Street W8 7LX
020 7229 3016
www.chegworth.com
Notting Hill LU
Mon-Fri 8am-9pm,
Sat 8am-8pm, Sun 9am-6pm

This rustic shop showcases an attractive range of organic produce from Chegworth Farm in Kent and other small British producers. In addition to Chegworth's famous apples (of which there are around 40 different varieties) Chegworth Farm's organic vegetables, including a wide range of salad leaves, are a popular draw.

The Grocer on Elgin

6 Elgin Crescent, W11 2HX
020 7221 3844
www.thegroceron.com
Ladbroke Grove & Notting Hill Gate LU
Mon-Fri 8am-8pm, Sat-Sun 8am-6pm

This large, sophisticated shop, with a café area at the back, specialises in posh traiteur meals, made from upmarket ingredients, vacuum-packed in stylish microwavable bags.

Harrison's

60 Pittshanger Lane, W5 1QY
020 8998 7866
www.harrisonswines.co.uk
Hanger Lane LU
Mon-Tues 9am-7pm, Wed 9am-8pm,
Fri-Sat 9am-9pm, Sun 11am-4pm

Run by Belinda Harrison, this appealing, family-owned delicatessen comes well stocked with good things to eat and drink: around 70 British and continental cheeses, Flour Station breads, olives and sweet treats. Also on offer is an impressive range of over 400 wines, directly imported by the Harrisons themselves, with Swiss wines a particular speciality.

Jeroboams

96 Holland Park, W11 3RB
020 7727 9359
www.jeroboams.co.uk
Holland Park LU
Mon-Fri 8am-8pm
Sat 9am-7pm, Sun 10am-6pm

In addition to its noted range of wines, this branch of Jeroboams offers a fine and extensive cheese counter and an impressive, wide-ranging selection of deli foods. Stock ranges from sweet and savoury biscuits, oils and vinegars to smoked salmon, blinis and sea urchin caviar.

Mortimer & Bennett

🏠 *33 Turnham Green Terrace, W4 1RG*
☎ *020 8995 4145*
🖥 *www.mortimerandbennett.co.uk*
🚇 *Turnham Green LU*
🕐 *Mon-Fri 8.30am-6pm, Sat 8.30am-5.30pm (also Sundays in December)*

Dan Mortimer's small, well-established shop is crammed with goodies, including 80-100 British and European farmhouse cheeses (many sourced directly), charcuterie, jams and olive oils. Chocolate, confectionary and biscuits are also well represented, with Dan keeping an eagle eye out for new, speciality treats to stock.

Mr Christians

🏠 *11 Elgin Crescent, W11 2JA*
☎ *020 7229 0501*
🖥 *www.mrchristians.co.uk*
🚇 *Notting Hill Gate LU*
🕐 *Mon-Fri 7.30am-6.30pm, Sat 7.30am-6pm, Sun 8am-3pm*

Founded in 1974 by Glyn Christian and Tim Dawson, this well-etablished deli is a local institution. Now owned by Jeroboam's, who have a smart wine shop next door, it does a roaring business selling traiteur dishes such as soups and quiches as well as breads, cheeses, cold meats and a host of treats.

Raoul's

🏠 8-10 Clifton Road, W9 1SZ

☎ 020 7289 6649

🖱 www.raoulsgourmet.com

🚇 Warwick Avenue LU

🕐 Mon-Fri 7.30am-8.30pm
Sat 7.30am-8pm, Sun 8.30am-6pm

Run with flair by Geraldine Leventis this attractive delicatessen, linked to the popular café, has a loyal local following. Spread over two rooms, Raoul's offers an interesting range of good things to eat, both savoury and sweet. The traiteur side is very popular, with customers returning for dishes such as salads, soups and pasta dishes, cheeses and own-made desserts such as tiramisu.

Tavola

🏠 155 Westbourne Grove, W11 2RS

☎ 020 7229 0571

🚇 Notting Hill Gate LU

🕐 Mon-Fri 10am-7.30pm, Sat 10am-6pm

Chef Alistair Little and his wife Sharon have created a delicious food shop, with dishes freshly cooked on the premises, ready to be taken home and enjoyed traiteur-style. The menu is seasonal, so summer brings gazpacho and crab cakes, while winter months see hearty Italian bean soups and pasta sauces. 'We're all about taste,' explains Sharon. There is also a discerningly selected range of groceries and edible treats.

South-West

Bluebird Epicerie

🏠 350 King's Road, SW3 5UU

☎ 020 7559 1140

🖱 www.bluebird-restaurant.com

🚇 Sloane Square LU, then 11, 19, 22, 49 bus

🕐 Mon-Fri 8am-9pm, Sat 9am-8pm,
Sun 9am-6pm

Linked to the elegant Bluebird restaurant, this stylish food shop sells own-baked breads and freshly made traiteur dishes as well as a select range of deli stock.

Brixton Cornercopia

🏠 5 Brixton Village Market,
Coldharbour Lane, SW9 8P2

☎ 07919542233

🖱 www.brixtoncornercopia.ning.com

🚇 Brixton LU/Rail

🕐 Wed 12noon-3pm, Thurs-Sat 12noon-
3pm and 6pm-11.30pm

This tiny corner shop, linked to the popular restaurant, is an advocate of localism, specialising in South London produce, from honey to jams made from locally foraged fruits and Brixton Pound sauce.

Cannon & Cannon

18 Market Row, Brixton Market, SW9 8LD
020 7501 9152
www.cannonandcanon.com
Brixton LU/Rail
Tues-Wed 11am-5.30pm,
Thurs-Sat 11am-10pm, Sun 11am-4pm

A new Brixton Market enterprise from British charcuterie specialists Cannon & Cannon, combining a deli section selling carefully-sourced British cheeses and charcuterie with an upstairs café area in which to sample the wares.

Elizabeth King

34 New King's Road, SW6 4ST
020 7736 2826
www.elizabethking.com
Parsons Green LU
Mon-Wed 8am-8.30pm,
Thurs-Sat 8am-9pm, Sun 8am-8.30pm

In a residential part of Fulham, this well-stocked, upmarket food shop, now linked to Bayley and Sage, offers a one-stop shop, carrying an extensive range of groceries, from basics to indulgences. Stock includes meat and fresh fish from Cornwall, fresh fruit and vegetables, 150 cheeses and charcuterie.

MacFarlane's

48 Abbeville Road, SW4 9NF
020 8673 5373
Clapham Common / Clapham South LU
Mon-Fri 10am-7pm
Sat 9am-6pm, Sun 10am-5pm

Tucked away on a residential Clapham side-street MacFarlane's has been described as 'South London's best-kept secret'. Despite its discreet location, the shop has built up a loyal local following. MacFarlane's is a textbook example of what a neighbourhood deli should be, filled with good things to eat and with the well-stocked cheese counter a particular highlight.

Partridges

2-5 Duke of York Square
King's Road, SW3 4LY
020 7730 0651
www.partridges.co.uk
Sloane Square LU
Daily 8am-10pm

Distinctly upmarket, as befits a business which has a Royal Warrant as Grocers to the Queen. This smart, spacious shop comes complete with a café and wine bar. Partridges offers an extensive range of stock, from grocery staples to luxuries, traiteur dishes and Christmas hampers. Saturdays sees the Partridges Food Market in the square outside the shop.

Partridges

🏠 *17-21 Gloucester Road, SW7 4PL*
☎ *020 7581 0535*
🖥 *www.partridges.co.uk*
🚇 *Gloucester Road LU*
🕐 *Daily 8am-11pm*

A smaller branch of the King's Road establishment, with a particular focus on American foodstuffs.

The Pieman

🏠 *16 Cale Street, SW3 3QU*
☎ *020 7737 7799*
🖥 *www.thepieman.co.uk*
🚇 *Sloane Square LU*
🕐 *Mon-Fri 6.30am-5pm,*
   Sat 6.30am-2.30pm

An appetising savoury smell of baking signals the presence of this small establishment, known locally for its own-baked pastries, own-made 'freezer foods' and snacks.

Rosie's Deli Café

🏠 *14e Market Row, SW9 8LD*
🖥 *www.rosiedelicafe.com*
🚇 *Brixton LU*
🕐 *Mon-Sat 9.30am-5.30pm*

Rosie Lovell's small, mellow café-cum-deli in the heart of Brixton Market has carved out a loyal following. Regulars come by to sample the fresh simple food or to buy foodstuffs – 'a hotch-potch of things we like,' laughs Rosie.

Trinity Stores

🏠 *5-6 Balham Station Road, SW12 9SG*
☎ *020 8673 3773*
🖥 *www.trinitystores.co.uk*
🚇 *Balham LU/Rail*
🕐 *Mon-Fri 9am-8pm,*
   Sat 9.30am-5.30pm, Sun 10am-5pm

Handily positioned for commuters by Balham Station, this relaxed deli-cum-café does a roaring trade. Customers pop in to enjoy a coffee and own-made cake or a light lunch. Stock ranges from fresh bread, cheeses and larder items.

Wild Caper

🏠 *11A-13 Market Row, SW9 8LB*
☎ *020 7737 4410*
🖥 *www.wildcaper.co.uk*
🚇 *Brixton LU*
🕐 *Mon-Sat 10am-5pm*

In a Brixton Market arcade, this austerely stylish deli-cum-café has been set up by Bridget Hugo and Giuseppe Mascol, founders of acclaimed pizzeria Franco Manca, a few doors down. On offer here are a discerningly-chosen, range of good things to eat and drink. Treats include Bread Bread's flavourful, wood oven sourdough breads, excellent Sicilian olive oil and fine Italian wines.

South-East

Bambuni

- 143 Evelina Road, SE15 3HB
- 020 7732 4150
- www.bambuni.co.uk
- Nunhead Rail
- Tues-Fri 9am-7pm,
  Sat 8.30am-6pm, Sun 10am-4pm

Warmly welcomed by locals, this informal deli-cum-café offers a range of carefully sourced food and drink, from cheeses and craft beers to competitively priced Shipton Mills flour. The family-friendly café, serving Volcano coffee and snacks, is a popular draw.

Sourced Market, see p.53

Beamish & McGlue

- 461 Norwood Road, SE27 9DQ
- 020 8761 8099
- www.beamishandmcglue.com
- Mon-Sat 9am-6pm

An exuberant bright blue façade marks this cheerful, unpretentious corner shop, run with friendly hospitality by Antonia Beamish and Casey McGlue. 'A delicious food shop' is Antonia's own description and indeed Beamish & McGlue is crammed with good things to eat and drink: crates of organic fruit and vegetables, artisanal breads, decent bacon, salamis and cheeses, wines sourced from growers. Customers pop in for a chat along with a slice of home-made cake or a sandwich with a coffee.

East Dulwich Deli

- 15-17 Lordship Lane, SE22 8EW
- 020 8693 2525
- www.eastdulwichdeli.com
- East Dulwich Rail
- Mon-Thurs 9am-7pm, Fri 9am-8pm
  Sat 9am -6pm, Sun 10am-4pm

This spacious shop, run by Tony Zuccola, houses an impressive range of foods, from basics to luxuries. Bread is from Born and Bread, the wholesale bakery set up by Tony Zuccola and Tracey Woodward.

El's Kitchen

71 Ladywell Road, SE13 7JA

020 7998 4889

www.elskitchen.co.uk

Ladywell Rail

Tues-Fri 8am-8pm, Sat 8am-6pm,
Sun 9am-4pm

Opened in 2010 by local Ladywell resident El
Thompson, this is, in El's words, 'a posh corner
shop, rather than an expensive deli'. Having
researched what locals would want to buy, El's
Kitchen is crammed with good things to eat, all
carefully chosen by El, from quiches and cakes
(freshly baked in the backroom kitchen) to
cheeses, charcuterie, fresh fruit and veg, wines
and good bread.

Franklin's Farm Shop

155 Lordship Lane,
East Dulwich, SE22 8HX

020 8693 3992

www.frankinsrestaurant.com/farmshop

East Dulwich (Rail)

Mon-Sat 9am-6pm, Sun 10am-5pm

An offshoot of Franklins restaurant next door
this attractive shop showcases ingredients
used in the restaurant kitchen such as fresh
fruit and veg from Kent farms and British
cheeses. Also on offer are ready meals
prepared in the restaurant.

Frog on the Green

119 Consort Road, SE15 3RU

020 7732 2525

www.frogonthegreen.com

Peckham Rye Rail

Mon-Sat 8.30am-7.30pm,
Sun 9am-6.30pm

John Gionleka's pretty, café-cum-deli,
attractively housed in a bright white corner
shop, has a loyal local following. Customers
can sit inside or in the front courtyard
enjoying coffee and sampling cakes, pastries
or savoury dishes such as spinach feta pie.
All the food is freshly made in the kitchen
downstairs and generously served. Also
on offer are a well-chosen range of keenly-
priced deli foods, including excellent olive oils,
charcuterie and dried pasta.

Good Taste Food and Drink

28 Westow Hill, SE19 1RX

020 8761 7455

www.goodtaste-fd.co.uk

Crystal Palace Rail

Mon-Sat 9am-6pm, Sun 11am-4pm

Run with infectious enthusiasm by Manish
Utton-Mishra who set up this shop in 2011,
this small food shop offers a carefully-
chosen range of good quality charcuterie,
craft beers and wines, with pride of place
going to the selection of artisanl cheeses,
Manish's particular passion.

Hills & Parkes

49 Honor Oak Park, SE23 1TB

020 8699 1996

www.hillsandparkes.com

Honor Oak Park Rail

Tues 7am-6.30pm.
Wed-Fri 7.30am-7pm,
Sat 9am-5pm, Sun 10am-4pm

Set up by local residents Emma Ring and Jacqui Roper, this elegantly styled deli focuses on a select range of carefully chosen stock, selling 'a few things we really like', including Emmett's bacon 'with the rind on', Dartmoor Chilli Farm products, a handful of cheeses and Blackbird bakery breads. Home-made cakes, salads, quiches and Egg Boss Scotch eggs are a popular draw, with a small café area offering customers a chance to enjoy a coffee and a snack.

Mimosa

16 Half Moon Lane, SE24 9HU

020 7733 8838

www.mimosafoods.com

Herne Hill Rail

Mon-Fri 9am-6pm,
Sat 9am-5.30pm, Sun 9.30am-2.30pm

This pretty Mediterranean deli-cum-traiteur-cum-café offers good things to eat, from pastries and cakes to own-made salads and dips

Beamish & McGlue

Romeo Jones

🏠 *80 Dulwich Village, SE21 7AJ*
☎ *020 8299 1900*
🖰 *www.romeojones.co.uk*
🚆 *North Dulwich Rail*
🕐 *Mon-Fri 8am-5pm, Sat-Sun 9am-6pm*

As befits its Dulwich Village location, this is a snazzy 'boutique food shop'-cum-café, specialising in artisanal foods from Britain and Italy.

East

A. Gold

🏠 *42 Brushfield Street. E1 6AG*
☎ *020 7247 2487*
🖰 *www.agoldshop.com*
🕐 *Mon-Fri 8am-4pm, Sat-Sun 10am-6pm*

Atmospherically housed in eighteenth-century premises, Philip Cundall's charming shop offers a carefully chosen range of British products with an eye for retro appeal, from Campbell's Tea (in wonderful mustard yellow tins) to sugar mice. Home-made foods to go include popular Scotch eggs and tasty own-made sandwiches.

Albion

🏠 *2-4 Boundary Street. E2 7DD*
☎ *020 7229 1051*
🖰 *www.albioncaff.co.uk*
🚆 *Liverpool Street, Old Street, LU/Rail*
🕐 *Daily 8am-11.30pm*

Located in a Terence Conran restaurant complex, this small, smart shop offers a select range of British foodstuffs. On the shelves can be found an appealing range of breads, cakes, biscuits and pastries – all baked on-site.

The Deli Downstairs

🏠 *211 Victoria Park Road, E9 7JN*
☎ *020 8533 5006*
🚌 *Bus 388*
🕐 *Mon-Tues 9am-5.30pm,*
Wed-9am-6.30pm, Thurs 9am-7pm,
Sat 9am-6pm, Sun 9am-4pm

Having begun life in the basement of The Ginger Pig's butchers Lauriston Road shop – hence the name – this family-run deli has expanded to its own shop, filled with good things to eat and drink. Stock ranges from fundamentals such as good bread and seasonal produce to treats such as Alder Carr 'fruit cream ices' and East End honey.

L'Eau à la Bouche

🏠 *36-37 Broadway Market, E8 4PH*
☎ *020 7923 0600*
🖰 *www.labouche.co.uk*
🚆 *London Fields Rail*
🕐 *Mon-Fri 8.30am-7pm,*
Sat 8.30am-5pm, Sun 9.30am-5pm

In a prime position on this picturesque street, Stephane Cusset's attractive deli-cum-café is hugely popular with locals. Saturdays see it thronging with customers drawn by the market on its doorstep enjoying a cup of quality coffee and a snack. Stock – including charcuterie and cheeses – is carefully chosen.

Food Hall

- 374-378 Old Street, EC1V 9LT
- 020 7729 6005
- Old Street LU
- Mon-Fri 8.30am-7pm,
  Sat-Sun 9.30am-5pm

Housed in a tiled former dairy, Food Hall stocks an expansive range of foods, with the emphasis on quality names such as Daylesford, Ginger Pig, and L'Artisan du Chocolat. A separate room houses British and European cheeses and charcuterie, while a café area caters to hungry customers.

Leila's

- 15-17 Calvert Avenue, E2 7JP
- 020 7729 9789
- Old Street LU/Rail
- Wed-Sat 10am-6pm, Sun 10am-5pm

Just by Arnold Circus, Leila McAlister's relaxed and individualistic shop-cum-café is a much-loved local institution. Spread over two premises, Number 15 (which was once a fruiterers) is now stocked

with an appealingly displayed range of good things to eat, from carefully chosen, seasonal produce to core staples, such as superior couscous. Next door, at Number 17, customers can sit at communal tables enjoying excellent coffee and simple dishes such as fried eggs with sage.

Verde & Co.

- 40 Brushfield Street, E1 6AG
- 020 7247 1924
- www.verde-and-company-ltd.co.uk
- Liverpool Street LU/Rail
- Mon-Fri 8am-8pm, Sat-Sun 11am-5pm

Just by Spitalfields Market, housed in a beautifully restored late eighteenth-century building owned by novelist Jeanette Winterson, Verde's evokes a different era. Boxes of lovingly arranged fruit and vegetables are on display outside and there is a cosy seating area by a stove inside its atmospheric interior. The shop is run with flair and enthusiasm by chef Harvey Cabaniss, who stocks a wide range of delicious treats from handmade chocolates to top-notch Italian staples such as dried pasta and fresh pesto.

Fishmongers

The Chelsea Fishmonger

N owadays, a fishmongers or 'wet fish shop' is all too rare a sight on London's high streets. This is such a shame, as fishmongers are essential for the enjoyment of fresh fish and seafood. Only an experienced fishmonger can ensure high quality fresh fish, as well as fillet and prepare it to your requirements. If you are lucky enough to have a good fishmongers near your work or home, make sure you use them – you'll taste the difference.

Central

The Chelsea Fishmonger

🖼 *10 Cale Street, SW3 3QU*
☎ *020 7589 9432*
🖱 *www.thechelseafishmonger.co.uk*
🚇 *Sloane Square LU*
🕐 *Tues-Fri 9.30am-5.30pm,*
   Sat 9.30am-4pm

Rex Goldsmith is the 'Chelsea Fishmonger'. His small, picturesque Chelsea Green fishmongers, with its tempting counter display of visibly fresh fish and seafood, has a loyal cosmopolitan clientele. From line-caught red mullet to Scottish langoustines, Rex prides himself on sourcing the best possible, seasonal fish and seafood. The majority of his stock comes from British coastal waters from trusted suppliers.

Moxon's

🖼 *17 Bute Street, SW7 3EY*
☎ *020 7591 0050*
🖱 *www.moxonsfreshfish.com*
🚇 *South Kensington LU*
🕐 *Tues-Fri 8.30am-7.30pm*
   Sat 8.30am-5.30pm

This smart, helpful South Kensington fishmongers, is noted for the quality and freshness of its fish and seafood, day boat sourced from around the British coast and much appreciated by the local French community. Stock is distinctly upmarket, ranging from sea trout and Dover sole to grocery stock including Japanese sushi ginger, Ortiz tuna, saffron and bottaraga.

North

Harry's Fine Food

🖼 *258 Kentish Town Road, NW5 2AA*
☎ *020 7485 0346*
🚇 *Kentish Town LU/Rail*
🕐 *Tues-Sat 9am-6pm*

This friendly, well-established shop, unusually combines a fishmongers with a butchers. It has an excellent range of carefully sourced, choice fish. Stock ranges from basics like herring and mackerel to upmarket fish such as turbot, wild sea bass and prime smoked salmon.

The Fishery

🏠 111 Stoke Newington High Street,
N16 0PH
☎ 020 7923 9471
🖥 www.the-fishery.co.uk
🚉 Rectory Road Rail
🕐 Mon-Sat 8am-6pm

An eye-catching display of carefully sourced fresh fish and seafood marks this friendly, family-run, Stoke Newington fishmongers.

France Fresh Fish

🏠 99 Stroud Green Road, N4 3PX
☎ 020 7263 9767
🚉 Finsbury Park LU/Rail
🕐 Mon-Sat 9am-7pm, Sun 11am-5pm

An eye-catching window display of brightly coloured tropical fish is an attractive feature of this long-established fish-shop. It is owned by the same Mauritian family who run the Chez Liline restaurant next door. Staff are friendly and happy to offer advice on the exotic stock.

Hampstead Seafoods

🏠 78 Hampstead High Street, NW3 1RE
☎ 020 7435 3966
🚉 Hampstead LU
🕐 Tues-Fri 7.30am-5pm, Sat 7.30am-4pm

Tucked away off the High Street, this small shop offers a good range of quality seafood.

Steve Hatt

🏠 88-90 Essex Road, N1 8LU
☎ 020 7226 3963
🚉 Angel LU
🕐 Tues-Thurs 8am-5pm, Fri-Sat 7am-5pm

An Islington institution, this popular fishmonger is knowledgeably run by Steve Hatt. There's an excellent range of fresh fish – everything from herring to swordfish – and the shop is also known for its own-smoked fish. Such is its following, that there is normally a queue waiting patiently.

La Petite Poissonnerie

🏠 75 Gloucester Avenue, NW1 8LD
☎ 020 7387 6101
🖥 www.lapetitpoissonerie.co.uk
🚉 Chalk Farm LU
🕐 Tues-Sat 9.30am-7.30pm,
Sun 10.30am-5.30pm

Nic Rascle's upmarket fishmongers, which comes complete with an eye-catching boat-shaped display-case, offers a fine selection of prime fish and has a loyal local following. Stock extends to Japanese groceries, reflecting the fact that Nic's wife is Japanese, with sushi classes also on offer. Knowledgeable and affable, Nic, who is also a chef, is happy to offer advice and cooking suggestions.

Poisson

7 Station Parade, Cockfosters Rd, EN4 0DL

020 8449 0335

www.poissonfish.com

Cockfosters LU

Tues-Sat 8am-5pm

A smart family-run fishmongers, established in 1959, offering an excellent assortment of fish and seafood, including luxuries such as monkfish, raw clams and scallops. Staff are helpful and are happy to take orders in advance.

Walter Purkis & Sons

17 The Broadway, N8 8DU

020 8340 6281

www.purkis4fish.com

Finsbury Park LU/Rail, then the W7 bus

Tues-Sat 8.30am-5pm

Right in the middle of Crouch End's bustling Broadway, this friendly, family-run fishmongers sells a great range of fish and seafood, including own-smoked fish smoked in the shop's own, veteran smokehouse, and has a loyal local following

Walter Purkis & Sons

52 Muswell Hill Broadway, N10 3RT

020 8883 4355

www.purkis4fish.com

Highgate LU, then 134 bus

Tues-Sat 8.30am-5pm

The Muswell Hill branch of a family-run fishmongers, offering an excellent range of fish and seafood including own-smoked fish smoked in the Crouch End smokehouse.

A. Scott & Son

94 High Road, N2 9EB

020 8444 7606

East Finchley LU

Tues-Sat 7.30am-6pm

This small, friendly fishmongers has a great range of fresh fish and seafood.

West

Copes Seafood Company

700 Fulham Road, SW6 5SJ

020 7371 7300

Fulham Broadway LU

Mon-Sat 9am-7.30pm, Sun 12noon-6pm

The sheer quality of the fresh, Cornish-caught fish on offer here has gained this fishmongers a notable reputation and loyal local following.

Covent Garden Fishmongers

- 37 Turnham Green Terrace, W4 1RG
- 020 8995 9273
- www.coventgardenfishmongers.co.uk
- Turnham Green LU
- Tues-Wed & Fri-Sat 8am-5.30pm
  Thurs 8am-5pm

Despite small premises, veteran fishmonger Phil Diamond's shop stocks a great range of upmarket fish and seafood, from monkfish and sea bass to clams and langoustines.

The Fish Shop

- 201 Kensington Church Street, W8 7LX
- 020 7243 6626
- Notting Hill LU
- Tues-Fri 9am-7pm, Sat 9am-5pm

This sleek annexe to the Kensington Place restaurant sells a select range of North Sea fish, plus tuna and swordfish. The majority of the fish is delivered from Cornwall fresh and whole, before being filleted on the premises.

Golborne Fisheries

- 75 Golborne Road, W10 5NP
- 020 8960 3100
- Ladbroke Grove LU
- Tues-Sat 8am-6pm

This bustling fish shop is a local institution, always busy with customers. The range of stock is enormous, from sea bass and bream to parrot fish, and prices are reasonable.

La Maree

- 76 Sloane Avenue, SW3 3DZ
- 020 7589 8067
- South Kensington LU
- Mon-Sat 8am-6pm, Sun 12noon-5pm

This tiny annexe of the Poisonnerie restaurant sells a small but select range of seafood, such as langoustines and scallops in their shells. Prices are high but so is the quality and the staff are very willing to offer advice and prepare the fish exactly to your requirements.

Poisson

- Unit 3, Devonshire House,
  201-211 Northfield Avenue, W13 9QU
- 020 8567 4507
- www.poisson-ltd.co.uk
- Northfields LU
- Open Tues-Fri 9am-6pm, Sat 9am-4pm

Simon Osborne's small, white-tiled fishmongers, established in 2009, carries a good range of upmarket fish and seafood, sourced predominantly from the British coast. In addition, ready-made fish dishes such as Poisson's popular, home-made fish pie or coquilles St Jacques (ready to bake at home), go down well with customers looking for a meal to go. There is also a small but useful range of foodstuffs, including fresh produce (such as parsley, fennel and leeks), French fish soup and fish stock.

South-West

Moxon's

- Westbury Parade, Nightingale Lane, SW4
- 020 8675 2468
- www.moxonsfreshfish.com
- Clapham South LU
- Tues-Fri 9am-8pm, Sat 9am-6pm

Right by Clapham South tube, Robin Moxon's immaculate, white-tiled fishmongers, much appreciated by locals, sells an excellent, upmarket range of carefully sourced fish. Stock ranges from sardines and mackerel to rod-and-line-caught sea bass, 'unsoaked scallops', razor clams and oysters.

South Coast Fisheries

- Northcote Road (corner of Shelgate Rd)
- Mon-Sat 9am-4pm

A fish van addition to Northcote Road's food stalls, offering an upmarket range of fish and seafood, from brown shrimps and scallops to sea bass and sea bream at competitive prices.

Sandys

- 56 King Street, TW1 3SH
- 020 8892 5788
- www.sandysfish.net
- Twickenham Rail
- Mon-Wed & Sat 7.30am-6pm, Thurs 7.30am-8pm, Fri 7.30am-7pm, Sun 9am-5pm

This large fishmonger, a well-established, family-run Twickenham institution, impresses with its range of stock. The shop's ethos is summed up by a tiled sign on the walls which reads, 'Welcome to Sandys where only the best is good enough'. Halibut, sea bass and langoustines sit alongside jellied eels and cod roes. Sandys also offers a range of poultry.

South-East

Billings

- 45 Sydenham Road, SE26 5EX
- 020 8659 2781
- www.shopbillings.co.uk
- Sydenham Rail
- Mon-Fri 9am-6.30pm, Sat 9am-5pm

This friendly shop enterprisingly offers both a range of fresh meat and fresh fish as well.

Coquillage

- 50 Tranquil Vale, SE3 0BD
- 020 8318 9982
- www.coquillage.co.uk
- Blackheath Rail
- Tues-Thurs 10am-5.30pm.
  Fri-Sat 9am-5.30am, Sun 11am-4.30pm

A small, pretty fishmongers offering a select range of fresh fish and seafood, sourced from British coastal waters, as well as smoked fish.

The Fishmonger

- The Rear of 26 Royal Hill, SE10 8RT
- 07880 541 485
- www.thefishmongerltd.com
- Greenwich Rail
- Tues-Sat 8.30am-5pm

Julian Pryke's snazzy, contemporary Greenwich fishmongers offers not only a range of high-quality seasonal fish and seafood, but other good things to eat – from condiments to fresh bread and herbs. Advice and recipe suggestions are happily offered.

Moxon's

- 149 Lordshop Lane, SE22 8HX
- 020 8299 1559
- www.moxonsfreshfish.com
- East Dulwich Rail
- Tues-Sat 9am-5.30pm

An attractive shop with impressively fresh fish and helpful staff. Robin Moxon sources prime fish and seafood caught around the British coast, from mackerel to plump crabs.

F.C. Soper

- 141 Evelina Road, SE15 3HB
- 020 7639 9729
- www.fcsoper.com
- Nunhead Rail
- Tues-Fri 9am-5.30pm
  Sat 8.30am-5.30pm, Sun 9am-2pm

This established fishmongers has a loyal following. The prime fresh fish is the draw, carefully sourced (much of it from Cornish day boats) and knowledgeably sold. Stock ranges from fish heads for stock to upmarket sea bass and scallops. Staff are friendly and happy to offer advice.

Whittakers

- 326 Norwood Road, SE27 9AF
- 07518 808 241
- www.whittakers.net
- West Norwood Rail
- Tues 9am-6pm, Thurs 9am-4.30pm,
  Fri-Sat 9am-5pm

Pauline Ivaldi runs this popular fishmongers with an infectious zest for fish and seafood, offering advice and recipe suggestions alongside a good range of fresh and smoked fish and seafood.

East

Fin and Flounder

📇 *71 Broadway Market, E8 4PH*
☎ *0783 8018395*
🖥 *www.finandflounder.com*
🚋 *London Fields Rail*
🕐 *Tues-Fri 10am-6.30pm, Sat 9am-5pm*

In a prime spot on Broadway Market, this friendly, contemporary fishmongers prides itself on offering sustainably-sourced fish and seafood. Advice and recipe suggestions are happily offered.

Jonathan Norris of Pimlico

📇 *207 Victoria Park Road, E9 JN*
☎ *020 8525 8999*
🖥 *www.jonathannorrisfishmonger.com*
🚋 *London Fields Rail*
🕐 *Tues-Fri 10am-7pm, Sat 9am-5pm*
　 Sun 12am-4pm

Jonathan's smart new fishmongers offers an excellent range of fish and seafood, with the focus on fish sourced direct from Cornwall. Stock ranges from hake and gurnard to lobsters, clams and sea urchins, as well as offering smoked fish, sauces and herbs. In a nod to his East End location, Jonathan also stocks jellied eels, cockles and winkles – particularly popular with Sunday shoppers.

Food Halls

The People's Supermarket

London's food halls range from grand, vintage establishments such as Fortnum and Mason to the stylish contemporary setting of Harvey Nichols. In recent years, a new take on the food hall concept is being offered by shops such as Greensmiths, just by Waterloo Station, aiming to give the high street food shopping experience under one roof, and The People's Supermarket, which offers a convenient, ethical alternative to supermarkets.

Central

Fortnum & Mason

181 Piccadilly, W1J 9EH
020 7734 8040
www.fortnumandmason.com
Piccadilly Circus LU
Mon-Sat 10am-9pm, Sun 12noon-6pm

Established in 1707, this grand, spacious store has long been noted for its upmarket foods and delicacies. An extensive range of foods is carried with the emphasis on quality and provenance, from prime fresh meat in the basement to invitingly packaged treats such as chocolates, biscuits, honeys and jams on the ground floor. Small British producers, from cheesemakers to biscuit producers, are well represented and traditional touches, such as the fact that one can buy whole pieces of assorted candied peel, are another appealing aspect. The in-house eateries range from a wine bar to a tea-room, offering shoppers a chance to sit and revive themselves.

Greensmiths

27 Lower Marsh, SE1 7RG
020 7921 2970
www.greensmithsfood.co.uk
Waterloo LU
Mon-Fri 8am-8pm, Sat 8am-6pm

Handsomely housed in a corner site, just a short distance from Waterloo Station, Greensmiths' aim is to offer the convenience of a supermarket combined with the quality and service of an old-fashioned high street. Owner Chris Smith has gathered together an impressive range of partners under one roof including butchers Ginger Pig, The Old Post Office Baker, Antica Coffee, fresh produce wholesalers Solstice and Waterloo Wine – all spaciously represented here. General grocery stock and a café serving up food freshly prepared on the premises complete the picture.

Harrods

- *87 Brompton Road, SW1X 7XL*
- *020 7730 1234*
- *www.harrods.com*
- *Knightsbridge LU*
- *Mon-Sat 10am-8pm, Sun 11-8pm*

The beautiful food halls – some complete with vintage tiling – recall Harrods' roots as a grocers and tea merchants. As one would expect, the range of foodstuffs stocked is enormous: from the eye-catching fresh fish display to exotic fruits and vegetables. Highlights of a visit to Harrods include the extensive charcuterie and cheese counters. There is an extensive selection of packaged foods with many exclusive brands including Harrods own label.

Harvey Nichols Food Hall

- *Knightsbridge, SW1X 7RJ*
- *020 7235 5000*
- *www.harveynichols.com*
- *Knightsbridge LU*
- *Mon-Sat 10am-8pm, Sun 12noon-6pm*

This stylish food hall, with its high-tech marketplace feel, offers an upmarket range of high-end food and drink.

John Lewis

- *Oxford Street. W1A 1EX*
- *020 7629 7711*
- *www.johnlewis.com*
- *Oxford Circus*
- *Mon-Sat 9.30am-8pm, Sun 12noon-6pm*

Housed in the basement, this roomy Waitrose foodhall offers a useful range of foodstuffs, including fresh fish, meat and poultry and fruit and vegetables. Particularly appealing elements include the range of breads and pastries and the aromatic walk-in cheese room.

Selfridges

- *400 Oxford Street, W1A 1AB*
- *0800 123 400*
- *Bond Street LU Marble Arch LU*
- *Mon-Sat 9.30am-10pm, Sun 10am-9pm*

Smart and spacious, the food hall at Selfridges reflects its cosmopolitan clientele with an impressively international range, from groceries to a globetrotting assortment of ready meals. From fundamentals such as meat, seafood and produce to treats such as Pierre Herme macaroons or artisanal chocolates, the emphasis is on quality food and drink.

The People's Supermarket

72-78 Lamb's Conduit Street, WC1 3LP

020 74301827/3

www.thepeoplessupermarket.org

Holborn/Russell Square LU

Mon-Sat 10am-8pm, Sun 10am-9pm

A social enterprise in retail form, this friendly, down-to-earth food shop was founded in 2010 with the aim of addressing the issue of the impact of supermarkets and empty shops on high streets. It is run as a co-op by its members, all of whom contribute time working in the shop, although you don't have to a member to shop here. While very much focused on being an accessible community shop, carrying everyday items, the stock is also selected with healthy and ethical criteria in mind, so, for example, alongside Coca Cola one finds Fairtrade Ubuntu and organic cola. A highlight is the extensive range of reasonably-priced fresh fruits and vegetables, ranging from curly cucumbers and various tomato varieties to Wye Valley asparagus, samphire and wild mushrooms. Food to go, such as soups and pasta bakes, freshly cooked each day in the on-site kitchen, is another popular draw.

Greengrocers

Andreas

S adly, traditional greengrocers are increasingly a rare sight on our high streets. A good greengrocer filled with carefully displayed fresh fruits and vegetables – with that wonderful scent of fruit in the air – is to be treasured

Andreas

- *4 Cale Street, SW3 3QU*
- *020 7589 5775*
- *www.andreasveg.com*
- *Sloane Square LU*
- *Mon-Fri 8am-5.30pm, Sat 8am-4pm*

This elegantly rustic greengrocers, a welcome addition to Chelsea Green's parade of independent shops, was opened by Andreas Georghiou, who thinks that this is the first time a new greengrocers has opened in Chelsea for decades. The attractively arranged stock features seasonal delights carefully and knowledgeably sourced by Andreas, from frais du bois, English asparagus and a wonderful array of tomatoes to quinces and wild mushrooms with helpful staff happy to offer advice.

Andreas

- *35 Turnham Green Terrace, W4 1PW*
- *020 8995 0140*
- *www.andreasveg.com*
- *Turnham Green LU*
- *Mon-Fri 8am-6pm, Sat 8am-5.15pm*

Very much a local institution, Andreas Georghiou's friendly, helpful greengrocers shop is noted for the range of produce and the quality. Sand-grown carrots, Roscoff carrots, coloured beetroots, sea vegetables – the list could go on. Andreas, Sophia and Darren are happy to help and offer guidance.

Blandford Fruit Store

- *25 Blandford Street, W1U 3DN*
- *020 7935 4262*
- *Bond Street LU*
- *Mon-Sat 9am-5pm*

A small, neat, green-painted greengrocer, run by Arif Halil, offering fresh produce and helpful service.

Clocktower Store

- *2 The Broadway, N8 9TP*
- *020 8348 7845*
- *Finsbury Park LU/Rail, then the W7 bus*
- *Mon-Fri 8.30am-7pm,*
  Sat 8.30am-6pm, Sun 10am-5pm

This well-established, bustling Cypriot greengrocer, just by Crouch End's landmark Clock Tower, offers an excellent range of seasonal produce, from bunches of fresh herbs to cherries, peaches and apricots.

D. McKay (Fruiterers) Ltd

🏠 *19A Harrington Road, SW7 3ES*
☎ *020 7584 1929*
🚇 *South Kensington LU*
🕐 *Mon-Sat 8am-5.30pm*

An upmarket range of fresh fruit, veg and take-away freshly squeezed juices are on offer at this down-to-earth establishment.

Michanicou Brothers

🏠 *2 Clarendon Road, W11 3AA*
☎ *020 7727 5191*
🚇 *Holland Park LU*
🕐 *Mon-Fri 9am-6.30pm, Sat 9am-5.30pm*

This long-established greengrocers, crammed with fresh produce, is known for both the range and quality of its stock. Service is brisk and knowledgeable.

Mrs Lovell's Greengrocer

🏠 *28 Highbury Park, N5 2AA*
🚇 *Arsenal LU*
🕐 *Mon-Sat 8am-6pm, Sun 8am-4pm*

A useful addition to the area's food shops, this offers a good range of fresh fruits and vegetables.

Newington Green Fruit and Veg

🏠 *109 Newington Green Road, N1 4QY*
☎ *020 7354 0990*
🚇 *Canonbury Rail*
🕐 *Daily 8am-10pm*

Down-to-earth and unpretentious, this well-established greengrocers is filled with a truly impressive range of fresh vegetables, fruits and herbs, from everyday basics such as onions and potatoes, to exotic novelties such as lemon grass or mangosteens. Prices are remarkably reasonable, service is friendly and efficient and the shop has a loyal local following, with customers waiting patiently in the invariable queue to be served.

Two Peas in a Pod

🏠 *85 Church Road, SW13 9HH*
☎ *020 8748 0232*
🚇 *Barnes Bridge Rail*
🕐 *Mon-Sat 7am-5.30pm, Sun 10am-1pm*

With its enticing display of fresh fruit and vegetables outside and array of fresh, upmarket produce inside the shop and friendly, helpful service, this fine example of an independent greengrocers has a loyal local following within Barnes.

Yeomans

🏠 *152 Regent's Park Road, NW1 8XN*
☎ *020 7722 4281*
🚇 *Chalk Farm LU*
🕐 *Mon-Sat 8am-7pm, Sun 10am-6pm*

A pretty and upmarket greengrocers-cum-juice bar, as befits its Primrose Hill location.

Earth Natural Foods

Health Food Shops

Nowadays, health foods and organic foods have become mainstream. London's health food shop scene features both veteran independents, such as the Haelan Centre in Crouch End to major retail chains such as Planet Organic and Daylesford Organic. Increasingly these stores act as alternative supermarkets, offering the opportunity for customers to do all their grocery shopping under one roof.

Central

Alara Wholefoods

- 58-60 Marchmont Street, WC1N 1 AB
- 020 7837 1172
- www.alarashop.com
- Russell Square LU
- Mon-Fri 9am-8pm, Sat 10am-7pm Sun 11am-6pm

Tucked away on a Bloomsbury side-street, this well-established, independent shop-cum-café offers an excellent range of foodstuffs, including Alara's well-known, own-brand muesli.

Planet Organic

- 22 Torrington Place, WC1E 7HJ
- 020 7436 1929
- www.planetorganic.com
- Goodge Street LU
- Mon-Fri 7.30am-9pm, Sat 9am-8pm, Sun 12noon-6pm

A large branch of Planet Organic, complete with a juice-bar and café area offering organic, vegan and vegetarian food.

Whole Foods Market

- 20 Glasshouse Street, W1B 5AR
- 020 7406 3100
- www.wholefoodsmarket.com
- Piccadilly Circus LU
- Mon-Fri 7.30am-9.30pm, Sat 9am-9.30pm, Sun 10am-9pm

A huge new West End store from the American chain, characteristically spacious and comprehensive, offering everything from fresh, organic produce to hand-rolled sushi.

Whole Foods Market

- The Barkers Building 63-97 Kensington High Street, W8 5SE
- 020 7368 4500
- www.wholefoodsmarket.com
- High Street Kensington LU
- Mon-Sat 8am-10pm, Sun 12noon-8pm

Housed in what was formerly Barkers department store, this flagship London store of the American health food chain is vast. It carries a correspondingly comprehensive stock of 'natural and organic' foodstuffs as well as an eat-in foodhall.

North

Bumblebee

⬚ *30, 32 & 33 Brecknock Road, N7 0BT*
☎ *020 7607 1936*
🖰 *www.bumblebeenaturalfoods.co.uk*
🚌 *Kentish Town LU/Rail, then the 393 bus*
🕐 *Mon-Sat 9am-6.30pm*

Spread out over a stretch of Brecknock Road, this long-established trio of shops – the Veg Shop, the Bakery and the Nut Shop – offers an excellent range of health foods, from fresh organic produce to vegetarian cheeses. Staff are friendly and helpful.

Earth Natural Foods

⬚ *200 Kentish Town Road, NW5 2AE*
☎ *020 7482 2211*
🖰 *www.earthnaturalfoods.co.uk*
🚌 *Kentish Town LU / Rail*
🕐 *Mon-Sat 8.30am-7pm*

A pleasant, spacious organic food shop, offering an impressive range of organic, vegan, biodynamic, gluten-free and wheat-free products. Staff are friendly and helpful.

Haelan Centre

⬚ *41 The Broadway, N8 8DT*
☎ *020 8340 4258*
🖰 *www.haelan.co.uk*
🚌 *Finsbury Park LU, then W7 bus*
🕐 *Mon-Sat 9am-6pm, Sun 12noon-4pm*

Just by Crouch End's Clock Tower, this corner shop is very much a local institution. The ground floor shop sells fresh organic produce and health-food groceries ranging from goat's milk to honey, while upstairs there is a health clinic.

Haelan Centre

⬚ *304 Park Road, N8*
☎ *020 8340 1720*
🖰 *www.haelan.co.uk*
🚌 *Finsbury Park LU, then the W7 bus*
🕐 *Mon-Sat 9am-6pm, Sun 12noon-4pm*

A branch of the established Crouch End health food institution, housed in an old-fashioned parade of shops at the foot of Muswell Hill.

Planet Organic

⬚ *64 Essex Road, N1 8LR*
☎ *020 7288 9460*
🖰 *www.planetorganic.com*
🚌 *Angel LU*
🕐 *Mon-Sat 8am-9pm, Sun 9am-9pm*

A branch of the organic supermarket chain.

Planet Organic

111-117 Muswell Hill Road, N10

020 8452 2910

www.planetorganic.com

Highgate LU, then 134 bus

Mon-Fri 8am-9pm
Sat 8.30am-9pm, Sun 10am-3pm

A branch of the organic supermarket chain.

Whole Foods Market

49 Parkway, NW1 7PN

020 7428 7575

www.wholefoodsmarket.com

Camden Town LU

Mon-Sat 8am-9pm, Sun 9am-9pm

A popular branch of the Whole Foods chain.

Whole Foods Market

32-40 Stoke Newington Church St,
N16 0LU

020 7254 2332

www.wholefoodsmarket.com

Stoke Newington Rail

Mon-Sat 8am-9pm, Sun 9am-9pm

A spacious branch of the Whole Foods chain.

North-West

The Organic Grocer

17 Clifton Road, W9 1SY

020 7286 1400

Warwick Avenue

Mon-Sat 8.30am-8.30pm,
Sun 10am-7pm

With its pale blue shelving and an attractive display of flowers, this pretty, well-established organic shop suits its Little Venice setting. Stock, as the name suggests, is predominantly organic, including Rhug Estate meat, organic fruit and veg, traiteur dishes and a range of store-cupboard staples.

West

As Nature Intended

201 Chiswick High Road, W4 2DR

020 8742 8838

www.asnatureintended.uk.com

Turnham Green LU

Mon-Fri 9am-8pm, Sat 9am-7pm,
Sun 10.30am-6.30pm

An 'organic supermarket' offering a comprehensive range of organic foodstuffs.

As Nature Intended

🏠 *17-21 High Street, W5 5DB*

☎ *020 8840 1404*

🖱 *www.asnatureintended.uk.com*

🚇 *Ealing Broadway*

🕐 *Mon-Fri 9am-8pm, Sat 9am-7pm,*
Sun 11am-6pm

A large, neatly-arranged shop offering a comprehensive range of organic foodstuffs.

Daylesford Organic

🏠 *208-212 Westbourne Grove, W11 2RH*

☎ *020 7313 8050*

🚇 *Notting Hill LU*

🕐 *Mon-Sat 8.30am-7pm, Sun 10am-4pm*

An elegant, spacious establishment housing a restaurant, café and shop offering a tasteful and upmarket range of organic foods.

Planet Organic

🏠 *42 Westbourne Grove, W2*

☎ *020 7221 7171*

🖱 *www.planetorganic.com*

🚇 *Bayswater LU, Queensway LU*

🕐 *Mon-Sat 7.30am-9pm,*
Sun 12noon-6pm

Planet Organic's first and largest store sells everything for a healthy lifestyle, from fresh juices at the juice bar to organic muesli. There is a large grocery section, a seafood and butchers counter, and a particularly extensive fresh produce section.

South-West

As Nature Intended

🏠 *186-188 Balham High Road, SW12 9BP*

☎ *020 8675 2923*

🚇 *Balham LU*

🕐 *Mon-Fri 9am-8pm, Sat 9am-7pm,*
Sun 10.30am-6.30pm

An established organic supermarket offering a wide selection of health foods.

Brixton Wholefoods Transatlantic

🏠 *59 Atlantic Road, SW9 8PU*

☎ *020 7737 2210*

🖱 *www.brixtonwholefoods.com*

🚇 *Brixton LU*

🕐 *Mon 9.30am-7pm, Tues-Thurs & Sat*
9.30am-5.30pm, Fri 9.30am-6pm

This well-established shop, founded in 1982, has a loyal following and is a friendly, laid-back establishment, so-named because its former premises were on the other side of Atlantic Road. Stock is extensive, from grains, nuts and pulses to a popular self-serve selection of around 350 herbs and spices (organic and non-organic).

Dandelion Foods

- 120 Northcote Road, SW11 6QU
- 020 7350 0902
- www.dandeliononline.co.uk
- Clapham Junction Rail
- Mon-Sat 9am-6pm, Sun 11am-4pm

Long established, this narrow shop is crammed with health foods, from a full range of Dove flours to organic baby foods. Lunchtime customers come by for the vegan, gluten-free soup, vegetarian lasagne and gluten-free cakes – all cooked in the kitchen at the back.

Daylesford Organic

- 44B Pimlico Road, SW1W 8LP
- 020 7881 8060
- www.daylesfordorganic.com
- Pimlico LU
- Mon-Sat 8am-8pm, Sun 11am-5pm

In an appropriately select neighbourhood, Daylesford's elegant white shop offers a ground-floor café area, bakery, grocery and basement butchers selling organic meat.

Whole Foods Market

- 305-311 Lavender Hill, SW11 1LN
- 020 7585 1488
- www.wholefoodsmarket.com
- Clapham Junction Rail
- Mon-Fri 9am-9pm,
  Sat 8.30am-7.30pm, Sun 12noon-6pm

This large branch of the US-based organic food specialists offers a characteristically extensive range of foodstuffs.

Here

- Chelsea Farmers Market
  125 Sydney Street, SW3 6NR
- 020 7351 4321
- Sloane Square LU
- Mon-Sat 9.30am-8pm,
  Sun 10am-6.30pm

A distinctly stylish health food shop, as befits its Chelsea setting. On offer is an attractively displayed range of organic foods.

Oliver's Wholefood Store

- 5 Station Approach, TW9 3PT
- 020 8948 3990
- www.oliverswholefoods.co.uk
- Kew Gardens LU
- Mon-Sat 9am-7.30pm,
  Sun 10am-7.30pm

This attractive airy shop boasts an impressive overall stock, including an excellent selection of fresh organic produce. Shelves offer an extensive range of groceries, from fundamentals such as organic grains and pulses to treats such as organic chocolate. Staff are friendly and helpful and the shop has a deservedly loyal local following.

South-East

Baldwin's Health Food Centre

- 171-73 Walworth Road, SE17
- 020 7703 5550
- www.baldwins.co.uk
- Elephant & Castle LU
- Mon-Sat 9am-6pm, Thurs 9am-7pm

A South London institution, this established business, founded in 1844, carries a truly impressive range of herbals remedies. They also have a good general organic and health food stock. Staff are knowledgeable, helpful and friendly, which may help explain why the business has thrived for so long.

SMBS Foods

- 75 Lordship Lane, SE22 8EP
- 020 8693 7792
- East Dulwich Rail
- Mon-Fri 9am-6.30pm,
  Sat 9am-6pm, Sun 10am-4.30pm

Kash Rao's splendidly eclectic shop has been selling organic foods since 1985. Stock ranges from fresh fruit and vegetables to grains and pulses, spices, ice cream, dairy products, meat and poultry. The stock is impressively wide-ranging and globe-trotting.

East

The Grocery

- 54-56 Kingsland Road, E2 8DP
- 020 7729 6855
- www.thegroceryshop.co.uk
- Liverpool Street/Old Street LU
- Mon-Sun 8am-10pm

The Grocery carries an extensive range of organic and Fairtrade foodstuffs and household goods. Under the vaulted ceilings, stock ranges from chilled organic soups and tofu to assorted coffees. An organic café area completes the picture.

Unpackaged at Arthaus

- 197 Richmond Road, E8 3NJ
- 020 8986 7933
- www.beunpackaged.com
- Mon-Sat 9am-8pm, Sun 9am-4pm
  Café/Bar: Mon 9am-8pm,
  Tues-Sat 9am-11pm, Sun 9am-10pm
- London Fields Rail

This new Hackney incarnation of Catherine Conway's much-loved, food shop comes complete with a café and aims to offer a social community hub. The shop ethos is to cut down on unnecessary food packaging by encouraging customers to bring their own containers and fill them with the carefully chosen range of good things to eat and drink.

Ice Cream

HERE COMES THE SUN... ?!
ENJOY IT IN STYLE!
AWOOOOOO!
GELUPO

Gelupo

Once it was hard to find good ice cream in the capital; a recent ice cream boom, however, has changed all that. Across London, artisanal ice cream businesses are being set up in a variety of forms, from experimental 'ice cream labs' to smart chains.

Amorino London

▢ *41 Old Compton Street, W1D 6HF*
✎ *www.amorino.com*
🚇 *Leicester Square or Piccadilly Circus LU*
☺ *Mon-Sat 11am-11pm, Sun 12noon-9pm*

This smart gelateria–cum–café (a London branch of an international chain) offers high-quality Italian–style ice cream. Flavours are classic – such as melon, pistachio or stracciatella (chocolate chip) and can be enjoyed in cups, cones or sandwiched in focaccine (brioche buns).
Branch: 67A King's Road, SW3 4NT

Chin-Chin Labs

▢ *49-50 Camden Lock Place, NW1 8AF*
📞 *07885 604284*
✎ *www.chinchinlabs.com*
🚇 *Camden Town LU*
☺ *Tues-Sun 12noon-7pm*

Tucked away in Camden Lock Market, Chin Chin Labs – with its playful laboratory-esque styling – is 'Europe's first nitro ice cream parlour'. Showmanship and entertainment is part of the package here, as owners Ahrash and Nyisha freshly make up each ice cream order, freezing it dramatically with liquid nitrogen. The results are notably smooth-textured ice creams, which can be topped with assorted toppings. Flavours range from classic Valrhona chocolate and Madagascan Vanilla to invented, innovative weekly creations such as basil choc chip.

Gelupo

▢ *7 Archer Street, W1D 7AU*
📞 *020 7287 5555*
✎ *www.gelupo.com*
🚇 *Piccadilly Circus LU*
☺ *Mon-Thurs 12noon-11pm,*
  Fri-Sat 12noon-12midnight,
  Sun 12noon-10pm

Set up by acclaimed Italian restaurant Bocca di Lupo (just over the road), this tiny gelateria, hidden away down a Soho side-street, offers an alluring range of in-house freshly-made gelati, sorbeti and granite. Quality is at the heart of the operation, from carefully sourced ingredients to the production in small batches, using a Cattabriga machine in order to create the desired texture. The range is of around 16 flavours, from classics such as the blood orange sorbet or hazelnut, to innovative, seasonally-inspired flavours such as rhubarb crumble, summer pudding or ricotta and sour cherry.

La Grotta Ices

Unit 12, Bermondsey Spa Terminus
between Spa Road and
Dockley Road, SE16
Sat 9am-2pm

Kitty Travers of La Grotta Ices has a cult following for her imaginative, exquisite fresh ices, noted for their bright, intense flavours, made in small batches from seasonal fruits and ingredients and with a high fruit content. Kitty's creative flavours include delights such as Raspberry and Peach Leaf or quince sorbet, with inspiration coming from what she finds at the market.

Marine Ices

8 Haverstock Hill, NW3 2BL
020 7482 9003
Chalk Farm LU
Tues-Sat 10.30am-11pm,
Sun 11am-10pm

A venerable gelateria set up by Gaetano Mansi in 1930 and still run by the Mansi family. I le had been a fruiterer and the family myth goes that he began making water-ices from left-over fruit. The business prides itself on its range of flavourful Italian ice creams made from good quality ingredients. Ice cream desserts have traditionally been purchased here for family occasions by London's Italian community.

Nardulli

The Pavement, Clapham, SW4 0JE
020 7627 1515
www.nardullisicecream.co.uk
Clapham Common LU
Winter: Mon-Fri 11am-9pm,
Sat-Sun 11am-10pm;
Summer: Mon-Thurs 12noon-10pm,
Fri 12noon-11pm, Sat 11am-11pm,
Sun 11am-10pm

Lorenzo Nardulli's friendly, down-to-earth Italian ice cream parlour offers traditional gelati and sorbeti in a range of flavours including classics such as fior di latte, straciatella, nutella and lemon.

Oddono's Gelati

4 Bute Street, SW7 3EX
020 752 0732
www.oddonos.com
South Kensington LU
Mon-Thurs, Sun 11am-11am,

This smart Italian gelateria, the first in what is now a small chain, offers its own ice cream, freshly made on the premises. Flavours range from refreshing sorbets, such as lemon, to richer milk-based gelati including chocolate, nocciola (hazelnut) and pistachio.

Ruby Violet

🏠 *118 Fortess Road, NW5*
🌐 *www.rubyviolet.co.uk*
🚇 *Tufnell Park LU*
🕐 *Daily 11am-7pm*

A small, friendly ice cream parlour, with a few seats in which to sit and sample home-made ice creams, sorbets and graniti from refreshing watermelon and mint granita to fashionable salted caramel.

Scoop

🏠 *40 Shorts Gardens, WC2H 9AB*
🕐 *020 7240 7086*
🌐 *www.scoopgelato.com*
🚇 *Covent Garden LU*
🕐 *Mon-Sun 11am-9pm*

Noted for their top-notch Italian-style ice cream and sorbets, this small gelateria offers an elegant assortment of flavours such as Nocciole (made using Piedmontese Tonda Gentile hazelnuts), Fiordilatte and Melon.
Branches: 53 Brewer Street, W1F 9UJ
16 Old Brompton Road, SW7 3DL

Gelupo

Markets

Brockley Market

Markets

One of the most exciting recent developments on London's food shopping scene has been the growing number of new, specialist food markets, following the trend set by Borough Market which brought quality food producers and importers face-to-face with the public. Many of London's down-to-earth, traditional street markets still survive – among them, Chapel Street Market, Portobello and Walthamstow – offering fresh produce at bargain prices.

Berwick Street Market

Berwick Street, W1F 0PH
Oxford Circus LU, Piccadilly Circus LU
Mon-Sat 9am-5pm

In the heart of Soho, Berwick Street is London's most central street food market. While it still offers a fresh fish stall and a handful of fruit and veg stalls, its latest incarnation is as host to a number of street food stalls.

Borough Food Market

Southwark Street, SE1 1TL
www.boroughmarket.org.uk
London Bridge LU/Rail
Thurs 11am-5pm, Fri 12noon-6pm, Sat 8am-5pm

Housed in Borough's wholesale market (atmospherically situated under the railway arches next to Southwark Cathedral) Borough food market has become a major attraction. Fundamental to its success is the range and quality of the food. Shoppers can choose from raw ingredients – scallops, grass-fed beef, wild mushrooms– to luxuries such as Joselito hams, artisanal European cheeses and great olive oils. Take-away foods are also available, from spicy chorizo sandwiches to Mrs King's proper pork pies. The nearby streets are also home to some great food shops, including Neal's Yard Dairy, Monmouth Coffee House and Konditor & Cook.

Broadway Market

Broadway Market, E8 4PH
www.broadwaymarket.co.uk
London Fields Rail
Sat 8.30am-4.30pm

This appealing Hackney market, inspiringly created by the local community, has rapidly become a roaring success. On offer is a characterful mix of stalls, the majority of which sell food, though clothing and crafts are also represented. On the food front, customers can choose from basics, such as excellent meat, fresh fruit and veg, cakes and breads, charcuterie, cheeses and a huge array of food-to-go, from falafels to roast hog rolls.

Brockley Market

Lewisham College Car Park,
Lewisham Way, SE4 1UT

St Johns Rail

www.brockleymarket.com

Sat 10am-2pm

Founded in 2011 by local food lover Toby Allen out of frustration at not being able to source good food locally, Brockley Market has quickly and deservedly achieved a keen following for its good food and relaxed, friendly atmosphere. Around 25 stalls offer a range of good things to eat, from excellent meat, fish and fresh produce to treats such as Egg Boss Scotch eggs, Moons Green charcuterie and cakes. Hungry visitors can enjoy a selection of street food snacks, from stalls Including Luardos and Tongue 'n' Cheek and a coffee hit from Dark Fluid's lovingly-made coffee.

Brunswick Centre Market

Brunswick Centre WC1N 1BS

Russell Square LU

Sat 10am-6pm

A popular weekly food market, offering an assortment of foods to go and good quality foodstuffs.

Chapel Market

Chapel Market, N1 9ER

Angel LU

Tues-Sat 9am-6pm, Thurs & Sun till 4pm

This down-to-earth Islington market is home to a number of reasonably-priced fresh food stalls, selling fruit and veg, fish and seafood and French cheeses.

Covent Garden Real Food Market

Covent Garden East Piazza, WC2E 8RF

Covent Garden LU

Thurs-Fri 10.30am-8pm,
Sat 10.30am-6pm

A cosmopolitan selection of food stalls, with the focus predominantly on food to go, appealing to hungry office workers and visiting tourists alike.

Hackney Homemade

St John's Church Gardens
(opposite M & S), E5 0PD

www.hackneyhomemade.com

Hackney Central Rail

Sat 11am-5pm summer
Sat 11am-4pm winter

Attractively situated in the leafy gardens of St John's Church, this offers an assortment of food to go and foodstuffs, from meat, game and produce to cheeses and cakes.

Maltby Street Market

⬚ *Maltby Street, SE1 3PA*
⬚ *www.maltbystmarket.com*
⬚ *London Bridge LU/Rail*
⬚ *Sat 9am-4pm*

On Saturdays the railway arches and the Ropewalk off Maltby St offer an appetising range of good things to eat and drink. Here you can find St John's Bakery with its sourdough loaves and legendary doughnuts, wholesaler Tony Booth's prime fruit and veg and Hansen & Lydersen's smoked salmon. In addition to food shopping, visitors can enjoy good food and drink at a number of local establishments including Jamoneria Bar Tozino and 40 Maltby Street, noted for its fine natural wines.

Portobello Market

⬚ *Portobello Road, W11 1LJ*
⬚ *Notting Hill Gate / Ladbroke Grove LU*
⬚ *Mon-Wed, Fri-Sat 8am-6pm,*
Thurs 8am-1pm

Best known for its antique market on a Saturday, Portobello also has a lively traditional street market throughout the week. Fruit and veg stalls, selling bargain-priced fresh produce, line the road between Elgin Crescent and Talbot Road.

Partridges Food Market

⬚ *Duke of York Square, SW3 4LY*
⬚ *www.partridges.co.uk*
⬚ *Sloane Square LU*
⬚ *Sat 10am-4pm*

Partridges, the well-established grocers, have enterprisingly set up a food market in the square outside their store. Saturdays see a cosmopolitan selection of around 50 food stalls, with everything from dainty hand-made chocolates or Colchester oysters to artisanal bread and prime British beef. There is also a cosmopolitan assortment of stalls offering foods to go, from Moroccan salads to Peruvian stews.

Real Food Market at the South Bank

🖼 *Southbank Centre, Royal Festival Hall, outside Canteen restaurant, Belvedere Road, SE1 8XX*

🖥 *www.realfoodfestival.co.uk*

🚌 *Waterloo LU/Rail*

🕐 *Fri 12noon-8pm, Sat 11am-8pm, Sun 12noon-6pm*

Bringing the opportunity for good food shopping to the cultural environment of the Southbank Centre, this weekly market comprises around 40 stalls. Foods on offer range from superior Label Anglaise chickens or Borough Cheese Company's more-ish Comte cheese to sweet treats such as macaroons and churros.

Ridley Road Market

🖼 *Ridley Road, E8 2LH*

🚌 *Dalston Kingsland Rail*

🕐 *Mon-Sat 9am-5pm,*

This much-loved, vibrant food market – spread along a long, pedestrianised Hackney street – offers an array of fresh fruit and veg, fish and seafood and meat at bargain prices, with regular market-goers queuing patiently at their favourite stalls to get what they want.

Venn Street Market

🖼 *Venn Street, SW4 0AT*

🖥 *www.vennstreetmarket.co.uk*

🚌 *Clapham Common LU*

🕐 *Sat 10am-4pm*

A popular addition to Clapham's food shopping scene with wet fish, rare breed meats, fresh produce and fine cheeses. There's also lots to eat on the move including hog roast from Moen & Sons

Walthamstow Market

🖼 *Walthamstow High Street E17 7JY*

🚌 *Walthamstow LU*

🕐 *Tues-Sat 8am-5pm*

Among the stalls at this huge, down-to-earth, busy street market – reputedly Europe's longest outdoor street market – are several offering cut-price fresh fruit and veg and kitchenware.

Farmers' Markets

Farmers' markets are an idea imported from America. Islington hosted the first of the capital's farmers' markets back in 1999 and there are now farmers' markets, spread across the city. London Farmers' Markets (www.lfm.org.uk) were the pioneers but they have been joined by City and Country Markets (www.wearecccfm.co.uk). There are also a few independents such as Growing Communities (www.growingcommunities.org) in Stoke Newington and Peckham Farmers' Market, which are locally organised and have a fantastic community atmosphere and great locally sourced food.

Shopping at farmers' markets is an excellent way to support local producers and source seasonal produce at its best. There is more on offer at farmers' markets, however, than simply fresh fruit and vegetables: meat, fish and shellfish, breads, cakes, cheeses and fruit juices are just some of the other foodstuffs to be found at the best of them

Central

Bloomsbury (LFM)
- *Torrington Square, Byng Place, behind ULU, WC1E 7HY*
- *Thursdays 9am-2pm*

Marylebone (LFM)
- *Cramer St car park, corner Moxton St, off Marylebone High St, W1U 4EW*
- *Sundays 10am-2pm*

Pimlico Road (LFM)
- *Orange Square, corner of Pimlico Road & Ebury St, SW1W 8UT*
- *Saturdays 9am-1pm*

South Kensington Market (LFM)
- *Bute Street, SW7 3EX*
- *Saturdays 9am-1pm*

North

Alexandra Palace (CCM)
- *Alexandra Palace, Muswell Hill, N10 3TG*
- *Sundays 10am-3pm*

Islington London (LFM)
- Chapel Market, Between Penton Street and Baron Street, N1 9PZ
- *Sundays 10am-2pm*

Parliament Hill (LFM)
- *William Ellis School, Highgate Road, NW5 1RN*
- *Saturdays 10am-2pm*

Stoke Newington (Indie)
- *in front of St Paul's Church, Stoke Newington High Street, N16 7UY*
- *Saturdays 10am-2.30pm*

West

Ealing (LFM)
🚪 *Leeland Rd, West Ealing, W13 9H*
🕐 *Saturdays 9am-1pm*

Hammersmith (CCM)
🚪 *Lyric Square, Hammersmith, W6 0QL*
🕐 *Thursdays 10am-3pm*

Notting Hill (LFM)
🚪 *Car park behind Waterstones, access via Kensington Place, W11 4EW*
🕐 *Saturdays 9am-1pm*

North-West

Queen's Park (LFM)
🚪 *Salusbury School, Salusbury Road, NW6 6RG*
🕐 *Sundays 10am-2pm*

Swiss Cottage (LFM)
🚪 *Eton Avenue, NW3 3EU*
🕐 *Wednesdays 10am-3pm*

West Hampstead (LFM)
🚪 *West Hampstead Thameslink station forecourt, NW6 2LJ*
🕐 *Saturdays 10am-2pm*

South

Mordern (CCM)
🚪 *Mordern Hall Park, Mordern Hall Road, SM4 5JD*
🕐 *Saturdays 10am-3pm*

South-West

Balham (LFM)
🚪 *Chestnut Grove Primary School, junction of Chestnut Grove and Hearnville Road, SW12 8JZ*
🕐 *Saturdays 9am-2pm*

Brixton (LFM)
🚪 *Brixton Station Road, SW9 8PA*
🕐 *Sundays 10am-2pm*

Parsons Green (LFM)
🚪 *New King's School, New King's Road, opposite Cristowe Road, SW6 4LY*
🕐 *Sundays 10am-2pm*

Twickenham (LFM)
🚪 *Holly Road Car Park, Holly Rd, TW1 4HF*
🕐 *Saturdays 9am-1pm*

Wimbledon Park (LFM)
🚪 *Wimbledon Park First School, Havana Road, SW19 8EJ*
🕐 *Saturdays 9am-1pm*

South-East

Eltham (CCM)
- Passey Place, Eltham, SE9 5DQ
- 3rd Sunday of every month, 10am-3pm

Blackheath (LFM)
- Blackheath Station Car Park, SE3 9LA
- Sundays 10am-2pm

Dulwich (CCM)
- Dulwich College, SE21 7LS
- Every 4th Sunday of the month

Eltham (CCM)
- Passey Place, SE9 5DQ
- Every 3rd Sunday of the month

Herne Hill (CCM)
- Railton Road,
  in front of Herne Hill station, SE24 0JN
- Sundays 10am-4pm

Lewisham (CCM)
- Old Road entrance, Lee, SE12 5SY
- 1st Saturday of the month, 10am-3pm

- Hilly Fields, SE4 1QA
- 2nd Saturday of the month, 10am-3pm

- Corner of Erlanger Rd &
  Arbothnot Road, SE14 5LS
- 3rd Saturday of the month, 10am-3pm

Oval (CCM)
- St Mark's Church, The Oval, SE11 4PW
- Saturdays 10am-3pm

Peckham (Indie)
- Peckham Square, SE15 5DT
- Sundays 9am-1pm

East

Broadgate (LFM)
- Finsbury Avenue Square,
  Broadgate, EC2M 2PG
- 2nd and 4th Thursday of each month,
  8am-2pm

Queen Mary (LFM)
- The Curve, Westfield Way,
  Queen Mary University of London,
  Mile End Rd, E1 4NS
- Thursdays 9am-2pm during term time

Walthamstow (LFM)
- Town Square by Selbourne Walk
  Shopping Centre, E17 7JN
- Sundays 10am-2pm

LFM = London Farmers' Market
CCM = City & Country Markets
Indie = Independent Market

Street Food

For too many years, London's street food scene consisted solely of dodgy hot dog vans, selling deeply dubious hot dog 'sausages' with greasy fried onions. Things have changed dramatically, however, and, aided by the rise of social media as an effective communications tool, London's street food scene is now vibrant and diverse, offering a chance to try some truly delicious food at affordable prices, carefully prepared by committed traders who are proud of what they do. London's many markets, from old-fashioned street markets to new food markets, are the place in which to find many of these traders.

Berwick Street Market

Berwick Street, W1F
Leicester Square or Oxford Circus LU

What was a dwindling traditional street food market is having new life breathed into it by the arrival of popular street food traders, such as the exuberant Pizza Pilgrims who, having travelled Italy in their little Piaggio Ape van in quest of the perfect pizza recipe, now sell Napoli-style pizza, with each pizza freshly and rapidly baked to order in the furnace-like pizza oven in the back of their (now very heavy) van.

The Rib Man

KERB at Kings Cross

www.kerbfood.com
Kings Boulevard, N1C
Kings Cross LU/Rail

A group of street food traders, headed by the dynamic Petra Barron, KERB is an energetic force on London's street food scene, on a mission to bring high-quality street food to the capital. Weekdays between 11am-2.30pm sees a daily-changing assortment of KERB traders at King's Boulevard (behind Kings Cross station) with offerings ranging from The Ribman's slow-roasted ribs to Tongue 'n' Cheek's Italian-inspired dishes showcasing underused cuts such as tongue or ox cheek. Check the website or follow them on Twitter @KERB_ for up-to-date news of what's happening where.

Lower Marsh Market

Lower Marsh, SE1
Waterloo LU/Rail

Just behind Waterloo Station, this street market offers a chance to enjoy some varied street food.

Whitecross Street Market

Whitecross Street, EC1
Barbican/Old Street LU

Weekday lunchtimes see this street lined with assorted street food traders, such as Luardos, noted for their generously-filled, flavourful burritos, sand Eat My Pies, selling own-made British dishes, including sweet and savoury pies, Scotch eggs and puddings.

Spices

I f you're hunting for spices, then bear in mind that many Asian shops carry a great range of spices, often at very reasonable prices.

Indian Spice Shop

🏠 *115-119 Drummond Street, NW1 2HL*
☎ *020 7916 1831*
🚇 *Euston LU/Rail*
🕐 *Mon-Sat 9.30am-9pm, Sun 10am-9pm*

Situated by Euston station, this long-established shop caters for both the local English and Indian communities. It is divided into an off-licence and corner shop on one side and an Indian grocers on the other. The range of spices carried here is impressive, ranging from black cardamoms to za'atar and smoked paprika.

The Spice Shop

🏠 *1 Blenheim Crescent, W11 2EE*
☎ *020 7221 4448*
🖥 *www.thespiceshop.co.uk*
🚇 *Ladbroke Grove LU*
🕐 *Mon-Sat 9.30am-6pm, Sun 12noon-5pm*

Birgit Erath founded this aromatic shop in 1995 and runs it with enthusiasm and energy. There is an impressive range of spices and herbs from all over the world and used for both culinary and medicinal purposes. A great place to stock up on spices when visiting Portobello Market.

Mail Order

Seasoned Pioneers

🏠 *Unit 8 Stadium Court, Stadium Road, Plantation Business Park, Bromborough, Wirral CH62 2RP*
☎ *0800 0682 348 (freephone)*
🖥 *www.seasonedpioneers.co.uk*

Mark Steene's spice company offers a carefully chosen range of over 200 spices, spice blends, flavourings, chillies and herbs, which range from the familiar to the gloriously obscure. Spices are dry-roasted in small batches in-house, carefully blended to offer authentic flavours and ingeniously packaged in funky re-sealable foil packets.

Steenbergs

🏠 *6 Hallikeld Close, Barker Business Park, Melmerby, Ripon HG4 5GZ*
☎ *01765 640 088*
🖥 *www.steenbergs.co.uk*

Axel and Sophie Steenberg's company offers a wide range of attractively packaged, good-quality Fairtrade and organic spices.

Tea & Coffee

Algerian Coffee Stores

Central

Algerian Coffee Stores

🏠 *52 Old Compton Street, W1D 4PB*
☎ *020 7437 2480*
🌐 *www.algcoffee.co.uk*
🚇 *Leicester Square LU*
🕐 *Mon-Wed 9am-7pm,*
Thurs-Fri 9am-9pm, Sat 9am-8pm

This Soho institution was set up in 1887 by an Algerian businessman but has now been run by the Crocetta family for decades. The fragrant scent of coffee and spices wafts out of the door – a clue to the extensive range of coffees and teas inside. Stock also includes an impressive range of tea and coffee equipment and delicious sweet treats to enjoy with your coffee. Customers can also grab an espresso or cappuccino to go.

H. R. Higgins

🏠 *79 Duke Street, W1K 5AS*
☎ *020 7629 3913*
🌐 *www.hrhiggins.co.uk*
🚇 *Bond Street LU*
🕐 *Mon-Fri 9.30am-6pm, Sat 10am-6pm*

Founded in 1942 by Harold Higgins (known as 'the coffee man'), this family-run business continues to sell quality teas and coffees. The huge copper caddies, beautiful old scales and knowledgeable, courteous service provide a glimpse into another retail era.

Monmouth Coffee Company

🏠 *27 Monmouth Street, WC2H 9EU*
☎ *020 7232 3010*
🌐 *www.monmouthcoffee.co.uk*
🚇 *Covent Garden LU*
🕐 *Mon-Sat 8am-6.30pm*

Founded in 1978, this small coffee shop, complete with a 'sampling room' in which to drink their coffee, was the first venture for Monmouth Coffee, a pioneer of quality coffee in Britain. The Monmouth Street establishment has now become a much-loved Covent Garden institution. Here one can choose from a discerningly-sourced range of own-roasted coffee beans, sourced from single farms, estates and co-operatives. The coffee is sold whole or freshly ground, while the tasting option remains popular.

Monmouth Coffee Company

🏠 *2 Park Street, SE1 9AB*
☎ *020 7232 3010*
🌐 *www.monmouthcoffee.co.uk*
🚇 *London Bridge LU/Rail*
🕐 *Mon-Sat 7.30am-6pm*

Right by Borough Market, in a prime corner site, this is an attractively spacious café-cum-coffee shop, with a seemingly perpetual queue of people waiting to buy a coffee. It offers Monmouth's range of excellent coffees, freshly roasted down the road at their roastery. Visitors can sit at a central table to enjoy their coffee along with a slice of baguette, jam and farmhouse butter or a selection of pastries.

Postcard Teas

9 Dering Street. W1S 1AG

020 7629 3654

www.postcardteas.com

Oxford Circus LU

Mon-Sat 10.30am-6.30pm

Just off teeming Oxford Street, this aesthetic tea shop is run with courteous charm by tea expert Tim d'Offay. It is a serene haven, much appreciated by its loyal regulars who return for teas ranging from fine, refreshing oolongs to Muscatel-flavoured Second Flush. Timothy's genuine fascination with tea has led him to spend many years visiting tea estates in countries around the world from, Japan to Sri Lanka. The beautifully-packaged leaf teas stocked here are a select choice that Timothy himself imports from small-scale, artisanal producers. Also for sale is a selection of exquisite tea ware from hand-crafted Japanese metal tea caddies to linen tea cloths. Although a shop rather than a café, customers can sit and sample teas – a very pleasurable experience.

Tea Palace

12 Covent Garden Market, WC2E 8RF

020 7836 6997

www.teapalace.co.uk

Covent Garden LU

Mon-Fri 10am-7pm, Sat-Sun 11am-6pm

In the heart of Covent Garden Market, this smart shop offers a stylishly-packaged range of teas and tisanes (herbal infusions).

North

Angelucci's

472 Long Lane, N2 8JL

020 8444 9211

www.angeluccicoffee.co.uk

East Finchley LU

Mon-Fri 8am-2pm

This veteran business was founded in 1929 by Mr Angelucci and is now run with courteous charm by his son and daughter – Andy and Alma Angelucci. For many years, Angelucci's was a Soho institution, with customers including General de Gaulle and Odette Churchill. Mark Knopfler of Dire Straits fame, immortalised Angelucci in his song 'Wild West End'. Now relocated to roomier premises in East Finchley, Angelucci continues to sells its excellent coffees, including Mokital, a special blend created by Mr Angelucci and served to this day in Soho's famous Bar Italia.

Camden Coffee Shop

🏠 *11 Delancey Street, NW1 7NL*
☎ *020 7387 4080*
🚍 *Camden Town LU*
🕐 *Mon-Wed & Fri 9.30am-5.30pm*
   Thurs 9.30am-2.30pm, Sat 9.30am-5pm

'Fresh roasted coffee' reads a simple sign outside this old-fashioned shop, established in 1950. Inside the store, George (who has run the business since 1978) roasts his coffees in batches in a small coffee-roaster, which turns noisily, filling the air with the rich scent of roasting coffee. The choice is confined to ten coffees, roasted from light to dark, and all very competitively priced. 'I'm the only coffee shop left like this,' remarks George thoughtfully. He's absolutely right.

W. M. Martyn

🏠 *135 Muswell Hill Broadway, N10 3RS*
☎ *020 8883 5642*
🚍 *Highgate LU, then 134 bus*
🕐 *Mon-Sat 9.30am-5.30pm,*
   Sun 12noon-4pm

The aroma of freshly-roasted coffee beans wafting down the Broadway marks the presence of this small, old-fashioned grocer's, which was established over 100 years ago. While best-known for its teas and coffees, the shop also stocks traditional groceries, from excellent dried fruits to sugar mice and bars of German marzipan. Staff are helpful and friendly.

East

Teasmith

6 Lamb Street, E1 6EA

020 7247 1333

Liverpool Street LU/Rail

www.teasmith.co.uk

Mon-Sun 11am-6pm

Housed in Spitalfields Market, this high-ceilinged 'tea bar' offers its customers a chance to savour fine teas, from green teas to aged Puers. Each tea is sampled in a number of infusions, making for a leisurely experience. Also on offer are patisserie and chocolates from chocolatier William Curley, such as matcha-flavoured financiers. Staff are friendly and helpful and happy to guide you through the intricacies of tea-making and drinking. There is also a fine selection of tea ware on sale.

Climpson & Sons

67 Broadway Market, E8 4PH

www.webcoffeeshop.co.uk

London Fields Rail

Showcasing Climpson's own-roasted coffee, this café sells a selection of coffee beans as well as offering coffees to drink. Weekends see it packed to the gills with keen coffee-drinkers.

Mail Order

Rare Tea Company

www.rareteacompany.com

Run with an infectious enthusiasm for tea by founder Henrietta Lovell, this boutique company offers a small but carefully sourced range of leaf teas. Products include fragrant green, white, and jasmine silver tip teas from China and Lost Malawi and an African single-estate black tea.

Union Hand Roasted Coffee

7a South Crescent, E16 4TL

020 7474 8990   fax 020 7511 2786

www.unionroasted.com

Coffee aficionados Jeremy Torz and Steven Macatonia of Union Hand Roasted were early pioneers of sustainably sourced, artisanal, high quality coffee in the UK, lovingly roasted in small batches in their East End London Roastery. They have a loyal following for their discriminatingly selected Arabica coffees which can be found in coffee bars, restaurants and delis across the capital. They pride themselves on their online mail order service, which means that coffee drinkers at home can also explore their extensive range of coffees, which are roasted to order and delivered direct, fresh from the Roastery.

Best Coffee

Where to go for a great cup of coffee...

London's coffee scene is buzzing, with new, lovingly run, independent coffee shops (many inspired by the coffee culture scene in Australia and New Zealand) springing up around the capital. Look out, too, for coffee enthusiasts Dark Fluid, who sell their coffees in various markets, including Brockley Market.

Allpress Roastery Café

58 Redchurch Street, E2 7DP
020 7749 1780
uk.allpressespresso.com
Shoreditch High Street LU

A roomy, laidback café on the same site as the Allpress Roastery, offering own roasted coffees to an appreciative crowd.

Dose Espresso

70 Long Lane, EC1A 9EJ
020 7600 0382
Barbican/Farringdon LU

James Phillips' appealingly coffee-focused bar, offering artisanal, ethical coffee.

The Espresso Room

⌨ *31-35 Great Ormond Street, WC1N 3HZ*
☎ *07760 714883*
🖊 *www.theespressoroom*
🚌 *Holborn or Russell Square LU*

A tiny Bloomsbury coffee shop, with a cult following for its excellent coffee.

Flat White

⌨ *17 Berwick Street, W1F 0PT*
☎ *07837 919099*
🖊 *www.flatwhitecoffee.com*

Oxford Circus or Tottenham Court Road LU Opened in 2005, this Aussie-style coffee house is known for its signature flat white. *Sister shop: Milk Bar, 3 Bateman Street, W1D 4AG*

Kaffeine

⌨ *66 Great Titchfield Street, W1W 7QJ*
☎ *020 7580 6755*
🖊 *www.kaffeine.co.uk*
🚌 *Oxford Circus LU*

An appealingly mellow coffee shop, inspired by Australia's and New Zealand's coffee house culture.

Monmouth Coffee

⌨ *27 Monmouth Street, WC2H 9EU*
☎ *020 7232 3010*
🖊 *www.monmouthcoffee.co.uk*
🚌 Covent Garden or Leicester Square LU

A pioneer of quality, carefully sourced coffee in the capital, this small, friendly coffee shop and 'sampling room' was established by Anita Le Roy in 1978 with Monmouth's coffee roasted on the premises right until 2007. *Branch: 2 Park Street, SE1 9AB*

Prufrock Coffee

⌨ *23-25 Leather Lane, EC1N 7TE*
☎ *020 7242 0467*
🖊 *www.prufrockcoffee.com*
🚌 *Chancery Lane LU*

Established by World Barista Champion, Gwylym Davies, this roomy coffee shop champions coffee making by siphon and is an excellent place for both coffee and coffee talk.

Taylor Street Baristas

⌨ *25 Old Broad Street, EC2N 1AR*
☎ *020 7256 8665*
🖊 *www.taylor-st.com*
🚌 *Bank LU*

Founded by three 'Aussie siblings', Taylor Street Baristas have grown into a small chain. This branch is a huge, buzzing coffee shop, offering their trademark excellent coffee as well as teas and pastries.

Wine, Beer & Spirits

Berry Bros & Rudd

In addition to wine shop chains, London is also home to some wonderful independent wine and spirits merchants. The stores range from venerable institutions to relaxed, innovative shops, all proud of the knowledgeable service which they offer.

Central

Amathus

🏠 *17-19 Leadenhall Market, EC3V 1LR*
☎ *020 7283 0638*
🖥 *www.amathusdrinks.com*
🚇 *Bank LU*
🕐 *Mon-Fri 9am-7pm*

Picturesquely located in Leadenhall Market, this spacious shop comes courtesy of an established, specialist drinks importer. Stock is consequently strong on spirits, such as aged rums, Van Wees genevers and Heering liqueurs, with wines also stocked. Staff are polite and helpful.
Branch: Hammer House,
113-117 Wardour Street, W1F 0UN

Berry Bros & Rudd

🏠 *3 St James Street, SW1A 1 EG*
☎ *0800 280 2440*
🖥 *www.bbr.com*
🚇 *Green Park LU*
🕐 *Mon-Fri 10am-6pm, Sat 10am-5pm*

Founded in 1698, Berry Brothers and Rudd has a venerable and fascinating history, starting life as a grocer's shop supplying the aristocracy, before moving into the wine trade. It is still owned and managed by members of both the Berry and Rudd families. The business began supplying wine to the British Royal Family in 1760 and currently holds two Royal Warrants. Entering the atmospheric, elegantly understated shop offers a glimpse of the past, including the huge scales on which notable customers such as William Pitt and Lord Byron were weighed, with their weight ceremoniously recorded. The cellars which were at one time home to Napoleon III are now used as a venue for wine tastings and lunches as well as for storing wine. Elegantly dressed staff offer courteous advice to in-store highlights, from fine wines to King's Ginger, a liqueur created by Berry Bros for King Edward VII. Despite the company's history they were early pioneers of on-line wine shopping and have an award-winning website.

French Bubbles

🏠 *22 Wellington Street, WC2E 7DD*
☎ *020 7240 1604*
🖥 *www.frenchbubbles.co.uk*
🚇 *Covent Garden LU*
🕐 *Tues-Sat 11am-11pm, Sun 11am-8pm*

Stefano Frigerio's intimate wine shop-cum-bistro offers a chance to buy diverse and characterful 'grower champagnes', discerningly sourced by Stefano from France's smaller, independent family-owned vineyards, with Stefano happy to offer advice and make suggestions.

Gerry's Wines and Spirits

- 74 Old Compton Street W1D 4UW
- 020 7734 4215
- www.gerrys.uk.com
- Leicester Square LU
- Mon-Thurs & Sat 9am-6.30pm, Fri 9am-7.30pm, Sun 12noon-6pm

Set up in 1984 by Michael Kyprianou, this characterful drinks emporium is a much-loved Soho institution. Noted especially for its range of spirits (200 different rums, 150 tequilas, 150 vodkas), the shelves here are lined with a colourful array of bottles, each neatly labelled with name and price. Photos of assorted happy customers testify to Gerry's popularity. Stock ranges from Pisco (much sought-after by Chilean and Peruvian expats) to Lillet Vermouth (featured in the film 'Casino Royal') and a huge range of flavoured syrups for making cocktails. The down-to-earth staff are friendly and helpful and take pride in tracking down the most obscure alcoholic request from their loyal customers.

GERRY'S ISN'T A LIQUOR SHOP, IT'S A SPIRITS MUSEUM!

74 Old Compton Street, Soho, W1D 4UW
Tel: 020 7734 2053/4215
info@gerrys.uk.com

Opening hours:
Mon-Sat 9am-6.30pm,
Sun 12noon-6pm

www.gerrys.uk.com

Milroy's of Soho

- 3 Greek Street, W1D 4NX
- 020 7437 9311
- www.milroys.co.uk
- Tottenham Court Road LU
- Mon-Sat 10am-7pm

This veteran whisky shop was set up in 1964 by brothers John and Wallace Milroy and soon became known to locals simply as 'the whisky shop'. Now part of the Jeroboams group, Milroy's stocks over 700 carefully sourced whiskies from around the world, with the emphasis on Highland single malts. Stock also includes fine wines and other spirits such as rums and Cognacs.

North

The Sampler

266 Upper Street, N1 2UQ

020 7226 9500

www.thesampler.co.uk

Angel, Highbury & Islington (LU)

Mon-Sat 11.30am-9pm,
Sun 11.30am-7pm

This relaxed and friendly wine shop offers customers a chance to sample over 1,000 assorted, carefully selected wines. Ten wine sampling machines rotate a range of 80 wines from sherries to fine wines. An additional lure is the extensive range of around 120 various grower Champagnes. *Branch: 35 Thurloe Place, SW7 2HP*

West

Moreno Wine Merchants

11 Marylands Road, W9 2DU

020 7286 0678

www.morenowinedirect.com

Warwick Avenue LU

Mon-Fri 4pm-8pm, Sat 12noon-8pm

This well-established, affable wine merchants specialises in Spanish wines, but also has wines from other countries too. The service here is excellent and they have a keen eye for up-and-coming producers.

Roberson's

348 Kensington High Street. W14 8NS

020 7371 2121

www.robersonwinemerchant.co.uk

Olympia LU

Mon-Sat 10am-8pm, Sun 12noon-6pm

Established in 1991, this smart, spacious wine shop is noted for its collection of quality Bordeaux and Burgundy wines. They also stock wines from other European countries among their 2,000 wines, with the emphasis on classic wines. Wine buffs can stock up their cellars from the 'Fine and Rare Wines' section, kept securely under lock and key, while bargain-hunters enjoy browsing the ongoing sales section. Wine tastings are an added attraction.

The Winery

4 Clifton Road, W9 1SS

020 7286 6475

www.thewineryuk.com

Warwick Avenue LU

Mon-Sat 11am-9.30pm,
Sun 12noon-8pm

This friendly, cheery shop showcases wines it has imported directly from small growers in France, Germany, Italy, Spain and California. Its wide range of new-wave, dry German Riesling and Pinot Noir is a particular speciality.

South

40 Maltby Street

40 Maltby Street, SE1 3PA

020 7237 9247

www.gergoviewines.com

London Bridge LU/Rail

Thurs 5.30pm-10pm,
Fri 5.30pm-10pm, Sat 11am-5pm

Discerningly chosen 'natural wines' – that is wines made from wine-growers who grow and make their wines as naturally as possible, without resorting to pesticides and bought-in yeasts – are on offer here at the railway arches warehouse of Gergovie Wines. In addition to buying wines to take home, there is an informal wine bar area in which to sample the wines and excellent, seasonal food, ranging from freshly sliced, fine charcuterie to purple-sprouting broccoli with Ortiz anchovy dressing.

Bedales

5 Bedale Street, SE1 9AL

020 7403 8853

www.bedaleswines.com

London Bridge LU/Rail

Mon-Tues 10am-10pm,
Wed 10am-10.30pm,
Thurs-Fri 10am-11pm, Sat 9am-10pm,
Sun 10am-7pm

Atmospherically housed in Borough Market, this relaxed wine shop and wine bar (the first in what is now a small chain) carries a diverse range of wines from around the world. The staff are friendly and helpful.

Kernel Brewery

Arch 11, Dockley Road Industrial Estate, SE16 3SF

020 7231 4516

www.thekernelbrewery.com

Bermondsey LU

Sat 9am-3pm

Founded in 2009 by Evin O'Riordain, this pioneering London-based micro-brewery is noted for its acclaimed range of lovingly-made beers, including London Pale Ale and London Porter. On Saturday mornings you can buy direct from the brewery and chat to the knowledgeable team.

Laithwaites

Arch 219-221, Stoney Street, SE1 9AA

020 7407 6378

www.laithwaites.co.uk

London Bridge LU/Rail

Mon-Thurs 10am-7pm, Fri 10am-9pm,
Sat 10am-8pm, Sun 12noon-6pm

Housed in Vinopolis, Tony Laithwaite's London wine shop offers an impressive range of knowledgeably sourced stock, with the emphasis on both quality and affordability. The friendly, knowledgeable staff are happy to offer advice.

Utobeer

📷 *Unit 24, Middle Row,*
    Borough Market, SE1 1TL
☎ *020 7378 6617*
🖱 *www.utobeer.co.uk*
🚇 *London Bridge Rail*
🕐 *Wed-Thurs 11am-6pm,*
    Fri 10am-6pm, Sat 9am-5pm

Founded by beer enthusiasts, this Borough Market shop showcases an extensive selection of beers from Britain and around the world, displaying around 700 out of a range of 2000 at any one time. Service is friendly and knowledgeable

South-West

Haynes Hanson & Clark

📷 *7 Elystan Street, SW3 3NT*
☎ *020 7584 7927*
🖱 *www.hhandc.co.uk*
🚇 *Sloane Square LU*
🕐 *Mon-Fri 9am-7pm, Sat 9am-4.30pm*

On a Chelsea side-street, this small, immaculate wine shop prides itself on sourcing directly from growers, with French wines – Burgundy, Bordeaux and Loire Valley – a particular forte. Service is courteous and well informed.

Jeroboams

📷 *50-52 Elizabeth Street, SW1W 9PB*
☎ *020 7730 8108*
🖱 *www.jeroboams.co.uk*
🚇 *Victoria LU*
🕐 *Mon-Fri 9.30am-7pm, Sat 10am-5pm*

This showcase shop of the noted wine merchants, London's largest independent wine merchants, is a smart affair, as befits its Belgravia surroundings. On offer here are around 500 fine wines, including excellent wines from Bordeaux, Burgundy and Champagnes. The courteous, knowledgeable staff are an added attraction. See the website for details of their other branches.

Lea & Sandeman

📷 *170 Fulham Road, SW10*
☎ *020 7244 0522*
🖱 *www.leaandsandeman.co.uk*
🚇 *Gloucester Road LU*
🕐 *Mon-Sat 10am-8pm*

Founded in 1988 by Charles Lea and the late Patrick Sandeman, this acclaimed independent wine shop (now with three sister shops) has always prided itself on sourcing interesting wines to the public.

95 Lauriston Rd
Hackney
E9 7HJ
020 8985 1549

49 Park Rd
Crouch End
N8 8SY
020 8347 7577

bottle apostle
wines to sample, buy and adore
www.bottleapostle.com

Market Row Wines

📠 20 Market Row,
Brixton Market, SW9 1LD

☎ 020 7274 2463

🚇 Brixton LU/Rail

🕐 Tues-Wed 12noon-5pm,
Thurs-Sat 12noon-9pm,
Sun 12noon-4pm

David Simpson's small, independent wine shop, which with its brick walls has an appealing wine cellar feel to it, has been greeted with delight by locals, thrilled at having a good wine shop in the neighbourhood. Stock is pared down and clearly displayed and Dave is happy to offer guidance.

Philglas & Swiggot

📠 21 Northcote Road, SW11 1NG

☎ 020 7924 4494

🌐 www.philglas-swiggot.co.uk

🚇 Clapham Junction Rail

🕐 Mon-Fri 11am-7pm, Sat 10am-6pm,
Sun 12noon-5pm

Founded in 1991, this friendly wine shop has carved out a loyal following among the local community. Always innovative, it offers a great range of quality wines and is renowned for its service.

*Branches: 22 New Quebec Street, W1H 7SB
64 Hill Rise, TW10 6UB*

The Wine Tasting Shop

📠 18 Hildreth Street, SW12 9RQ

☎ 020 8616 8658

🌐 www.thewinetastingshop.co.uk

🚇 Balham LU/Rail

🕐 Mon-Sat 11am-9pm, Sun 12noon-5pm

Julia Michael's friendly and accessible wine shop offers a great range of wines, with the focus on lesser-known, reasonably-priced wines from innovative growers. As the shop's name suggests, wine-preserving technology means that these can be sampled for a small price before purchasing.

East

Bottle Apostle

🏠 *95 Lauriston Road, E9 7HU*
☎ *020 8985 1549*
✎ *www.bottleapostle.com*
🚇 *Mile End LU*
🕐 *Tues-Fri 12noon-9pm*
   Sat 10am-8pm, Sun 10am-6pm

This friendly, innovative wine shop, welcoming wine novices as well as wine experts, offers self-service wine sampling, with prices for the samples ranging from a few pence to a few pounds. The globe-trotting stock ranges from beers and ciders to wines and spirits and the friendly staff are happy to offer advice and suggestions. *Branch: 49 Park Road, N8 8SY 020 8347 7577*

Noble Fine Liquor

🏠 *27 Broadway Market, E8 4PH*
☎ *020 7254 9737*
✎ *www.wearenoble.co.uk*
🚇 *London Fields Rail*
🕐 *Tues-Fri 12noon-8pm, Sat 10am-9pm, Sun 12noon-8pm*

This new wine shop addition to bustling Broadway Market specialises in 'terroir-focussed' wines from Italy and France and craft beers from the UK.

Wine Tastings

If you'd like to learn more about wine, then there are a number of wine-tasting classes and courses in the capital.

• Berry Brothers and Rudd offers an extensive range of wine courses, from one-day events to evening classes. *(www.bbr.com)*

• Jeroboams offer a range of informal wine-tasting events, held at Milroy's in Soho. *(www.jeroboams.co.uk)*

• Wine expert Michael Schuster, much acclaimed for his teaching, offers courses at Bordeaux Index in Hatton Garden. *(www.schuster.f9.co.uk)*

• The Wine & Spirit Education Trust offer a range of wine courses and qualifications. *(45 Bermondsey St, SE1 3XF, 020 7089 3800, www.wsetglobal.com)*

• Vinopolis are renowned for the wine tastings and master classes held at their smart South Bank headquarters. *(www.vinopolis.co.uk)*

Cookery schools and classes are booming in the capital, with a recent trend being the rise of enterprising individuals teaching classes on subjects dear to their hearts. Whether you want to spend a few hours learning how to make fresh pasta or spend months mastering professional culinary techniques, there's bound to be something to suit you. A useful guide to cookery courses is www.lookingtocook.co.uk. Here are some tasters of what's on offer.

Billingsgate Seafood Training School

Billingsgate Market Trafalgar Way, E14 5ST

020 7517 3548

www.seafoodtraining.org

Canary Wharf DLR/LU

From how to identify truly fresh fish to filleting and cooking fish, the Billingsgate Seafood Training School, led by the capable C.J. Jackson and based at bustling Billingsgate Market, is a mine of piscine information. Cookery classes here are admirably hands-on and informative. The guided tours offer a fascinating insight into this historic market.

Catalan Cooking

www.catalancooking.co.uk

Spanish food aficionado Rachel McCormack teaches small, informal, hands-on classes focused on regional Spanish dishes.

Cookery School

15B Little Portland St, W1W 8BW

020 7631 4590

www.cookeryschool.co.uk

Oxford Circus LU

This friendly, informal cookery school offers a wide-ranging, seasonal selection of classes and courses. Founder Rosalind Rathouse aims to pass on her passion for and knowledge of food and cookery and the varied programme offers students the chance to learn everything from thrifty cooking to knife skills.

Le Cordon Bleu London

15 Bloomsbury Sq, WC1A 2LS

020 7400 3900

www.lcblondon.com

Holborn LU

The London branch of this famous French cookery school offers a programme of diplomas and certificates. Pupils learn through both demonstrations and practice.

Cucina Caldesi

118 Marylebone Lane, W1U 2QF
020 7487 0750
www.caldesi.com
Bond Street LU

Run by restaurateurs Giancarlo and Katie Caldesi, this friendly cookery school specialises in Italian cookery. There are classes and courses on subjects from making fresh pasta to Tuscan cuisine.

Culinary Anthropologist

www.culinaryanthropologist.org
Trained chef and self-termed 'food nerd' Anna Colquhon, author of *Eat Slow Britain*, offers small, hands-on cookery classes with themes such as Seasonal Preserving, Homemade Bread for Busy People and New Nordic Cuisine for the Home Cook.

Denise's Kitchen

www.jewishcookery.com
A chance to learn about Jewish cookery from chef and cookery writer Denise Phillips. Hands-on classes range from Sephardi Favourites to Pesach Baking.

Divertimenti

33-34 Marylebone High Street, W1U 4PT
020 7935 0689
www.divertimenti.co.uk
Baker Street LU

This well-established kitchenware store is also known for its cookery classes, which take place in the downstairs Cookery Theatre. Teachers are drawn from the world of food and include well-known chefs and food writers, with classes on themes from street food to sugarcraft.

Leiths School of Food and Wine

16-20 Wendell Road, W12 9RT
020 8749 6406
www.leiths.com
Stamford Brook LU

This well-established cookery school offers both 'Professional Courses' and 'Enthusiasts' Courses'. There is a wide-ranging syllabus offering both courses in Practical Cookery and classes in subjects such as Knife Skills and Seasonal French Cooking.

Angela Malik Cookery School

- 6 Churchfield Road, W3 6EG
- 020 8992 5011
- www.angelamalik.co.uk

Angela Malik's hands-on cookery school offers a lively programme of cookery classes on subjects ranging from Thai Express Lunches to Indian Home Cooking.

Recipease

- 92-94 Notting Hill Gate, W11 3QB
- 020 3375 5398
- www.jamieoliver.com/recipease
- Notting Hill Gate

This jaunty, spacious venture, spread over two floors and manned by friendly staff, is Jamie Oliver's flagship 'Recipease' combining a cookery school, café and deli. Classes here are informal affairs, yet clearly and effectively taught, with customers learning new life skills such as how to make great fresh pasta or how to fillet fish.
Branch: 48-50 St John's Road, SW11 1PR

Recipease

- 48-50 St John's Road, SW11
- 020 3006 0001
- www.jamieoliver.com/recipease
- Clapham Junction LU
- Mon-Fri 9am-9pm, Sat 8am-8pm
  Sun 9am-6pm

TV chef Jamie Oliver is behind this spacious, characteristically enterprising venture, which combines a cookery school, meal-assembly points and food and kitchenware shops. Customers can pop in for ready-made meals, prepared in the on-site kitchen or try some of the freshly made bread.

Sabrina Ghayour

- www.sabrinaghayour.com

Famed for her supper clubs, Sabrina Ghayour also offers cookery classes exploring the delights of Persian cuisine.

Sarah Moore

- www.sarahmoore.co.uk

Experienced caterer and champion of an ethical and sustainable approach to food, Sarah Moore offers intelligently-conceived, hands-on cookery classes for small groups focused on understanding ingredients.

Sozai Limited

- 5 Middlesex Street, E1 7AA
- 020 7458 4567
- www.sozai.co.uk
- LU/Rail Liverpool Street

A new, specialist Japanese cookery school offering classes by Japanese chefs and cookery teachers on subjects from sushi and tempura to ramen and okonomiyaki.

cookeryschool
at little portland street

15B Little Portland Street,
London, W1W 8BW
Tel: 020 7631 4590
info@cookeryschool.co.uk
www.cookeryschool.co.uk

Cookery School at Little Portland Street is a hidden gem in the heart of central London offering classes and courses for all food lovers from beginners to experienced cooks, as well as hosting bespoke corporate events from team building to client entertaining. Committed to sustainability, the school runs on green energy and sources seasonal, organic ingredients.

www.cookeryschool.co.uk

African & Caribbean

Brixton Market

In his monumental book, *Staying Power*, Peter Fryer points out that the first Black presence in Britain dates back to Roman times, when Black men were among the conscripts in the Roman army. The growth of a domestic Black community, however, was connected with Britain's slave trade, which was started in 1562-3 by the first 'triangular voyage' between Britain, Africa and the West Indies. The demand for sugar and the labour-intensive sugar cane plantation system in the Caribbean encouraged the slave trade's growth, making it enormously profitable to those running it.

Africans came to Britain as slaves until the slave trade was outlawed in 1807. Before this date some free Blacks, such as seamen, servants and street entertainers were established in Britain, with the London community living mainly along the Thames in Limehouse. Records such as that of freed slave Ukawsaw Gronniosaw, give a vivid picture of ill-treatment and discrimination, which forced many into destitution. After 1807 the Black community in Britain declined, although Black loyalists returned after fighting in the American War of Independence, and some seamen settled after serving in the Napoleonic Wars (1792-1815). In the late nineteenth century a small community of Somali seamen settled in the London docks.

The coming of the First World War meant a change of attitude towards the Black community. Instead of being rejected for work on racial grounds, their help was now needed in the munitions factories. Black seamen also filled the gaps in the Merchant Navy caused by conscription. By 1919 there were 20,000 Black people in Britain. But once the war was over the picture changed again, with the seamen's unions closing the door firmly against any Black labour.

A similar pattern occurred in the late 1940s and 1950s when, as Britain struggled to rebuild its war-torn economy, a call went out to the Commonwealth for workers to come to the 'Mother Country'. The 1948 Nationality Act granted British citizenship to people living in Britain's current and former colonies. For many West Indians this was an opportunity to be seized; unemployment was high in the West Indies and in 1951 a hurricane added to Jamaica's problems. Corporations such as London Transport actively recruited labour in Barbados in 1956, and by 1966 had also turned to Trinidad and Jamaica. Between 1945 and 1958, over 125,000 West Indians emigrated to Britain.

The different stages of African immigration into London in the post-war years have been triggered by the ebb and flow of African politics. The 1950s and 1960s saw an influx of West Africans made up largely of students and lawyers. During the 1970s, African and Asian Ugandans fled Idi Amin, while recent years have seen an increase in immigration from Ghana, Zaire and Ethiopia. There is also a South African community in London, with Wimbledon (nicknamed 'WimbleDurban') a focal residential area for South African ex-pats.

There is no single centre for the African community in London, with pockets of different African nationalities scattered throughout the capital. For the West Indian community, however, there are focal points such as Brixton, Hackney and, during the 1960s and 1970s, Notting Hill. Many of the first post-war Jamaican immigrants who sailed over on the 'Empire Windrush' settled in Brixton, a formerly prosperous suburb which had become cheap and run-down. This community attracted further Jamaican immigrants during the 1950s and 1960s. Notting Hill, in which mainly Trinidadians settled, still hosts the famous Carnival. What originated as a 1964 Bank Holiday street party for local children has since developed into Europe's largest open -air street festival with the costume parades, floats and rhythmic steel drums all derived from Trinidad's own spectacular Carnival.

African & Caribbean Cuisine

'African food' is a blanket term covering a huge number of countries, each with their own characteristic cuisines. Ethiopian cuisine, for example, is marked by its richly spiced dishes and its use of teff, a grain so small that there are 2,500-3,000 seeds to the gram. Teff is traditionally used to make Ethiopia's staple flatbread – injera, which has a characteristically sour tang. South Africa's cuisine reflects its history of colonization and immigration, featuring dishes of Dutch, German, Indian and Cape Malay origins. Certain staples, such as maize, cassava, plantain and beans, are shared across different African countries and crop up in Black cuisine in many parts of the world. Dried foods, such as smoked or salted fish and meat, are another common element in the African kitchen, reflecting the need to preserve food before the days of refrigeration or canning. Many of these ingredients are now used to add a distinctive flavour to dishes.

West African slaves brought their cuisine to the West Indies and its influence is still marked in today's Caribbean cooking. Many of the staples are the same (several brought from Africa): cassava, yams, taro, plantain and groundnuts. Dishes in common include coo-coo (cornmeal pudding) and fufu, the latter being a Fanti word used on the Cape Coast. In West Africa fufu is pounded yam, plantain and cassava dough dipped into a soup, while in Jamaica fufu now means both the pounded yam and the soup. The slaves' restricted diet also included salted meat and fish and these are still popular, although the latter is now something of a luxury.

Caribbean cooking is very much a melting pot of a cuisine, influenced by a series of colonisers and immigrants. Chillies were brought from South America by the Spanish colonisers and 'escovished fish' (fresh pickled fish) originated from the Spanish dish escabeche. The arrival in Trinidad of indentured workers from India means that dishes like roti and curry goat are popular there today.

The fertility of the Caribbean islands meant many plants could be introduced successfully. Many foods were introduced from other countries, such as breadfruit, now a staple, which was introduced by Captain Bligh. Fresh seafood is characteristic of West Indian cuisine and increasingly fish such as colourful snappers are becoming available in Britain.

Glossary

Ackee: a red-skinned fruit that is only safe to eat when the fruit is fully ripe. The white, fleshy base called an aril is the part that is eaten. Fresh ackee is very rarely found in the UK but it is available in tins. Saltfish with ackee is one of Jamaica's famous dishes. The Latin name of the fruit, Blighia sapida, is a tribute to Captain Bligh, who introduced it to Jamaica.

Agbono: sometimes spelt ogbono, this is the inner kernel of the African bush mango. The kernel is the size and shape of an almond but browner and much harder. Available both whole and ground.

Allspice: peppercorn-sized berries, with a flavour that combines cloves, cinnamon and nutmeg – hence the name.

Annatto: small, orange-red seeds, used to add colour and flavour.

Arrowroot: a starch extracted from the underground stem of a water-plant.

Avocado: this green-skinned, soft-fleshed fruit is called 'pear' in the Caribbean.

Bananas: green bananas, which are the unripe fruit of certain varieties, and ripe yellow bananas are treated as both a vegetable and a fruit in Caribbean and African cuisines.

Biltong: a South African cured meat, usually sold in strips, made by marinating, spicing and drying meat. Nowadays, beef is widely used to make biltong, but it can be made from many other meats including wild game.

Bitter leaf: A distinctively flavoured African leaf, related to the lettuce family. Available dried or frozen.

Boerewors: 'farmer's sausage' – a South African sausage, made to many different recipes but often made using a mixture of beef and pork and characteristically flavoured with coriander seeds, cloves and nutmeg.

Breadfruit: a football-sized fruit with thick, green, pimply skin and creamy flesh, used both as a starchy vegetable and in pies and puddings.

Callaloo: green leaves of the dasheen plant, used to make a famous soup of the same name. Available tinned and fresh.

Cassava: large, brown, hand-shaped tubers of the cassava plant, also called manioc or yucca. Bitter cassava, despite the fact it contains toxic prussic acid which must be removed by either cooking or pressing, is a staple food. Yellow-fleshed sweet cassava is eaten as a vegetable. Dried, ground cassava is used in Africa to make gari. Ground cassava meal is used in the West Indies to make a type of bread and the flavoured juice of grated cassava is used to make cassareep, a key ingredient of pepperpot.

Catfish, dried: small blackened fish, with a distinctive large head, used to add flavour to soups and stews in West African cooking.

Cho-cho (christophene, chayote): a pear-sized member of the squash family, with a wrinkled skin ranging in colour from white to green, and watery white flesh.

Cho-cho

Coconut: coconut flesh and milk are widely used in Caribbean cookery.

Cornmeal: coarsely or finely ground dried corn kernels.

Crayfish, dried: although called 'crayfish' in Africa, these are a type of shrimp. Used whole or ground as flavouring.

Custard apple: apple-sized fruit with a knobbly, green skin. The white, sweet pulp has a custard-like texture, hence the name.

Dasheen: potato-sized fibrous tubers with white starchy flesh. Some varieties of dasheen have an acrid taste.

Eddoe: a small, rounded fibrous tuber with white starchy flesh.

Egusi: pumpkin seeds, which are available shelled, either whole or ground. Egusi is used in West African cooking, providing a nutty texture in soups and stews.

Fish: *flying fish*, a distinctive 'winged' fish; *king fish*, a firm-fleshed 'meaty' fish, often sold as steaks; *parrot fish*, a brightly-coloured fish with a beaky head; *snapper*, a popular, firm-fleshed fish, available in colours from grey to pinkish-red; and *trevalli*, a large, firm-fleshed oily fish. *Jacks* is the name given to the smaller fish of the same family.

Gari: coarsely-ground cassava, an African staple.

Guava: small, yellow-green, hard-skinned fruit with pinkish flesh filled with small seeds. It has a distinctive fragrance and is eaten raw or used to make jams and jellies.

Guinep: small, round, green fruit which grows in bunches. The pink flesh has a delicate flavour.

Okra

Irish moss: white, curly seaweed from which an eponymous drink is made. Available either dried or ready to drink.

Jackfruit: a large, green fruit with a pimply skin, similar in appearance to breadfruit.

Kenke: West African dumpling, made from fermented maize flour wrapped in corn husks or banana leaves and cooked.

Ortanique

Landsnails: giant snails, sold either alive, frozen, tinned or smoked. If bought alive, keep them and feed them on lettuce leaves for a few days before cooking to make sure they have excreted anything toxic.

Mango: this large, kidney-shaped fruit, with its succulent orange flesh and sweet, resiny flavour, comes in numerous varieties. One of the best-known West Indian varieties is the Julie mango.

Okra (ladies fingers, ochroes): finger-sized, ridged, tapering green pods, introduced into the Caribbean from West Africa.

Ortanique: a cross between an orange and a tangerine, this looks like an orange with a flattened end.

Palm hearts: tender palm tree hearts, usually found tinned.

Palm oil: a thick, orange-red oil, made from the fruit of the oil palm, which adds flavour and colour to African dishes.

Pawpaw: long, oval fruit, with soft orange flesh, varying in skin colour from green to orange.

Peppers: among the hottest and most flavourful of the peppers used in African and Caribbean cooking is the squat, rounded Scotch bonnet pepper, available in green, yellow and red varieties.

Pepper sauce: the sauce comes in a variety of textures from liquid to paste, but is always hot!

Pigeon pea (gunga): ridged pea pods, with every pea in its own section. Unusually, the peas within a single pod vary in colour from cream through green and brown. Available fresh, tinned or dried.

Plantain: similar in appearance to green bananas, plantain have starchy flesh and are cooked and eaten as a vegetable. They can be chipped, boiled or cooked in stews.

Plantain

Pomelo: often called shaddock, after the merchant ship captain who introduced the fruit to the Caribbean, this is a large, thick-skinned citrus fruit, similar in flavour to grapefruit.

Saltfish: preserved foods such as salted fish were brought over to the Caribbean to feed the plantation workers. It is now something of a luxury item. Stockfish is a popular salted fish.

Sapodilla (naseberry): a fruit very similar in appearance to kiwi fruit, with a brown, furry skin. Inside it has pinky-brown, granular flesh with a few glossy pips and a distinctive sweet flavour.

Sorrel (rosella): the red sepals of a flowering plant, used either fresh or dried to make a dark-red, aromatic drink, traditionally at Christmas.

Soursop: a large, oval-shaped fruit with a thick, green, spiny skin. The pinkish-white flesh inside is custard-textured with a delicate, tart flavour.

Sugar cane: similar in appearance to bamboo, this plant has played a considerable part in Caribbean history as the sugar cane plantations demanded extensive labour, provided by slaves. Short lengths of the woody stalk are either chewed and sucked for their sweet refreshing juice.

Sweet potato: a sweet-fleshed tuber, available in many varieties.

Sweet Potato

Yam: a family of large, brown-skinned, starchy tubers, which come in many varieties, both yellow and white-fleshed.

Food Shops

For the best range of African and Caribbean foodstuffs, head to bustling markets such as Brixton Market in South London or Ridley Road Market in East London.

Central

Randsavers

⊡ *Unit 3 The Arches*
   Villiers Street, WC2N 6NG
☎ *020 7839 6415*
🖱 *www.southafricanshop.co.uk*
🚌 *Charing Cross/Embankment LU*
🕐 *Mon-Fri 10am-7pm, Sat 10am-6pm,*
   Sun 11am-5pm

Tucked away under the railway arches, the South African flag signals this roomy, subterranean shop, crammed with South African foodstuffs, from imported soft drinks to cereals and confectionary. The shop is best-known for its range of competitively-priced biltong, sold from wet to dry.

North

Engocha

⊡ *143 Fortess Road, NW5 2HR*
☎ *020 7485 3838*
🚌 *Tufnell Park LU*
🕐 *Daily 10am-8.30pm*

This tiny, frankincense-scented Ethiopian food shop has a meat counter and a small stock of basics, including spices and tef (an Ethiopian grain). Home-made injeera (Ethiopian bread) is particularly popular.

France Fresh Fish

⊡ *99 Stroud Green Road, N4 3PX*
☎ *020 7263 9767*
🚌 *Finsbury Park LU/Rail*
🕐 *Mon-Sat 9.30am-7pm, Sun 11am-5pm*

An eye-catching window display of tropical fish such as parrot fish marks out this established tropical fish shop. Chez Liline, the Mauritian fish restaurant is next door.

K. M. Butcher's Grocer's

⊡ *29 Stroud Green Road, N4 3EF*
☎ *020 7263 6625*
🚌 *Finsbury Park LU/Rail*
🕐 *Mon-Sat 8am-8pm, Sun 8am-6pm*

A large store selling an extensive range of African and Caribbean foodstuffs, with groceries ranging from store-cupboard staples to fresh goat's meat.

Stroud Green Food Store

🏠 *65 Stroud Green Road, N4 3EG*
☎ *020 7272 0348*
🚌 *Finsbury Park LU/Rail*
🕐 *Daily 8am-8pm*

A neatly-arranged store with an attractive display of fresh fruit and vegetables outside, including breadfruit, mangoes, plantain and bunches of thyme, and grocery staples inside.

Walthamstow Market

🏠 *Walthamstow High Street E17 7JY*
🚌 *Walthamstow LU*
🕐 *Tues-Sat 8am-5pm*

Among the stalls at this huge street market – reputedly Europe's longest outdoor street market – are several selling African and Caribbean ingredients.

West

Portobello Road Market

🏠 *Portobello Road, W10 5TD*
🚌 *Notting Hill Gate LU*
🕐 *Mon-Sat 9am-5pm*

Alongside the antique shops and fashionable boutiques, is a traditional street market selling fruit and vegetable, with many of the stalls here selling West Indian produce such as yams, Scotch bonnet peppers and okra.

Shepherd's Bush Market

🏠 *Uxbridge Road, W12 7JA*
🚌 *Goldhawk Road or Shepherd's Bush LU*
🕐 *Mon-Wed, Fri-Sat 9am-5pm,*
    Thurs 9am-1pm

Once a more food-orientated market, among the fabric, lingerie and kitchenware stalls, however, one can find stalls selling Caribbean produce such as yams, mangoes and plantain.

South-East

G. Baldwin & Co.

🏠 *171-173 Walworth Road, SE17 1RW*
☎ *020 7703 5550*
🖱 *www.baldwins.co.uk*
🕐 *Mon-Sat 9am-6pm*

Established in 1844 and a South London institution, Baldwin's is known among Britain's African and Caribbean community for its iconic sarsaparilla drink.

Choumert Road Market

🏠 *Choumert Road, SE15 4SE*
🚌 *Peckham Rye Rail*
🕐 *Mon-Sat 9am-3pm*

Off Rye Lane – itself lined with African and Caribbean butchers, fishmongers and grocers – this street market offers stalls selling tropical fish and staple produce.

East Street Market

⊡ *East Street, SE17 1EL*
🚇 *Elephant and Castle LU*
🕐 *Tues-Fri 8am-5pm,*
  Sat 8am-6.30pm, Sun 8am-2pm

Just off the Walworth Road, this traditional street market is home to several stalls selling African and Caribbean produce, while among the shops lining East Street include halal butchers, African and Caribbean food shops and a fishmonger selling tropical fish.

South-West

Brixton Market

⊡ *Brixton Station Road, Pope's Road,*
  SW9 Atlantic Road, Electric Lane
  and Electric Avenue, SW9 8JX
🚇 *Brixton LU/Rail*
🕐 *Mon-Tues, Thurs-Sat 8am-5.30pm,*
  Wed 8am-1pm

This is the best market in London for Caribbean and African foodstuffs. Spread out through streets and arcades are a number of African and Caribbean food shops, butchers, fishmongers and market stalls. Produce is piled high including yams, Scotch bonnet peppers, green and yellow plantains, breadfruit, mangoes, limes and bunches of thyme. Fishmongers here sell a colourful array of tropical fish while the butchers (some with signs advertising 'meat so tender you don't need teeth') offer goat, offal, cow's feet and pig's trotters. Saturday is the busiest market day with shoppers exchanging greetings, catching up on news and bargaining.

The Savanna

⊡ *Barry House*
  20-22 Worple Road, SW19 4DH
🖱 *www.thesavanna.co.uk*
🚇 *Wimbledon LU/Rail*
🕐 *Mon-Sat 10am-8pm, Sun 11am-7pm*

South African foodstuffs and drinks, from maize meal to wines, are on offer here at this bright, neat shop.

Tooting Market

⊡ *Upper Tooting Road, SW17 0SN*
🚇 *Tooting Broadway LU*
🕐 *Mon-Sat 10am-6pm, Sun 10am-4pm*

This covered market offers a selection of African and Caribbean foodstuffs, both fresh and store cupboard.

East

Queen's Market

⊡ *Green Street, E13 9BA*
  (on the corner of Queens Road)
🚇 *Upton Park LU*
🕐 *Tues, Thurs-Sat 8am-5pm*

This huge, multi-cultural East End market houses a number of stalls and shops selling Caribbean foodstuffs, tropical fish and halal meat, often at very competitive prices.

Ridley Road Market

▪ *Ridley Road, E8 2NP*
🚌 *Dalston Junction Rail*
🕐 *Tues-Sat 9am-5pm*

A large, bustling street market, long known for its West Indian and African food stalls and shops, selling everything from meat, such as goat's meat and pig's trotters, and tropical fish to groceries and fresh fruit and vegetables.

Mail-Order

Jollof Pot

✎ *www.jollofpot.co.uk*

This Ghanaian catering company also sells Ghanaian spices and taster boxes mail-order.

Tobia Teff

✎ *www.tobiateff.co.uk*

An opportunity to buy teff, the ancient Ethiopian grain used to make injera, the traditional Ethiopian flatbread. The grain is so small that its name 'teff' comes from the Arabic 'teffa' meaning 'lost'.

Eating Places

Central

Jerk City ££

▪ *189 Wardour Street, W1F 8ZD*
☎ *020 7287 2878*
✎ *www.jerkcity.co.uk*
🚌 *Tottenham Court Road LU*

A small, relaxed café specialising in classic Caribbean dishes including saltfish and ackee and jerk chicken.

North

Cottons £££

▪ *55 Chalk Farm Road, NW1 8AN*
☎ *020 7485 8388*
✎ *www.cottonscamden.co.uk*
🚌 *Camden Town or Chalk Farm LU*

Attractively decorated in bright tropical colours this funky restaurant serves up generous portions of excellent Caribbean food such as mixed jerk grilled fish or curried goat. Drinks include cocktails, sorrel and a serious range of rums in the Rum Shack.

Hummingbird ££

84 Stroud Green Road, N4 3AN
020 7263 9690
Finsbury Park LU/Rail

This veteran Trinidadian restaurant is a relaxed place in which to try classic Trinidadian dishes such as rotis and rice and peas, accompanied by delicious punches.

Lalibela ££

137 Fortess Road, NW5 2HR
020 7284 0600
www.lalibelarestaurant.co.uk
Tufnell Park LU

This friendly, well-established restaurant offers a chance to enjoy lovingly prepared classic Ethiopian dishes such as 'wot', richly-spiced stews and injeera, the flat sour bread with which one scoops up and eats the wot. Finish off with Ethiopian coffee, a leisurely experience during which one inhales the fragrance of the freshly roasted beans, heated in a heavy metal saucepan, before being presented with a pottery flask of the freshly made coffee served with aromatic burning frankincense on the side.

Mango Room £££

10-12 Kentish Town Road, NW1 8NH
020 7482 5065
www.mangoroom.co.uk
Camden Town LU

Very much a Camden Town institution, this is a bright, attractive restaurant serving great, Caribbean food, from salt cod fritters with apple chutney to Creole snapper fillet with mango and green peppercorn sauce.

Queen of Sheba ££

12 Fortess Road, NW5 2EU
020 7284 3947
www.thequeenofsheba.co.uk
Kentish Town LU/RTail

A hospitable, well-established Ethiopian restaurant, offering dishes such as tibs firfir and misir we't.

Spinach and Agushi £

Exmouth Market EC1R 4QA
www.spinachandagushi.co.uk

This streetfood stall offers a chance on weekday lunchtimes to sample Ghanaian dishes, such as jollof rice and spicy stews.

West

Spinach and Agushi £

Portobello Road Market, W10 5TD
Notting Hill Gate LU
www.spinachandagushi.co.uk

This Ghanaian streetfood stall offers a chance on weekday lunchtimes to sample Ghanaian dishes, such as jollof rice and spicy stews

South-East

Bubba's Restaurant ££-£££

⊞ 7A Station Rise, SE27 9BW
☎ 020 8674 4114
✑ www.bubbasrestaurant.co.uk
🚌 Tulse Hill Rail

Warmly recommended by local residents, Bubba's showcases Michelin-starred chef Anthony Cumberbatch's talents, offering elegant versions of traditional Caribbean dishes and an appealing range of cocktails.

South-West

Asmara ££

⊞ 386 Coldharbour Lane, SW9 8LF
☎ 020 7737 4144
🚌 Brixton LU/Rail

This small, homely restaurant serves up delicious, carefully cooked Eritrean food.

East

Jungle Braai £-££

⊞ 28 Osborn Street, E1 6TD
✑ www.junglebraai.com
☎ 020 7247 0073
🚌 Aldgate East LU

A South African restaurant serving up South African barbecue dishes such as grilled boerewors sausages and piri-piri chicken.

Cookbooks

My personal recommendations of cookbooks for this cuisine, including both new titles and out-of-print classics:

Creole Caribbean Cookery
Kenneth Gardiner
A nicely written book with appetising recipes.

Caribbean and African Cookery
Rosamund Grant
A well-written, informative and readable cookbook.

A Taste of Africa
Dorinda Hafner
A look at African and Caribbean cookery, written with exuberance.

Caribbean Cooking
Elizabeth Lambert Ortiz
An excellent look at Caribbean cuisine.

Caribbean Food Made Easy
Levi Roots
An attractive & accessible Caribbean cookbook by the creator of Reggae Reggae Sauce.

Asian London

Patel Brothers

The term 'Asian' covers what was once the Indian subcontinent but is today Bangladesh, India, Pakistan and Sri Lanka. An Asian presence in Britain can be traced back to the seventeenth and eighteenth centuries. Some early settlers were performers but many were servants brought back from India by the newly prosperous nawabs. Through the East India Company others came as lascars, Indian seamen.

A fascinating book, *Across Seven Seas* (edited by Caroline Adams), describes how many of these lascars were from one small, land-locked part of Bengal called Sylhet. There was a tradition in rural India of men leaving their villages to work and support their family. Work as seamen was offered at large ports such as Calcutta. In the words of Haji Kona Miah, "The Sylhet people were in the ship because these people follow each other, and some went there and others saw them and thought they could get jobs too". The serangs, agents who chose workers for the ships, preferred to employ people from their own village or locality. Once Sylhetis became serangs, a pattern of using Sylheti sailors was established.

Those who settled in London lived in the East End, near the docks. For many of them earning a living was difficult and in 1858 the 'Strangers Home for Asiatics, Africans and South Sea Islanders' was opened in West India Dock Road, Limehouse. The major growth in the Bengali community came this century in 1956, when passports were finally granted and thousands of people came to London. By 1962, the number of Bengali immigrants living in the East End had swelled from approximately 300 to 5,000.

Of course, it was not only Bengali seamen to come to London: doctors, politicians and lawyers were also among the immigrants. Indeed, three men pivotal to India's independence studied law in London at the turn of the century: Mohandas Karamchand (later Mahatma) Gandhi, Mohammed Ali Jinnah and Jawaharlal Nehru. In 1892 Dabadhai Naoroji, a campaigner for Indian rights, was elected as Britain's first Asian MP by a majority of three votes.

It was in the period following the Second World War that the Asian presence in Britain expanded considerably, the 1948 Nationality Act granted the right of British citizenship to Britain's colonies and former colonies. After Indian Independence the violent partition of India and Pakistan left thousands dispossessed. Britain officially encouraged mainly unskilled workers from India and Pakistan to come to Britain and by 1958 there were around 55,000 Asians in Britain. The next wave of immigration came in the late 1960s when Asians were expelled from Uganda, and in 1972, when Idi Amin expelled nearly 30,000 Ugandan Asians who arrived in Britain within the space of three months.

The Asian community today, like the complex Indian subcontinent, is made up of people from different countries who speak different languages and practice different faiths. Certain areas in London are linked to particular groups. Brick Lane, which over the centuries has housed different waves of immigrants, is now predominantly Bengali, the Sylhet seamen who first settled there having paved the way for others. The history of Brick Lane is encapsulated in the story of one building on Fournier Street, built as a Huguenot chapel in 1774, it later became a Methodist chapel, in 1898 it was converted into a Jewish synagogue, and nowadays it functions as the London Jamme Masjid mosque.

Wembley is a Gujarati area, while Southall is predominantly Punjabi and

Patel Brothers

Sikh. There are various theories about Southall's roots. One is that workers brought in to construct the new airport at Heathrow settled near their worksite. Alternatively, it is thought that work was provided for Asian labourers in local factories and the community grew up around this. Southall today is a thriving community with everything from Sikh temples to bookshops and restaurants. In South London Tooting houses a diverse Asian community, including Sri Lankans, East African Asians, Pakistanis and Gujuratis. A Sri Lankan community is also found in Harrow, in West London. London's Hindu community, meanwhile, is justly proud of 'Shri Swaminarayan Mandir' (020 8965 2651), the traditional Hindu temple recently built in Neasden. The gleaming white marble temple, which rises like a mirage in an urban desert just off the North Circular, is unique in Europe as an example of traditional Indian temple construction. It is made from blocks of limestone and marble which were hand-carved in India then shipped over and assembled in London. There is an adjourning Haveli (community centre) decorated with intricate wooden carvings, where visitors to the temple complex are courteously welcomed.

Asian Cuisine

The term 'Indian cuisine' is a catch-all phrase, covering the diverse cuisines of India, Pakistan, Bangladesh and Sri Lanka and a spectrum of regional, religious and cultural differences. The hallmark of all Indian cuisine is the emphasis on spices and herbs. These numerous flavourings, from aromatic crocus stamens (saffron) to pungent resin (asafoetida), are used in intricate and varying ways: dry-roasted, fried in hot oil or mixed with other spices to form a masala (spice mix). Underlying their culinary use is an ancient belief in the health-giving properties of spices. In the Holy Hindu Scriptures, the medicinal properties of herbs and spices are listed. Turmeric and cloves both have antiseptic properties. Asafoetida, a digestive which prevents flatulence, is added to lentil dishes. Spices are divided into 'warm', generating internal heat, and 'cool', lessening it.

Underneath this culinary umbrella are diverse cuisines influenced by religion (the main Indian faiths being Hinduism, Islam, Buddhism, Jainism and Sikhism), geography and culture. Religions have laid down rules and taboos as to what can or cannot be eaten. For example, the Hindus will not eat beef as the cow is sacred. Some Hindus are vegetarian, while for strict vegetarians even the flavourings associated with meat (garlic and onion) are not allowed. For Muslims, pork is a forbidden meat.

When describing Indian cuisine in regional terms, it is possible to draw a crude north-south boundary, although there are exceptions. Flat wheat breads such as paratha and chapati are a staple in the north while rice is the staple in the south. Northern cuisine was influenced by Mogul rulers who came down to India through Persia. The Persian influence is apparent in the subtle spicing, the use of nuts and in dishes such as pullao, a descendant of the pilaff. From this luxurious court cuisine came techniques used today: korma (braising in a thick, often nut-based sauce); pot-roasting (in a traditional charcoal stove); and kebab, kofte and tandoori (dishes cooked in a tandoor oven). The Indian food that is most frequently served in restaurants is based on this Mogul cuisine. In Southern Indian cookery the coconut palm has an influential role, with sweet coconut milk used in many dishes. Rice is eaten not just as a grain but is ground, mixed with dal, and used to make light pancakes called dosai. As in other hot climates, fermentation is a well-used culinary technique.

Glossary

Angled loofah: a green gourd with distinctive raised ridges running down its length and a bitter flavour.

Asafoetida (heeng): a pungent brown resin, valued for its digestive properties, sold in either lump or powder form.

Bitter gourd (karela): a knobbly-skinned, cucumber-shaped green gourd with a distinctive bitter flavour and digestive properties.

Bitter Gourd

Bottle gourd (dudi): a large, smooth, bottle-shaped, green-skinned gourd with marrow-like flesh.

Cardamom: a fragrant spice pod sold whole, hulled or ready-ground. The small green or white cardamoms are used in both sweet and savoury dishes while the larger wrinkled black cardamom is used only in savoury dishes.

Carom (ajwan): a tiny seed spice, like miniature fennel seeds, with a medicinal scent and sharp, thyme-like flavour.

Chayote (chow-chow): A pear-sized, wrinkled, green-skinned squash with a single large seed and marrow-like flesh.

Chenna: a ricotta-like curd cheese.

Chickpea flour (gram or besan): ground chickpeas are the basis for many breads and fritters. Madhur Jaffrey recommends fridge storage.

Chick–peas (channa): fresh chickpeas are small, puffy green pods which need peeling to reveal the kernel.

Chikoo (sapodilla): similar looking to kiwi fruit with fine brown, furry skin, pinky-brown granular flesh, glossy pips and a distinctive sweet flavour.

Chillies: sold both fresh and dried. Fresh green chillies and dried red chillies are used in Indian cookery to add both pungent heat and a distinctive flavour.

Chilli powder: a hot red powder made from ground, dried red chillies.

Cluster beans (guar): fine, straight green beans.

Coconut milk: a thick white liquid made from grated coconut flesh and not, as is sometimes thought, from the cloudy liquid inside the coconut which is called 'coconut water'. Home-made coconut milk can be made by blending together dessicated coconut with hot water, then sieving it. Alternatively, tinned coconut milk is a convenient, ready-to-use product; Madhur Jaffrey recommends the Chaokoh brand. Creamed coconut or coconut milk powder needs diluting before use.

Coriander: both the aromatic green leaves (similar in appearance to flat-leafed parsley) and small rounded seeds are used extensively in Indian cookery.

Cumin: small, greenish, finely-ridged oval seeds, similar to caraway seeds, with a distinctive, slightly sharp flavour, widely used in Indian cookery. Black cumin, which is rarer, has a more pronounced herbal flavour.

Curry Leaves

Curry leaf: a spicy-smelling leaf which resembles a small bay leaf. It's usually sold dried but sometimes branches of fresh curry leaves are available.

Dal: a generic term covering the three types of pulses (lentils, beans and peas) used in Indian cookery: *chana dal*, small yellow split peas; *masoor dal*, tiny pink split lentils (sometimes called red split lentils); *moong dal*, yellow split mung beans (sold both skinned and unskinned); *rajma dal*, red kidney beans; *toovar dal*, a large split yellow pea; *urad dal*, ivory-coloured hulled black gram beans (used in Southern Indian vegetarian cookery in dishes such as pancakes and fried dumplings).

Moong Dal

Drumsticks: long, green, ridged pods with thick skin, fibrous pulp and a distinctive flavour. Usually available tinned but sometimes found fresh.

Fennel: aniseed-flavoured, greenish ridged seeds, valued as a digestive. Candied fennel seeds are eaten after a meal.

Drumstick

Fenugreek (methi): both the small, stubby, hard, yellow seeds and the spicy-smelling, bitter green leaves are used in Indian cookery. The seeds have a strong, bitter flavour and are used in pickles. The dark green trefoil leaves, which look similar to clover, are sold both fresh and dried.

Fenugreek

Fish: *hilsa*, a prized freshwater fish from Bangladesh; *pomfret*, a flat, round-shaped and white-fleshed fish.

Garam masala: a fragrant spice mix, available in many versions.

Ghee: clarified butter with a nutty flavour. Because of the clarification, ghee can be used for deep frying and stored at room temperature.

Ginger: this knobbly, lightbrown root is a key flavouring prized for its aromatic flavour and digestive qualities.

Green Mango

Guava: a fruit resembling a small, knobbly pear, with a distinctive aroma, pinkish flesh and several small, hard seeds.

Hyacinth bean (seim): a broad-podded, thick-skinned, curved green bean; a member of the hyacinth bean family.

Jackfruit: a huge fruit with a thick, green studded skin. The creamy-textured flesh inside is eaten as a vegetable when unripe and as a fruit when ripe.

Jaggery: a pale brown sugar with a nutty flavour, made from sugar cane juice or palm sap. Used in Indian sweets.

Kohlrabi: a pale green or purple bulbous vegetable, resembling a sprouting turnip – but with a more delicate flavour.

Kokum: a variety of mangosteen, sold in dried pieces and used as a souring agent.

Lemon crystals: light-coloured crystals used as a souring agent.

Mango: a kidney-shaped fruit, with succulent orange flesh and a sweet, resiny flavour, and enormously popular in India. Tart, green unripe mangoes are used to make pickles, chutneys and relishes while orange-red ripe mangoes are eaten on their own or used in desserts. Over a thousand varieties are grown in India, but the Alphonso mango is one of the best known in Britain.

Mango powder (amchoor): sour, beige-coloured powder made from dried, unripe mangoes, used to add a tart flavour to food.

Mustard oil: a pungent yellow oil, made from mustard seeds.

Mustard seeds: tiny, black round seeds, often used in pickles.

Okra (bhindi, ladies fingers): a tapering, ridged green pod which exudes a sticky juice when cooked.

Okra

Onion seed (kalonji or nigella): tiny tear-shaped black seeds – not related to onions. Used primarily in pickles but also on tandoori naan bread.

Panch phoran: a Bengali five-spice mix, containing cumin, fennel, onion seeds, fenugreek and black mustard seeds.

Paneer: a firm white cheese, made from pressed Indian curd cheese called chenna (similar to ricotta).

Panch Phoran

Patra: large, green taro leaves which are spread with a gram flour paste, rolled and steamed to make a dish called 'patra'.

Phalooda (falooda): transparent, thread-like noodles made from wheatberry starch and flavoured with pine or rose essence, used in desserts, to garnish kulfi or in a drink of the same name.

Pistachio: green-fleshed, delicately-flavoured nuts, used in Indian sweetmeats and ice cream or as a nibble.

Pointed gourd (parwal): this is a small, green squash (sometimes striped with white)

Pomegranate seeds (anardana): dried pomegranate kernels, used to add sourness.

Poppadums (papar): small round wafers made from split-peas and flavoured with garlic or spices. When fried in hot oil they puff up and become crispy.

Poppy seed (khas khas): white poppy seeds, used ground to thicken sauces.

Rice: the most famous and expensive of rice varieties grown in India is basmati, with its nutty aroma and flavour

Rose essence: a delicate rose-scented essence used in desserts. Rose water is a diluted form of rose essence.

Saffron: the dried stigmas of a crocus variety, sold as both thread and powdered.
Sevian: fine golden-brown wheat vermicelli, used in desserts.

Snake gourd: a long, narrow, twisted green gourd with marrow-like flesh.

Spiny bitter gourd (kantola): a small, spiky, egg-shaped relation of the bitter gourd.

Sweetmeats: many Indian sweetmeats are made from milk boiled down slowly until it thickens (rabadi) or until it takes on a fudge like consistency (khoya). Varieties include: *barfi*, a crumbly Indian fudge often flavoured with nuts; *gulub jamun*, deep-fried dumplings in syrup; *halwa*: nuts, fruits and vegetables cooked with ghee and sugar to a firm texture; *jalebi*: bright orange, crisp batter squiggles filled with syrup; *kulfi*, ice cream made from slow-cooked milk which gives a slightly grainy texture; and *rasmalai*: delicate, soft chenna dumplings served in *rabadi* (slow-cooked milk).

Tindola

Tamarind: a brown fleshy pod with a sour-sweet flavour, used as a souring agent. Both tamarind pulp and paste are available.

Taro: the term applies to a whole range of fibrous tubers, recognisable by their brown hairy skins and white starchy flesh.

Tinda: a small, rounded member of the marrow family, with pale green skin and white flesh.

Tindola (tindori): walnut-sized 'ivy' gourds with variegated markings and a crisp, crunchy texture.

Turmeric (haldi): a small-fingered, orange-fleshed root from which comes the powdered yellow spice powder of the same name.

Vark: fine edible foil, made from ground silver or gold, used to adorn dishes on special occasions.

White radish (mooli): long, thick white radish, with a mild flavour, used to stuff parathas in Pakistani cooking.

Yard-long beans: exceedingly long, thin green beans.

Yoghurt: traditionally made from buffalo milk, Julie Sahni suggests stirring a little soured cream into normal yoghurt to reproduce the necessary tangy flavour.

Food Shops

The range of stock in Asian food shops is huge, from fresh fruits and vegetables to staples like dals and flours. Often the emphasis is on bulk-buying and stocking up with large sacks of basmati or huge packets of spices.

Central

If you're looking for Indian ingredients in central London, then head to Drummond Street, a quiet side-street by Euston Station, home to some veteran Indian restaurants and a handful of food shops.

Ambala

⊞ *112-114 Drummond Street, NW1 2HN*
☎ *020 7387 7886 / 3521*
✎ *www.ambalafoods.co.uk*
🚌 *Euston LU/Rail*
🕐 *Daily 9am-9pm*

Ambala have been selling Asian sweets since 1965, when their first small shop opened on this quiet backstreet. Ambala is now a thriving chain and the original shop has been revamped in bright colours with marble counters. Customers return again and again for excellent fudge-like barfis, sticky jalebi and takeaway packets of rasmalai. Savoury snacks include crisp vegetable samosas and packets of Bombay mix.

Indian Spice Shop

⊞ *115-117 Drummond Street, NW1 2HL*
☎ *020 7916 1831*
🚌 *Euston LU/Rail*
🕐 *Mon-Sat 9.30am-9.30pm,
Sun 10am-9pm*

Catering for both the local English and Indian communities, Indian Spice is divided into an off-licence-cum-corner shop on one side and an Indian grocer's on the other. It offers a truly impressive range of spices, as well as other groceries including chutneys, papads and dals, plus huge sacks of basmati and fresh produce outside.

North

Ambala

⊞ *61 Turnpike Lane, N8 0EE*
☎ *020 8292 1253*
✎ *www.ambalafoods.co.uk*
🚌 *Turnpike Lane LU*
🕐 *Daily 9am-9pm*

A branch of the established Indian sweet company.

Goodeats

⊞ *124 Ballards Lane, N3 2PA*
☎ *020 7349 2373*
🚌 *Finchley Central LU*
🕐 *Mon-Sat 9am-7pm*

This well-established, neatly arranged foodstore has an excellent range of stock. In addition to a good selection of Indian groceries, there is a fresh fruit and vegetable section selling produce such as fresh methi and patra.

Q Stores

⌨ *19 Lodge Lane, N12 8JG*
☎ *020 8446 2495*
🚇 *Woodside Park LU*
🕐 *Mon-Sat 9.30am-5.45pm,*
   Sun 10am-1pm

Tucked away just off North Finchley's busy high street, this long, narrow shop has a good, neatly-arranged selection of fresh Indian produce, from mangoes to mustard seed, plus store-cupboard staples.

North-West

Wembley's Ealing Road has long been noted for its range of Asian food shops including enormous greengrocers. Be warned, however, that it becomes very busy over the weekend and finding a parking space can be a challenge. Kingsbury also has a useful cluster of Asian food shops, including grocers, confectioners and halal butchers.

Fudco

⌨ *184 Ealing Road, HA0 4QD*
☎ *020 8902 4820*
🚇 *Alperton LU*
🕐 *Daily 10.30am-6.30pm*

As importers and packagers, Fudco are a major supplier of foodstuffs from spices to dried fruits. Their own grocer's shop stocks an impressive range all neatly displayed.

Gayatri

⌨ *467 Kingsbury Road, NW9 9DY*
☎ *020 8206 1677*
✒ *www.gayatri.co.uk*
🚇 *Kingsbury LU*
🕐 *Mon-Fri 10.30am-6.30pm,*
   Sat 10.30am-6pm, Sun 9am-4pm

Warmly recommended by Gujurati friends, this sweet shop produces a range of traditional vegetarian sweets (such as tutti frutti burfi and shrikhand) plus savoury nibbles. It is especially noted for its Diwali specialities, doing huge business in the run-up to Diwali.

Kingsbury Fruit and Veg Ltd

⌨ *477-481 Kingsbury Road, NW9 9EA*
☎ *020 8905 0295*
🕐 *Daily 10am-7pm*

This large store carries a comprehensive range of stock, from fresh fruit and vegetables to store cupboard groceries.

Royal Sweets

- 280 Ealing Road, HA0 4LL
- 020 8903 9359
- Alperton LU
- Tues-Sun 10am-7pm

A friendly branch of the established Asian confectioners, selling brightly coloured halvas and savoury nibbles.

Sira Fruit–Veg

- 288 Ealing Road, HA0 4LL
- 020 8903 5769
- Alperton LU
- Daily 8am-8pm

A roomy shop with a large fresh fruit and vegetable section, including okra, fresh curry leaves and bunches of methi. In addition, there is a selection of basic Asian groceries.

V. B. & Sons Cash and Carry

- 738 Kenton road, HA3 9QX
- 020 8206 1770
- Kingsbury LU
- Mon-Sat 9am-6.45pm, Sun 10am-4pm

A large, well-established shop offering an impressive range of stock. They have their own-label, from pulses and flours to frozen vegetables and savouries such as kachoris.

V. B. & Sons Cash and Carry

- 218 Ealing Road, HA0
- 020 8902 8579
- Alperton LU
- Mon-Fri 9.30am-6.45pm, Sat 9am-6.45pm, Sun 11am-5pm

A huge, neatly-arranged store, aromatic with spices and bustling with customers tracking down the numerous special offers. V.B. specialises in groceries, with a wide range of spices, nuts, dried fruits, dals and flours. The freezer section contains yucca and mogo chips, samosas and samosa pastry.

Wembley Exotics

- 133-135 Ealing Road, HA0 4BP
- 020 8900 2607
- Alperton LU
- Daily 24 hours

Mounds of chillies, root ginger and peanuts under an awning mark this cavernous self-service store, which specialises in fresh produce. Inside is a staggering array of Asian fruits, vegetables and herbs, from guvar beans and pigeon peas to fragrant guavas, fresh tamarind and bunches of methi.

West

South Harrow Food and Wines

- 🏢 234-236 Northold Road, HA2 8DU
- ☎ 020 8423 6321
- ✐ www.southharrowfoodandwine.co.uk
- 🚌 South Harrow LU
- 🕐 Mon-Sat 7.30am-11pm,
  Sun 7.30am-10.30pm

An impressive range of Sri Lankan ingredients is on offer here at this family-run Sri Lankan supermarket, from fresh produce to groceries, including the company's in-house Harin brand.

South-West

The main highway through Tooting is lined with a real variety of Asian food shops (halal butchers, greengrocers, foodstores and sweetshops). There is also a tempting choice of eateries, ranging from veteran South Indian vegetarian to Pakistani restaurants offering halal meat dishes.

Ambala

- 🏢 48 Upper Tooting Road, SW17 7PD
- ☎ 020 8767 1747
- ✐ www.ambalafoods.co.uk
- 🚌 Tooting Bec LU. Tooting Broadway LU
- 🕐 Daily 9am-9pm

A branch of the established Asian sweet manufacturers.

Bhavins

- 🏢 193-197 Upper Tooting Road, SW17 7TG
- ☎ 020-8672 4462
- 🚌 Tooting Bec LU, Tooting Broadway LU
- 🕐 Daily 9am-9pm

Recommended by Indian food lover, Pek Choo, this large, bustling shop is particularly noted for its excellent, wide-ranging selection of fresh tropical fruits and vegetables, from seasonal varieties of Indian and Pakistani mangoes and custard apples to drumsticks and patra. If you're in a culinary rut when it comes to fruit and vegetables, come here!

Dadu's Cash & Carry

- 🏢 190-198 Upper Tooting Road, SW17 7EW
- ☎ 020 8672 4984
- 🚌 Tooting Bec LU, Tooting Broadway LU
- 🕐 Mon-Sat 9am-7pm, Sun 10am-6pm

This huge store has an extensive stock of competitively-priced Asian foodstuffs, from assorted pulses, flours and condiments to a freezer section crammed with everything from samosas to parathas.

Daily Fresh Foods

🖃 *152 Upper Tooting Road, SW17 7ER*
☎ *020 8767 7861*
🚌 *Tooting Bec LU, Tooting Broadway LU*
🕐 *Daily 8am-8pm*

As the name suggests, there's an eye-catching display of fresh fruit, vegetables and herbs on offer here. Inside is a halal counter and a grocery section offering a limited choice of basics.

Deepak Food and Wine

🖃 *953 Garratt Lane, SW17 0LR*
☎ *020 8767 7819*
🚌 *Tooting Broadway LU*
🕐 *Mon-Sat 9am-7.30pm, Sun 10am-4pm*

An enormous supermarket with an extensive range of Asian foodstuffs, particularly strong on store-cupboard staples such as spices, pulses and chutneys.

Niru Convenience

🖃 *82 Tooting High Street, SW17 0RN*
☎ *020 8672 3200*
🚌 *Tooting Bec LU, Tooting Broadway LU*
🕐 *Mon, Wed 8am-10pm,*
Tues, Thurs, Sun 8am-11pm

This long, narrow shop offers a good range of Sri Lankan ingredients, from fresh produce such as drumsticks and curry leaves to store-cupboard essentials such as hopper mixtures and assorted flours.

Patel Brothers

🖃 *187-191 Upper Tooting Road,*
SW17 7TG
☎ *020 8672 2792*
🖘 *www.patelbros.co.uk*
🚌 *Tooting Bec LU, Tooting Broadway LU*
🕐 *Daily 9am-6.30pm*

Founded in 1973 by Mr Patel, and still run by the Patel family with Mr and Mrs Patel manning the tills, this well-established business was the first Asian food store on Upper Tooting Road. Stock ranges from fresh produce to pickles, curry pastes and spices, ghee and tinned foods. A side-room is devoted mainly to rice, pulses and flours, including the Patels' own-line of flour.

Pooja Sweets

🖃 *168-170 Upper Tooting Road,*
SW17 7ER
☎ *020 8672 4523/8682 5148*
🖘 *www.poojasweets.com*
🚌 *Tooting Bec LU/Toorting Broadway LU*
🕐 *Mon-Sun 9am-9pm*

This smart establishment offers an extensive array of over 100 sweets and savouries, from assorted ladoo to chat.

Southall

Southall, in London's western suburbs, is a busy Indian shopping area full of sari shops, jewellers, halal butchers, greengrocers and stalls selling everything from mobile phones to freshly-fried jalebi. Southall also has several large-scale cash-and-carry stores, where the emphasis is on bulk-buying.

Chhappan Bhog

- 1 The Broadway, UB1 1JR
- 020 8574 7607
- www.chhappanbhog.co.uk
- Southall Rail
- Daily 10am-8pm

This small sweet shop comes complete with an outside stall selling freshly-fried jalebis and samosas. Inside, a colourful selection of assorted sweets is on display.

Dokal & Sons

- 133-135 The Broadway, UB1 1LW
- 020 8574 1647
- www.dokalandsons.co.uk
- Southall Rail
- Daily 9am-8pm

What appears at first glance to be a small corner shop widens out into a huge store and is filled with a comprehensive stock of groceries such as chutneys, flours, tinned vegetables, nuts and spices and is run with friendly enthusiasm by Mr Dokal and his family, who established this business in 1970.

Moti Mahal

- 94 The Broadway, UB1 1QF
- 020 8574 7682
- www.motimahal.co.uk
- Southall Rail
- Daily 10am-11pm

Food writer Roopa Gulati highly recommends the jalebis (freshly fried in a stall outside) and the kulfi ice creams from this established Southall eaterie.

Quality Foods

- 47-61 South Road, UB1 1 SQ
- 020 8917 9188
- www.quality-foods.co.uk
- Southall Rail
- Mon-Sat 7am-7.30pm,
  Sun 12noon-6pm

This store is recommended by food writer Roopa Gulati. It is a huge, spacious store with an impressive stock ranging from fresh produce such as round dudhi, white turmeric and bunches of saag to store cupboard items such as huge 2.5kg tins of chick peas and beans. Gulab, the in-house brand, is extensively stocked.

Sira Cash and Carry

⌨ *128 The Broadway, UB1 1QF*
☎ *020 8574 2280*
🚌 *Southall Rail*
🕐 *Daily 8am-8pm*

Established in 1969, this friendly shop carries a range of stock including flours, pulses, spices and chutneys. In addition there is an excellent, extensive greengrocery with an aisle of fruit including chikoo, limes, guavas and tiny green mangoes for pickling.

Sira Cash and Carry

⌨ *43 South Road, UB1 1SW*
☎ *020 8571 4529*
🚌 *Southall Rail*
🕐 *Daily 8am-9pm*

Usefully comprehensive, this spacious shop stocks fresh fruit and vegetables, grocery items, confectionery and kitchenware.

Sira Supermarket

⌨ *Amrit House, Springfield Road,*
    Hayes UB4 0JT
☎ *020 8569 1112*
✎ *www.siras.co.uk*
🕐 *Mon-Sat 8am-9pm, Sun 12noon-6pm*

Billed as 'the biggest Asian supermarket in London', this huge, brightly-lit, spic-and-span wholesale store comes complete with colourful murals, statues, piped music and an Ayurvedic clinic upstairs. The range of goods is extensive, including fresh produce, a confectionary counter from Royal Sweets, a butchers counter selling halal lamb, mutton and chicken, freezers full of Bangla fish and an extensive range of Sri Lankan foodstuffs. The fresh jalebi stall is also a popular feature. Weekends see the store filled with shoppers stocking up, some from as far away as Bournemouth and Oxford.

East

Focal points for Asian shopping in the East End are Brick Lane (home to a large Bengali community), while, further east, Green Street and Queens Market in Newham is also a great place to find Asian groceries.

Ambala

⌨ *55 Brick Lane, E1 6PU*
☎ *020 7247 8569*
🚌 *Aldgate East LU*
🕐 *Mon-Sat 10am-8pm,*
    Sun 9.30am-7.30pm

A branch of the well-established Indian sweet manufacturers, offering sweet and savoury snacks.

Banglacity

⌨ *86 Brick Lane, E1 6RL*
☎ *020 7456 1000*
🚌 *Liverpool Street LU/Rail*
🕐 *Daily 10am-9pm*

Set back slightly from Brick Lane, this cavernous supermarket is filled with a comprehensive, competitively priced range of Asian foodstuffs, from fresh produce to frozen food.

Green Street, E7

This long East End road has a mash shop and an assortment of Asian stores, selling everything from wedding saris to bargain boxes of mangoes and sweets.

Bharat

⌨ *4-6 Carlton Terrace, Green Street,*
    E7 8LH
☎ *020 8472 6393*
🚌 *Upton Park LU*
🕐 *Daily 9am-8pm*

This large store is aimed at those who buy in bulk, stocking items such as huge 15 litre tins of ghee and 10-kg sacks of basmati. The freezers are jammed with Indian fast food. Fresh fruit and veg can be found at Bharat's small sister shop, over the road at No. 263.

Queen's Market

⌨ *Green Street, E7*
    (on the corner of Queen's Road)
🚌 *Upton Park LU*
🕐 *Tues, Thurs-Sat 9am-6pm*

Handily positioned right by Upton Park tube, this large, keenly-priced, down-to-earth market, offering everything from fresh fish to household goods, bustles with shoppers stocking up and looking out for bargains. The presence of a local Asian community is reflected in a number of halal butchers and stalls offering a huge range of Asian fruit and vegetables.

Taj Stores

⌨ *112-14a Brick Lane, E1 6RL*
☎ *020 7377 0061*
✎ *www.tajstores.co.uk*
🚌 *Aldgate East LU*
🕐 *Daily 9am-9pm*

An impressively comprehensive food store, serving the local Bengali community, this spacious veteran Asian food shop was founded in 1936. It combines a halal meat counter, a greengrocery section and a mini-supermarket selling grocery items such as pulses and spices.

Eating Places

The British love affair with Indian food continues unabated. Asian eateries in London range from the cheap and cheerful to the luxuriously expensive. There are several simple cafés listed below, offering remarkably good value, while the glamorous restaurants offer a taste of sophisticated, contemporary Indian cuisine.

Central

Diwana Bhel Poori House £

121 Drummond Street, NW1 2HL
☎ *020 7387 5566*
🚌 *Euston LU/Rail*

Tucked away behind Euston station this well-established, unpretentious South-Indian vegetarian restaurant serves up dosai, idlee and thali at remarkably reasonable prices.

Great Nepalese ££

48 Eversholt Street, NW1 1DA
☎ *020 7388 6737*
✎ *www.great-nepalese.co.uk*
🚌 *Euston LU/Rail*

A Euston institution, established in 1982 popular with loyal regulars and hungry commuters. In addition to curry house fare it serves a selection of Nepalese specialities.

Indian YMCA £

41 Fitzroy Square, W1T 6AQ
☎ *020 7387 0411*
🚌 *Warren Street LU*

The appetising smell of Indian cooking wafts out from this large building, adding character to its institutional air. On offer is good home-style food at student prices in a canteen atmosphere.

Malabar Junction ££

107 Great Russell Street, WC1B 3NA
☎ *020 7580 5230*
✎ *www.malabarjunction.com*
🚌 *Tottenham Court Road LU*

A rather drab frontage hides a large, airy restaurant complete with a glass-roofed dining room. South-Indian cuisine is the speciality here, from tangy idlee (steamed rice and black gram cakes) to spicy Keralan fish curry.

Mela ££-£££

152-156 Shaftesbury Avenue, WC2H 8HL
☎ *020 7836 8635*
✎ *www.melarestaurant.co.uk*
🚌 *Leicester Square LU*

Warmly recommended by Indian friends, this informal, colourful restaurant serves up an assortment of heartily flavourful dishes, from spiced mutton chops to lobster stir-fried with black pepper.

Raavi Kebab
Halal Tandoori £-££

🏠 *125 Drummond Street, NW1 2HL*
☎ *020 7388 1780*
🚌 *Euston LU/Rail*

This small, unpretentious halal restaurant (an alcohol-free zone) serves up very reasonably priced dishes including tasty, chilli-spiced kebabs, freshly grilled over charcoal.

Ragam ££

🏠 *57 Cleveland Street, W1T 4JN*
☎ *020 7636 9098*
✍ *www.ragamindian.co.uk*
🚌 *Goodge Street LU, Warren Street LU*

A small, modest and friendly restaurant serving remarkably good value, flavourful food including South-Indian dishes such as avial or uthappam, and delicious breads.

Rasa Samudra ££££

🏠 *5 Charlotte Street, W1*
☎ *020 7637 0222*
🚌 *Goodge Street LU*

An attractive Indian restaurant, specialising in Keralan seafood dishes. Dishes such as kingfish and green mango curry and crab in coconut milk are both recommended.

Rasa W1 £££

🏠 *6 Dering Street, W1T 1RE*
☎ *020 7629 1346*
✍ *www.rasarestaurants.com*
🚌 *Oxford Circus LU, Bond Street LU*

Keralan vegetarian cuisine is on offer here, giving diners the chance to try distinctive spiced dishes such as green banana and mango curry and cashew nut patties. Round off your meal with Keralan desserts such as banana dosa (pancakes) or pal payasum (cashew rice pudding).

Sagar ££

🏠 *17a Percy Street, W1T 1DU*
☎ *020 8741 8563*
🚌 *Goodge Steet/Tottenham Court Rd LU*

A South Indian vegetarian café, known especially for its delicious dosais and idlis.

Veeraswamy £££

🏠 *99 Regent Street, W18 4RS*
☎ *020 7734 1401*
✍ *www.realindianfood.com*
🚌 *Piccadilly Circus LU*

London's oldest Indian restaurant, established in 1926, has long since shed its Raj image. Owned by the Chutney Mary team it has become a sleek example of new-wave Indian restaurants, complete with a lushly colourful décor, smartly dressed staff and a menu featuring well-prepared regional dishes.

North

Majjo's £

- 1 Fortis Green Road, N2 9JR
- ☎ 020 8883 4357
- 🚌 East Finchley LU

This small, smart, friendly take-away serves up superior Pakistani home-cooking. The meat is halal and there is a range of more unusual vegetarian dishes such as patra. Sample tastes are offered to those trying to choose from the array of dishes available.

Rani ££

- 7 Long Lane, N3 2PR
- ☎ 020 8349 4386/2646
- ✎ www.rani.uk.com
- 🚌 Finchley Central LU

Authentic Gujarati vegetarian cuisine. All dishes, from the home-made chutneys to the breads, are carefully prepared and the menu offers dishes such as banana methi and tindora curry.

West

New Asian Tandoori Centre (Roxy) ££

- 114-118 The Green, Southall, UB2 4BQ
- ☎ 020 8574 2597
- 🚌 Southall Rail

This large, spic-and-span, informal Punjabi eatery offers both take-away food and an eat-in restaurant. Prices are cheap and this is a great place for group eating, allowing you to sample lots of dishes.

Ram's £

- 203 Kenton Road, HA3 0HD
- ☎ 020 8907 2022
- ✎ www.ramsrestaurant.co.uk
- 🚌 Kenton LU/Rail

Known for its Gujurati vegetarian cuisine, this long-established restaurant is warmly recommended by food writer Roopa Gulati.

Sagar ££

- 157 King Street, W6 9JT
- ☎ 020 8741 8563
- 🚌 Hammersmith LU

Food writer Roopa Gulati recommends this South Indian vegetarian café, which has made a name for itself for its delicious dosais and idlis.

Zaika ££££

- 1 Kensington High Street, W8 5NP
- ☎ 020 7795 6533
- ✎ www.zaika-restaurant.co.uk
- 🚌 High Street Kensington

This sumptuous restaurant offers creative and innovative Indian cuisine to match its glamorous décor.

North-West

Sakonis £

⌨ 119-121 Ealing Road, HA0 4BP
☎ 020 8903 9601
🚌 Alperton LU

This bright, cheery vegetarian diner attracts queues of would-be diners (many of them in family groups), waiting patiently by the paan stall and take-away counter to sit down in the back room. The menu promises a wide range of snacks, mains, drinks and desserts: seriously chilli-hot dosai, chilli paneer, falooda, chikoo ice cream and delicious, salty-sweet freshly-squeezed lime juice.

South-West

Apollo Banana Leaf £-££

⌨ 190 Tooting High Street, SW17 0SF
☎ 020 8696 1423
🚌 Tooting Broadway LU

This popular, long-established restaurant offers a chance to sample South Indian and Sri Lankan food at remarkably reasonable prices.

Chennai Dosa £-££

⌨ 33 Upper Tooting Road, SW17 7TR
☎ 020 7351 3113
🖱 www.chennaidosa.com
🚌 Tooting Bec LU

A roomy branch of this thriving restaurant chain, specialising in dosa and idli and known for its innovative '5-foot family dosa'. In addition, the menu offers an extensive range of meat, poultry, fish and vegetarian dishes.

Chutney Mary ££££

⌨ 535 King's Road, SW10 0SZ
☎ 020 7351 3113
🖱 www.chutneymary.com
🚌 Fulham Broadway LU

This large, glamorous restaurant, complete with an attractive conservatory dining area, serves top-notch Indian cooking in an enjoyably buzzy atmosphere. The menu features classic Indian dishes and offers carefully chosen regional specialities.

Jaffna House £

⌨ 90 Tooting High Street, SW17 0RN
☎ 020-8672 7786
🖱 www.jaffnahouse.co.uk
🚌 Tooting Broadway LU

A small, down-to-earth café known for its range of affordable Sri Lankan dishes. Here you can enjoy anything from pittu and hoppers with sambol to sea food kotthu.

The Painted Heron ££££

- 📖 *112 Cheyne Walk, SW10 0DJ*
- ☎ *020 7351 5232*
- ✍ *www.thepaintedheron.com*
- 🚌 *Sloane Square LU*

This elegant, modern Indian restaurant specialises in refined contemporary dishes, using fresh and unusual ingredients to elegant effect.

Sree Krishna £-££

- 📖 *192-194 Tooting High Street, SW17 0SF*
- ☎ *020 8672 4250*
- ✍ *www.sreekrishna.co.uk*
- 🚌 *Tooting Broadway LU*

Established in 1973, this restaurant is full of enthusiasts who appreciate both the good South Indian vegetarian food and the reasonable prices.

The Star of India £££-££££

- 📖 *154 Old Brompton Road, SW5 0BE*
- ☎ *020 7373 2901*
- ✍ *www.starofindia.eu*

Gloucester Road LU

Reza Muhammad's sophisticated Indian restaurant offers a taste of elegant contemporary Indian cuisine.

East

Café Spice Namaste ££££

- 📖 *16 Prescott Street, E1 8AZ*
- ☎ *020 7488 9242*
- ✍ *www.caféspice.co.uk*
- 🚌 *Aldgate East LU, Tower Hill LU*

Chef Cyrus Todiwala is committed to bringing true Indian cookery, in all its variety, to the London restaurant scene. From within a brightly-decorated old courthouse he serves up an extensive menu, including many unusual Goan and Parsee dishes.

Halal Restaurant £-££

- 📖 *2 St Mark Street, E1 8DJ*
- ☎ *020 7481 1700*
- ✍ *www.halalrest.co.uk*
- 🚌 Aldgate East LU

Lovingly immortalised by The Gentle Author in his Spitalfields Life blog, this long-running restaurant, established in 1939, serves a range of classic dishes such as mutton curry to bhindi bhaji at very reasonable prices.

Lahore Kebab House £

- 📖 *2 Umberston Street, E1 1PY*
- ☎ *020 7488 2551*
- 🚌 *Aldgate East, Whitechapel LU*

This modest-looking restaurant has acquired a cult following, serving up gutsy Punjabi food to an appreciative audience.

Cookbooks

My personal recommendations of cookbooks for this cuisine, including new books and out-of-print classics:

Curry Lovers
Roopa Gulati
A slender but appetizing Indian cookbook, offering delicious recipes from tamarind chutney to an elaborate lamb biriyani.

Madhur Jaffrey's Indian Cookery
Madhur Jaffrey
A clearly-written, accessible introduction to this great cuisine.

Madhur Jaffrey's Ultimate Curry Bible
Madhur Jaffrey
This wonderful cookbook lives up to its grandiose title, with Madhur Jaffrey exploring all kinds of curry, from fish curry in Singapore to Pakistani-style kofta curry. The recipies are both appetising and achievable.

Reza's Indian Spice
Reza Mahammad
A collection of stylish yet accessible recipes, pitched as 'Eastern recipes for Western cooks', from restaurateur Reza Mahammad.

Fifty Great Curries of India
Camellia Panjabi
A beautifully-presented, illustrated guide which takes readers through the art of making curries clearly and in detail. Recipes range from classic dishes, such as Goanese pork Vindaloo, to less familiar ones such as Gujurati mango and yoghurt curry.

India Cookbook
Pushpesh Pant
An encyclopedic tome of 1,000 recipes from across India, including many less familiar ones, such as Drumstick Sambhar or Bajare Ki Roti (millet roti). A useful book for exploring Indian cuisine.

The Calcutta Kitchen
Simon Parkes and Udit Sarkhel
An attractive collection of recipes and writing, offering an appetising insight into Bengali cuisine.

Classic Indian Vegetarian Cooking
Julie Sahni
An inspirational book filled with appetising recipes conveying the less well-known world of Indian vegetarian cuisine in all its subtlety.

Chinese London

New Loon Moon

The original points of entry for the Chinese community in Britain were Liverpool and London: the ports into which Chinese seamen with the East India Company arrived and settled. The Limehouse area, near the docks in the East End, was London's first 'Chinatown', with the first immigrants arriving during the eighteenth century when Britain's tea trade with China was booming. Sailors jumped ship and set up businesses running laundries, shops or becoming ship's chandlers. In the 1950s, the development of the laundromat and the domestic washing machine badly affected the laundry business, so catering became an alternative source of work.

Limehouse was practically destroyed in the Blitz, and post-war restrictive regulations imposed on non-British workers by the Seamen's Union hit affected Chinese seamen hard. So, both alternative livelihoods and accommodation had to be found. Soho, a run-down, derelict area with a bad reputation and low property prices, saw an influx of Chinese around the Gerrard Street area in the 1950s. The first Chinese restaurants in Soho were chop-suey outlets, opened in the 1940s to cater for American GIs and British servicemen who had acquired a taste for Chinese food overseas. Restaurants catering specifically for the growing Chinese community also opened in the area. The Communist revolution in China in 1949 meant a further wave of immigration from China into Britain in the 1950s and 1960s, mostly from the British colony of Hong Kong. As a result, the Chinese community in Soho expanded further.

The area bounded by Shaftesbury Avenue, Leicester Square, Charing Cross Road and Wardour Street is a rectangle of predominantly Chinese shops, businesses, gambling clubs and restaurants. Gerrard Street, now pedestrianised, comes complete with Chinese-style arches and pagoda-style phone boxes.

Two annual festivals have become major events in London, attracting people from outside the Chinese community. Chinese New Year, according to the Chinese lunar calendar, takes place either in late January or early February, and is celebrated with gifts to children of 'ang pow', money in lucky red envelopes, and a lion dance procession. Special dishes appear on menus in the restaurants. Each year is attributed to one of the twelve animals in the Chinese zodiac – with the Year of the Dragon being especially auspicious – and the New Year celebrations feature the animal to which the year belongs. The autumnal Moon Festival, around September, is marked by special moon cakes and a lion dance. During both these festivals, Chinatown is filled with Chinese of all generations, colourful lanterns and decorations and street-stalls selling snacks and gifts.

Chinese Cuisine

This ancient cuisine is both complex and various. Underlying it are the 'yin and yang' principles, translated in culinary terms into hot, cold and neutral, with ingredients allocated different properties. A huge range of ingredients is used, with nothing wasted. There is an old saying that 'A Cantonese will eat anything with four legs except for a piece of furniture and anything that flies apart from a kite'. Textures play an important role in Chinese cooking and include some that are foreign to Western sensibilities, with slippery, jelly-like textures being prized.

Each of China's regions has its own characteristic cuisine, influenced by climate and the availability of ingredients. It's customary, however, to group China culinarily into four broad geographical groups: Peking/Northern, Shanghai/Eastern, Sichuan/Western and Cantonese/Southern. The cuisine of the North is distinguished by its use of grains other than rice, such as wheat, corn and millet, in the form of breads, noodles, dumplings and pancakes. Because the ancient Imperial Court was situated in Peking, elaborate dishes such as Peking Duck are characteristic of this cuisine. The Mongols introduced lamb, which is eaten more widely here than in other parts of China.

Eastern cuisine is famous for its fresh fish and seafood. Rich, sweet seasonings are a hallmark and popular techniques include stir-frying, steaming, red-cooking (slow simmering in soy sauce) and blanching. Sichuan cooking, from the provinces of Hunan, Yunnan and Sichuan in Western China, is marked by its use of fiery chillies, garlic, ginger and Sichuan peppercorns producing a vigorous, strongly flavoured cuisine. Two regional foodstuffs are aromatic peppercorns and chilli-pickled mustard plant.

Cantonese cuisine is the best-known Chinese cooking outside China, because of the large numbers of Chinese from southern Canton who emigrated in the nineteenth century. Strong, overwhelming flavourings are

avoided and, instead, a harmonious blend of colours, textures and flavours is sought. Stir-frying epitomises Cantonese cooking, with the freshness and colours of ingredients retained and a minimum of seasonings added. Dim sum, the small steamed and fried dumplings eaten at lunchtime, are another Cantonese speciality.

Glossary

Agar agar: a vegetarian setting agent obtained from seaweed which does not require refrigeration to set. Available either in powdered form or translucent strands.

Azuki beans: small red beans, used primarily in cakes and desserts and available both whole and in sweetened paste form.

Bamboo shoots: fresh bamboo shoots are occasionally available. Tinned bamboo shoots, either whole or sliced, are easily found.

Bean curd (doufu): a soya bean product which has always been a valuable source of protein in Chinese cooking. Fresh ivory-coloured bean curd has a firm custard texture and bland flavour. It is sold in the chilled section, packed in water. Deep-fried bean curd has a golden colour and spongy texture and is found in packets in the chilled section. Bean curd 'cheese', either red or white, is fermented bean curd with a strong, salty taste and is sold in jars. Dried bean-curd sheets are sold in packets.

Bean sprouts: white crispy sprouts of the mung bean; also available are the larger, nuttier soya bean sprouts, which should be cooked before eating.

Beche-de-mer: sea cucumber or sea slug, it is sold dried and prized as a delicacy.

Bird's nest: the key ingredient of the famous delicacy, bird's nest soup. The nests of a cave-dwelling species of swallow are coated with a gelatinous saliva and it is this which gives the soup its prized consistency. The nests are sold either whole or in fragments for high prices.

Black Beans

Black beans: small black soya beans, fermented with salt and spices, with a pungent flavour.

Chilli oil: a transparent oil, tinted red from chillies, sold in small bottles and with a powerful chilli kick.

Chinese broccoli (gaai laan): a thick-stalked vegetable with large rounded leaves and white flowers.

Chinese cabbage (bok choy): similar in appearance to Swiss chard, with dark green

Chinese Glossary

Temple

SALTED BLACK BEANS

leaves and thick white stems. Green bok choy, with green leaves and stems, is also available.

Chinese chives: long, dark green, flat leaves, with a stronger and more pungent odour and flavour than English chives; also sold blanched and complete with buds.

Bok Choy

Chinese cinnamon: cassia bark, sold in sticks similar to cinnamon but larger and rougher with a stronger flavour.

Chinese flowering cabbage (choi sum): a leafy vegetable with rounded leaves, small yellow flowers and long stems.

Chinese leaves: a large tight head of white-green crinkly leaves with a crunchy texture; widely available.

Chinese mushrooms: black, dried shitake mushrooms with distinctive meaty flavour. Prices vary according to the size and thickness of the caps.

Chinese sausages: these resemble small, fatty salamis, but they must be cooked before eating. There are two sorts: pork and pork and liver, the latter being darker in colour. They are found in packets or hanging up in bunches with other dried meats.

Coriander: this green herb, similar in appearance to flat-leaved continental parsley but with a distinctive sharp flavour, is one of the few herbs used in Chinese cooking.

Five-spice powder: fragrant, golden-brown powder made from five or sometimes six ground spices, with the four base spices being star-anise, Chinese cinnamon, cloves and fennel seeds. Sichuan peppercorns, ginger and cardamom are the additions.

Ginger: an aromatic root available fresh.

Glutinous rice: rounded rice grains with a sticky texture when cooked, used in both sweet and savoury dishes.

Golden needles: long dried buds of the tiger-lily flower.

Longan: a small brown-skinned fruit, related to the lychee, with translucent flesh and glossy black seed (also known as 'dragon's eye' fruit). Available either tinned or fresh.

Lotus leaves: the large leaves of the water-lily plant, available dried and used to wrap food for cooking.

Lotus root: a crunchy root with a decorative tracery of holes, available fresh, in sausage-like links, or tinned.

Mooli: a large, long white radish, with crispy white flesh.

Mustard Greens (gaai choi): a green large-leafed plant. The bitter varieties are pickled rather than cooked.

Noodles: *cellophane noodles* (also known as beanthread, glass or transparent noodles): fine thread-like noodles made from mung beans which need soaking before they can be easily cut; *egg noodles*: made from wheat flour, egg and water, distinguished by their yellow colour; *rice noodles* and *vermicelli* are dried, white noodles of varying

Egg Noodles

widths made from rice flour which need soaking before use; *river rice noodles* (sarhor noodles) are made from ground rice and water, steamed in thin sheets and cut into strips. Fresh-river rice noodles are sold in clear packets, and usually stored near the chilled section.

Potato flour: fine white flour, made from cooked potatoes, used as a thickener.

Rice vinega: mild vinegars, ranging from delicate white rice vinegar to sweet red rice vinegar and rich black rice vinegar.

Rice wine: made from glutinous rice, yeast and water, this is used for both drinking and cooking.

Sauces: *chilli bean sauce*, a hot, spicy, dark sauce made from soya beans and chillies; *chilli sauce*, a bright red sweet chilli sauce; *hoisin sauce*, a thick, brown fruity sauce; *oyster sauce*, a thick, brown sauce made from

Oyster Sauce

oysters; *soy sauce*, a dark brown salty liquid made from fermented soya beans (available as thin, salty Light Soy Sauce or as thicker, sweeter Dark Soy Sauce); and *yellow bean sauce*, a thick, brown sauce made from fermented yellow beans.

Sesame oil: a nutty, golden-coloured oil made from sesame seeds.

Shrimps, dried: small, shelled, dried pink shrimps, with a strong salty flavour.

Spring roll wrappers: white paper-thin wrappers, available in different sizes. Found in either the chilled or freezer sections.

Star-anise: dark brown, star-shaped pod with a distinctive liquorice flavour and scent.

Water Spinach

Straw mushrooms: cone-shaped mushrooms, usually available canned.

Sichuan peppercorns: fragrant, reddish-brown 'peppercorns', which are the dried berries of a shrub.

Sichuan pickled vegetables: mustard green tubers, pickled in salt and hot chillies, which are a speciality of Sichuan province.

Tangerine peel: in its dried form, in dark-brown pieces, this is used as a flavouring in Chinese cooking.

Thousand-year-old eggs: preserved duck eggs, with a pungent flavour, which are in fact only about a hundred days old.

Water chestnuts: the crunchy bulbs of a waterplant. Fresh, brown-skinned bulbs are sometimes found, but tinned water chestnuts are easily available.

Water spinach (ong chai): a triangular-leafed plant with a mild, spinach-like flavour.

Winter melon: a large green gourd with white flesh, available whole or in pieces, and often used to make soup.

Wonton skins: small squares of yellow egg-noodle dough, used to wrap up dumplings. Found in either chilled or freezer sections.

Wood ears: black, crinkled, dried fungus with a beige underside.

Food Shops

For decades, Gerrard Street and its side-streets have housed Chinese food shops, an important and thriving part of London's Chinese community. Dotted around London, there are also a number of huge Chinese cash-and-carry stores, stocking an impressive range of ingredients.

Central

Loon Fung Supermarket

⊡ 42-44 Gerrard Street, W1D 5QG
☎ 020 7437 7332
✎ www.loonfung,com
🚌 Leicester Square LU
🕐 Daily 10am-8pm

Loon Fung is the oldest and largest Chinese supermarket in Soho, occupying a key position on Gerrard Street and always bustling with customers. Boxes of fresh fruit from kumquats to longans, are displayed outside on the pavement with a large fresh vegetable section inside. A butcher's counter sells a range of Chinese pork cuts, plus more unusual items such as duck and chicken feet and duck tongues. The shop's size means that it offers a comprehensive range of store-cupboard staples.

New China Gate

⊡ 19 Newport Place, WC2H 7HP
☎ 020 7287 8969
🚌 Leicester Square LU
🕐 Daily 11am-9.30pm

A small food shop offering a limited range of both fresh fruit and vegetables outside and store-cupboard ingredients inside.

New Loon Moon Supermarket

⊡ 9a Gerrard Street, W1D 5PL
☎ 020 7734 9940
✎ www.newloonmoon.com
🚌 Leicester Square LU
🕐 Daily 10.30am-8pm

In the centre of Gerrard Street, this veteran food shop catches the eye with an attractive display of consistently good quality fresh fruit and vegetables, from Chinese greens such as gai lan or ong choi to longans. Inside, the busy shop expands both downstairs and upstairs to stock a huge range of Chinese foodstuffs, from frozen dumplings to fresh noodles, tofu and fishballs, bottled sauces, dried store-cupboard staples.

Newport Supermarket

⊡ 28-29 Newport Court, WC2H 7 PQ
☎ 020 7494 9222
🚌 Leicester Square LU
🕐 Daily 10am-9.45pm

A corner shop with a small assortment of fresh produce and an eclectic stock of ingredients, from condiments to noodles.

Oriental Delight

⌨ *14 Gerrard Street, W1D 5PT*
☎ *020 7439 1183*
🚌 *Leicester Square LU*
🕐 *Mon-Sun 11am-8pm*

The ground floor of this corner shop is crammed with Chinese biscuits, sweets and snacks. The roomy downstairs basement stocks an array of tinned, bottled and jarred Chinese foodstuffs, from sauces to canned fruits.

See Woo

⌨ *19 Lisle Street, WC2H 7BE*
☎ *020 7439 8325*
✍ *www.seewoo.com*
🚌 *Leicester Square LU*
🕐 *Daily 10am-8pm*

This large, sprawling shop has an excellent, comprehensive stock of chilled, frozen, dried, tinned and bottled ingredients. There is a large fresh fruit and vegetable section, which regularly features more unusual items. A basement room contains Chinese bowls of all sizes, woks, steamers and other Chinese cookware.

Young Cheng Fish Shop

⌨ *4 Dansey Place, W1D 6EY*
☎ *020 7387 0672*
🚌 *Leicester Square LU*
🕐 *Daily 10am-8pm*

Tucked away down a Chinatown alleyway, this offers a range of fresh and frozen seafood, Including sea bass and live crabs and lobsters.

North

Loon Fung

⌨ *111 Brantwood Road, N17*
☎ *020 8365 1132*
🚌 *Bus 123, W3 or White Hart Lane Rail*
🕐 *Mon-Sat 9.30am-6.30pm*
   Sun 11am-5pm

A Tottenham-based branch of the veteran Chinese business, this carries an extensive range of Chinese ingredients, from fresh vegetables and frozen seafood to store-cupboard ingredients such as sauces and dried noodles.

Wing Yip

⌨ *395 Edgware Road, NW2 6LN*
☎ *020 8450 0422*
🚌 *Colindale LU*
🕐 *Mon-Sat 9.30am-8pm,*
   Sun 11.30am-5.30pm

This enormous superstore at Staples Corner is the place for bulk-buying Chinese food, with shoppers using trolleys rather than baskets. It has an impressive and comprehensive range of Chinese ingredients. As well as aisles of canned, bottled, chilled and frozen produce, there is a fresh fish and seafood counter, a fresh produce section and a kitchenware section.

West

Costcutter Oriental Supermarket

- ⊡ 28 Queensway, W2 3RX
- ☎ 020 7243 2618
- 🚌 Bayswater/Queensway LU
- 🕒 Daily 8.30am-9pm

This roomy supermarket offers a selection of Chinese and Oriental ingredients, from fresh produce to frozen, dried, canned and bottled foodstuffs and beverages.

Loon Fung

- ⊡ 1 Glacier Way, Alperton, Middlesex HA0 1HQ
- ☎ 020 8810 8188
- ✎ www.loonfung.com
- 🚌 Alperton LU
- 🕒 Mon-Sat 9.30am-7pm, Sun 11am-5pm

A large Chinese cash-and-carry stocking an impressive range of Chinese foodstuffs.

South-West

Wing Tai Supermarket

- ⊡ 13 Electric Avenue, SW9 8JY
- ☎ 020 7738 5898
- 🚌 Brixton LU/Rail
- 🕒 Mon-Sat 10am-7pm

This roomy store is particularly strong on bottled, tinned and frozen goods, while also offering a small fresh produce section and fresh fish counter.

South-East

Daily Fresh Supermarket

- ⊡ 48 East Street, SE17 2DN
- ☎ 020 7701 6622
- 🚌 Kennington LU
- 🕒 Daily 9am-8pm

A small shop carrying a basic range of Chinese ingredients, including fresh fish and seafood such as live lobsters.

See Woo Cash and Carry

- ⊡ Furlong House Horn Lane, SE10 0RT
- ☎ 020 8293 9393
- ✎ www.seewoo.com
- 🚌 Westcombe Park Rail
- 🕒 Daily 9.30am-6.30pm

A cavernous Chinese cash-and-carry store stocking an extensive range of Chinese foodstuffs.

Wing Tai Supermarket

🏠 *Unit 11A The Aylsham Centre,*
   Rye Lane, SE15
☎ *020 7635 0714*
🚌 *Peckham Rye Rail*
🕐 *Mon-Fri 9am-9pm, Sat-Sun 10am-8pm*

A friendly down-to-earth shop with stock ranging from fresh fish to noodles and Thai fragrant rice.

Wing Tai Supermarket

🏠 *52-54 Denmark Hill, SE5 8RS*
☎ *020 7737 6788*
🚌 *Denmark Hill Rail*
🕐 *Mon-Fri 9am-9pm, Sat-Sun 10am-8pm*

Despite its slightly ramshackle appearance, a good range of Chinese foodstuffs can be found here.

East

Loon Fung

🏠 *Factory Road, Silvertown E16 2EJ*
☎ *020 7055 1888*
🖊 *www.loonfung.com*
🚌 *North Woolwich Rail*
🕐 *Mon-Sat 9.30am-6.30pm*
   Sun 11am-5pm

A spacious Chinese superstore carrying an ample range of Chinese foodstuffs, complete with a reasonably-priced noodle bar in which to have a meal.

CHINESE LEAVES

绍菜

£1.45

Chinese Bakeries

London's Chinatown is home to a number of Chinese bakeries, offering freshly baked sweet and savoury buns and pastries. Many of them also offer a café area in which to sit and sample their wares.

Chinatown Bakery

- 7 Newport Place, WC2H 7JR
- ☎ 020 7287 7995
- Leicester Square LU
- Daily 9.30am-9pm

This small, cheery bakery offers a range of reasonably-priced buns and cakes to go.

Far East

- 13 Gerrard Street, W1D 5PS
- ☎ 020 7437 6148
- Leicester Square LU
- Daily 10am-7pm

Recently revamped, during the day this is a bakery-cum-tea-shop offering Chinese breakfast dishes and Chinese cakes and pastries. At night it operates as a restaurant.

Golden Gate Cake Shop

- 13 Macclesfield Street, W1D 5EJ
- ☎ 020 7287 9862
- Leicester Square LU
- Daily 10am-6pm

This well-established Chinese bakery offers a good range of sweet and savoury buns as well as cakes and mango puddings.

Golden Gate Dessert House

- 110 Shaftesbury Avenue, W1D 5EJ
- ☎ 020 7494 3886
- Leicester Square LU
- Daily 10am-7pm

A bright red façade and eye-catching window display of colourful iced cakes mark out this theatreland cake house-cum-bakery.

Kowloon Chinese Café Cake Shop

⌖ *29 Gerrard Street, W1D 6JH*
☎ *020 7437 1694*
🚌 *Leicester Square LU*
🕐 *Daily 10am-7pm*

This bakery-cum-café does brisk business in Chinese buns and cakes which can be eaten in or taken away

Sun Luen

⌖ *4 Little Newport Street WC2H 7JJ*
☎ *020 7437 0251*
🚌 *Leicester Square LU*
🕐 *Daily 10am-6.30pm*

A down-to-earth, well-established bakery and café offering a selection of sweet and savoury goods.

Wonderful Patisserie

⌖ *45 Gerrard Street, W1D 5QQ*
☎ *020 7734 7629*
🚌 *Leicester Square LU*
🕐 *Daily 11am-7pm*

This bright and cheerful cake shop, with its iced confections much photographed by visitors to Chinatown, offers a wide range of Chinese cakes and biscuits.

Eating Places

For many years, London's Chinese restaurants offered predominantly Cantonese food. As a result several places offer excellent dim sum – an assortment of steamed and fried dumplings traditionally served at lunchtime – which are a speciality of Canton. Today, however, Chinese restaurant cuisine is beginning to reflect China's regional diversity with restaurants and cafés offering Fujianese or Sichuan dishes beginning to appear.

With Chinatown over-run by tourists, standards have slipped in many of its restaurants, though there are some offering reasonable food. If you enjoy good Chinese cuisine, then you should also head for Bayswater, where a cluster of excellent Chinese restaurants attracts enthusiastic and discerning diners.

Central

Baozi Inn £-££

⌖ *25 Newport Court, W1 7JS*
☎ *020 7287 6877*
🚌 *Leicester Square LU*

Hidden down a narrow alleyway, this small café serves up gutsy streetfood-inspired snacks such as chilli oil-slathered Chengdu dumplings and their own delicious plump buns.

Bar Shu £££

- 28 Frith Street, W1D 5LF
- 020 7287 6688
- www.bar-shu.co.uk
- Leicester Square LU

Upmarket and atmospheric, Bar Shu offers a chance to sample Sichuan's famously chilli-hot cuisine, serving classic dishes such as Dan Dan noodles or Pock-marked Old Woman's Beancurd.

Café de HK £-££

- 47-49 Charing Cross Road, WC2H 0AN
- 020 7534 9898
- Leicester Square LU

One of a new wave of more contemporary, casual eateries opening up in Chinatown – good for a quick one-dish meal.

Four Seasons ££

- 12 Gerrard Street, W1D 5PR
- 020 7494 0870
- www.fs-restaurants.co.uk

A Chinatown stalwart, run with businesslike efficiency and famous for its roast duck.

Golden Dragon ££

- 28-29 Gerrard Street, W1D 6JW
- 020 7734 2763
- www.goldendragonlondon.com
- Leicester Square LU

Big and bustling, this is a quintessential Chinatown restaurant, known especially for its dim sum and so particularly busy at Sunday lunchtime.

Hakkasan £££-££££

- 8 Hanway Place, W1T 1HD
- 020 7927 7000
- www.hakkasan.com
- Tottenham Court Road LU

Intriguingly situated down a back-alley, restaurateur Alan Yau's glamorous Michelin-starred restaurant comes complete with night-club like décor, cocktail bar and dainty dim sum.

Imperial China ££

- White Bear Yard, 25A Lisle Street, WC2 7BA
- 020 7734 3388
- www.imperial-china.co.uk
- Leicester Square LU

Picturesquely tucked away in a courtyard, this smart Chinatown restaurant offers classic Cantonese cuisine, including traditional lunchtime dim sum.

Joy King Lau ££

- 3 Leicester Street, WC2H 7BL
- 020 7437 1132
- www.joykinglau.com
- Leicester Square LU

A Chinatown veteran, spread out over a number of floors in a Soho townhouse. Friendly and efficient, It offers a extensive Cantonese menu, with the lunchtime dim-sum especially popular.

New World ££

- 1 Gerrard Place, W1
- 020 7434 0396
- www.newworldlondon.com
- Leicester Square LU

Vast and invariably busy, New World is very much an old-style Chinatown restaurant. What makes it stand out from the crowd, is that it is one of the few serving dim sum from trolleys, rather than à la carte.

Phoenix Palace ££-£££

- 3-5 Glentworth Street, NW1 5PG
- 020 7486 3515
- www.phoenixpalace.co.uk
- Baker Street LU

This spacious restaurant is perpetually filled to the brim with diners and is an impressively smooth-running operation, noted for its high-quality dim sum and a la carte menu.

Royal China ££-£££

- 24-26 Baker Street, W1U 7AB
- 020 7487 4688
- www2.royalchinagroup.biz
- Baker Street LU

This spacious, smart Chinese restaurant is noted for the quality of its food, particularly for its excellent lunchtime dim sum, so arrive early, especially at the weekend, if you want to nab a table.

Shanghai Blues £££-££££

- 193-197 High Holborn, WC1V 7BD
- 020 7404 1668
- www.shanghaiblues.co.uk
- Holborn LU

For sheer glamour, this strikingly-decorated restaurant is hard to beat. The menu offers an upmarket selection of dim-sum and mains, with the emphasis on luxurious ingredients such as fresh scallops, sea bass, lobster and fillet steak.

Yauatcha ££-£££

- 15 Broadwick Street, W1F 0DL
- 020 7494 8888
- www.yauatcha.com
- Oxford Circus LU

Set up by restaurateur Alan Yau, this basement restaurant is a stylish establishment, complete with a tropical fish tank, a light-studded ceiling and embroidered turquoise-coloured seating. Jewel-like dim sum, such as vegetarian shark's fin with gold leaf, look as good as they taste, with fresh seafood prominent. The ground floor serves exquisitely presented East-West fusion patisserie and a fine selection of teas.

North

Yum Cha ££

🔲 27-28 Chalk Farm Road, NW1 8AG
☎ 020 7482 2228
🖉 www.yumchasilksandspice.co.uk
🚌 Chalk Farm LU

This restaurant specialises in dim sum, offering respectable versions of classic dishes such as steamed barbecued pork buns or pan-fried turnip paste.

West

Four Seasons ££

🔲 84 Queensway W2 3RL
☎ 020 7229 4320
🚌 Bayswater LU, Queensway LU

A Queensway veteran, this straightforward restaurant offers traditional Chinese dishes and is particularly famous for its roast duck.

Golden Palace ££

🔲 146-150 Station Parade,
     Harrow HA1 2AT
☎ 020 8863 2333
🚌 Harrow-on-the-Hill LU/Rail

A well-established Cantonese restaurant, particularly popular for its dim sum.

Royal China ££-£££

🔲 13 Queensway, W2 4QJ
☎ 020 7221 2535
🚌 Bayswater LU, Queensway LU

Such is the fame of the dim sum here that, at the weekend, queues start forming before the restaurant opens at noon. Inside, the large, roomy dining area is decorated with shiny black tiled walls festooned with golden lacquerwork and masses of mirrors. Service is efficient, which is just as well considering how busy it gets. The dim sum dishes are spot on, from delicate mangetout dumplings (filled with pea-shoots) to soft, spongy char siu bau.

East

Shanghai ££

🔲 41 Kingsland High Street, E8 2JS
☎ 020 7254 2878
🖉 www.shanghaidalston.co.uk
🚌 Dalston Kingsland Rail

What was formerly a pie and mash shop, complete with traditional tiles, has now been transformed into a busy Chinese restaurant. Good dim sum and bargain lunchtime specials pull in the punters.

Cookbooks

My personal recommendations of cookbooks for this cuisine, including new books and out-of-print classics:

The Chinese Kitchen
Deh-Ta Hsiung
Offering a useful insight into Chinese cuisine, this is an attractive, well-illustrated book. There is extensive information on Chinese ingredients and an appealing range of recipes.

Classic Chinese Cookbook
Yan-Kit So
A classic Chinese cookbook by a wonderful food writer who knew how to share her knowledge in the most accessible way. This is both lucidly written and well-illustrated with mouthwatering, workable recipes.

Complete Chinese Cookbook
Ken Hom
A substantial collection of Hom's clearly-written, accessible recipes, arranged by type of foodstuff.

Every Grain of Rice
Fuchsia Dunlop
A characteristically well-researched and appetising collection of everyday recipes, mainly from Southern China, from a food writer noted for her expertise on Chinese cuisine.

Exploring China
Ken Hom and Ching He Huang
As the title suggests, this cookbook from two well-known Chinese TV chefs, contains a wide-ranging collection of regional recipes from around China, featuring both traditional and innovative dishes.

Heart and Soul
Kylie Kwong
Kylie Kwong's appetising book combines personal recollections with tasty, clearly written recipes

Sichuan Cookery
Fuchsia Dunlop
This elegantly and knowledgeably written cookbook offers a fascinating insight into Sichuan cuisine.

French London

Maison Bertaux

London's first serious experience of the French was when it fell under Norman rule following the 1066 Conquest. French became the language both of the Court and local government. London saw an influx of merchant traders from northern France and a number of religious orders, including the influential Knights Templar, established themselves in the city.

The next major increase in London's French community was due to the arrival of French-speaking Protestants, known in France as 'Huguenots', who came to England to escape Catholic persecution. In France, the limited privileges granted to Huguenots by the 1598 Edict of Nantes were gradually eroded, with restrictions placed on Protestant worship. In 1680 many Huguenots fled, and Charles II offered them asylum in 1681. Four years later in France, the Edict of Nantes was revoked and Protestant churches were ordered to be destroyed. Following this, between 40,000 and 50,000 Huguenots moved to England, with half of them thought to have settled in London. By the year 1700, Huguenots formed around five per cent of London's population.

Spitalfields and Soho were the two main areas in London in which the Huguenots settled. Spitalfields (also home to a community of Flemish weavers) attracted the Huguenot weavers, who eventually contributed to a prosperous period in the British silk industry. In Soho, where the Huguenots took over a chapel built for Greek Christians and used it until 1822, the new immigrants were craftspeople, such as watch and clockmakers, bookbinders and gold and silversmiths.

Our popular perception of the French as stylish and fashionable was apparent even then, with a 1700 report declaring, 'The English have now so great an esteem for the workmanship of the French refugees that hardly any thing vends without a gallic name'. Huguenot merchants, alongside other immigrants, played an important part in London's financial life. When the Bank of England was setup in 1694, several of the founder directors were Huguenots. In addition to influencing crafts and business, Huguenot academics played a notable role in the worlds of science and technology, with many joining the Royal Society.

London's French community were joined by subsequent groups of refugees, with an influx of royalists fleeing the 1789 French Revolution, and political refugees escaping the 1870 Commune.

Gradually, further institutions catering to French expats were set up, from a chapel in the French Embassy to French schools in Lisle Street in 1865. In 1867, the French Hospital and Dispensary in Shaftesbury Avenue was established, while 1893 saw the completion of the French Protestant Church in Soho Square. Paul Villars wrote in 1905 in 'Living London' of the French community that 'In London, as in France, they use the café as a club' – the Café Royal was a favourite haunt. During the eighteenth and nineteenth centuries, however, the French community slowly became assimilated into English society. Huguenot families such as the Courtaulds and Oliviers became established members of British society. Today, Spitalfields' Georgian houses and Huguenot names like Fournier Street are reminders of the area's former prosperity under the silk merchants.

During the Second World War, Soho, once home to the Huguenots, became a focal point for the French Resistance, with the York Minster pub acting as the headquarters of the Free French Forces. Generally known 'the French pub' it has now been renamed the French House; General de Gaulle used to shop for his coffee at Angelucci's around the corner on Frith Street.

Today, London is home to a large French community, estimated at between 300,000 and 400,000. Traditionally, the heartland of this Gallic presence was elegant, affluent South Kensington, with the French Lycée on Cromwell Road and the French Institute at Queensberry Place providing two focal points, served by a cluster of French bookshops, cafés and patisseries. Nowadays, however, the French community are dispersed through the capital, while a recent trend is the arrival of bi-lingual French and English schools, such as CFBL in Kentish Town, offering London's French residents the opportunity to embrace both cultures.

French Cuisine

French cuisine has been highly influential throughout Europe, with Britain especially living in its shadow. As the current edition of the Larousse Gastronomique baldly states, 'At the beginning of the twentieth century, French cookery gained supremacy throughout the world.' Today the language of the kitchen continues to be French, from 'chef' to culinary terms such as 'sauté'.

Still a predominantly agricultural country, France has retained many of the regional ingredients such as cheeses, hams and herbs which give its cuisine character and flavour; local markets still abound selling locally-grown seasonal produce. Standards of produce have remained high and the simple pleasures of life, such as a decent loaf of bread and some good cheese, are easily found.

An enduring regionalism means that even in the twenty-first century local dishes are cherished, rather than discarded in a mass move towards uniformity. As a result, French cuisine contains wonderfully contrasting strands: from the Mediterranean flavours of Provençal cooking, laden with tomatoes, basil and olive oil, to the cream, cider and calvados based dishes of Normandy.

French cooking can be divided broadly into 'haute cuisine', the cookery of grand restaurants and hotels; 'cuisine du terroir', regional cooking found in provincial restaurants; and 'cuisine grand-mère', the everyday food found in people's homes and in cheap, down-to-earth bistros. Haute cuisine has influenced chefs and cookery schools around the world. Naturally, it has followed trends and fashions. In the 1970s and 1980s 'nouvelle cuisine' – a move away from the over-rich dishes of the classic cuisine – was highly influential, although reviled in some quarters for its affectation. In contrast, regional and home cooking continues to stick to a traditional repertoire of classic French dishes, such as cassoulet or tarte tatin.

Glossary

Anchovy (anchois): a small sea fish, generally available salted in cans or jars, filleted or whole. The distinctive salty, fishy flavour of anchovies plays a key part in dishes like tapenade and pissaladière.

Bayonne ham: a famous salt-cured, smoked ham, originally from Bayonne but now manufactured all over France.

Butter: beurre d'Isigny from Normandy, sold both unsalted and salted, is highly prized in French pastry-cooking.

Banon

Calvados: a spirit distilled from cider traditionally from Normandy. Pays d'Auge Calvados is a particularly high-quality brand.

Capers: the unopened buds of a Mediterranean shrub, used pickled either in brine or vinegar as a distinctive sour flavouring.

Celeriac (céleri-rave): the white, firm-textured, bulbous root of a variety of celery with a distinctive nutty flavour.

Cep (cèpe): a brown-capped, thick-stemmed edible wild boletus mushroom, valued for its rich flavour and meaty texture.

Cheeses: French cheeses are one of the glories of French cuisine. There are hundreds of different French cheeses, with the following only a tiny selection. *Banon*, a soft, small, round cheese, traditionally wrapped in chestnut leaves; *Beaufort*, a Gruyère-like hard cow's milk cheese from the mountain pastures of the Savoie; *Brie*, a circular, soft, unpressed cow's milk cheese, with its origins in the thirteenth century; *Brie de Meaux* is a classic brie, farm-made from unpasturised milk; *Camembert*, a round, flat, soft cheese, traditionally from Normandy; *chèvre*, goat's milk cheese (mi-chèvre refers to cheeses made with a mixture of goat's and cow's milks); *Comte*, a Gruyère-type cow's milk cheese from the Jura mountains; *crottin de chavignol*, a soft goat's milk, cheese made in Sancerre, shaped like a small flattened ball; *explorateur*, a mild, cylindrical, triple-cream cow's milk cheese; *Fourme d'Ambert*, a semi-soft, cow's milk veined cheese; *fromage frais*, fresh curd cheese made from cow's milk, used in cooking; *Livarot*, a soft Normandy cow's milk cheese; *lucullus*, a soft, cylindrical cow's milk cheese; *Munster*, a soft cheese from the Alsace with an orange-red rind; *Pont l'Eveque*, a square-shaped, soft cow's milk cheese from Normandy; and *Roquefort*, a famous veined, semi-soft sheep's milk cheese, ripened for three months in the limestone caves of Les Causses.

Chervil: a subtle-flavoured green herb, with fine fronds, resembling a delicate continental parsley.

Crème fraîche: soured cream containing a minimum of 30% butterfat.

Dandelion (dent-de-lion, pissenlit): a jagged-leafed, wild meadow plant, dismissed as a weed in England but eaten when young as a salad leaf in France.

Lard de poitrine: a fatty version of streaky bacon used for flavouring dishes such as stews; also available smoked.

Marrons glacés: sweet, glazed, syrup-poached chestnuts, eaten as a costly sweetmeat and used in desserts. Available whole, in pieces or in purée form.

Marrons glacés

Mustard (moutarde): pale yellow Dijon mustard made from black or brown mustard seeds, verjuice and white wine; mild, aromatic dark-brown Bordeaux mustard; and grainy-textured Meaux mustard made from mixed mustard seeds.

Olive oil: Although a small producer, France's olive oil is well-regarded, with the best thought to come from Provençe.

Pâtés: *pâté de campagne*, coarse-textured pâté; pâté de foie, containing 15% pork liver and 45% fat.

Purslane (pourpier): a green salad vegetable with rounded, clover-shaped leaves.

Puy lentil: a prized small, green-brown lentil which retains its shape and has a good flavour when cooked.

Rocket (roquette): a peppery, jagged green salad leaf; a traditional element of Provençal mesclun (a wild leaf salad).

Salt cod (morue): dried, salted cod which needs pre-soaking before cooking and which is used in classic dishes such as brandade.

Saucisson sec: Dried sausages including: *Jésus*, a large, pork sausage; *saucisson d'Arles*, made from pork and beef; *saucisson de campagne*, made with pork, fat, garlic and spice; *rosette*, a slowly-matured pure pork sausage.

Sausages: *andouillette*, a thick, bumpy sausage, sometimes smoked; *boudin blanc*, a creamy white sausage containing meat such as veal, chicken or pork; *boudin noir*, a dark-skinned blood sausage made from pig's blood; *cervelas*: a short, stocky pork sausage; *merguez*, a spicy red-coloured Algerian lamb and beef sausage; *Toulouse*: a popular pork cooking sausage, used in cassoulet.

Shallot: a small, russet-skinned, mild member of the onion family.

Snails (escargot): an edible gastropod mollusc, enjoyed by the Gauls, available canned or frozen and sometimes found fresh.

Sorrel: a green, leafy herb with a distinctive sour flavour, used to flavour soups, omelettes and salads.

Shallots

Tarragon: a fine-leafed green herb with a distinctively aromatic, faintly aniseed flavour.

Truffle (truffe): rare and costly black and white tubers, with a distinctive aroma and flavour. Black Périgord truffles are particularly prized.

Vanilla sugar: vanilla-flavoured caster sugar, available commercially but easily made at home by placing two or three vanilla pods in a jar of caster sugar and leaving it to infuse.

Wine vinegar: red and white wine vinegars are key flavourings in French cookery, essential in salad dressings. Orleans wine vinegars are particularly valued.

Food Shops

As one would expect from a country famous for its baking, many of London's best French food shops are elegant patisseries. These stores offer Londoners the welcome chance to enjoy decent croissants, delectable cakes and excellent bread.

Central

Comptoir Gascon Food Hall

- ⌖ *61-63 Charterhouse Street, EC1M 6HJ*
- ☎ *020 7608 0851*
- ✑ *www.comptoirgascon.com*
- 🚍 *Farringdon LU/Rail*
- 🕐 *Tues-Sat 9am-10pm*

This handsome shop boasts an excellent pedigree, linked as it is to the Michelin-starred restaurant Club Gascon. Pride of place here goes to an array of home-made foie gras – the sweet wines stocked here are specifically chosen as good accompaniments to foie gras. Own-made traiteur dishes range from pig's cheek in Armagnac to Gascony pies. On-site bakers produce top-notch viennoserie, a range of breads, cakes and pastries – including canele, a speciality from South Western France.

La Fromagerie

- ⌖ *2-4 Moxon Street, W1U 4EW*
- ☎ *020 7935 0341*
- ✑ *www.lafromagerie.co.uk*
- 🚍 *Baker Street LU*
- 🕐 *Mon-Fri 8am-7.30pm, Sat 9am-7pm, Sun 10am-6pm*

Discreetly positioned just off Marylebone High Street, Patricia Michelson's attractive food shop is filled with good things to eat. As the name suggests, cheeses are the shop's forte, stocked in a separate, temperature-controlled cheeseroom. Here can be found between 100 and 150 seasonal farmhouse cheeses, many of which are French with Alpine cheeses, such as Beaufort, being a speciality. Patricia, whose passionate enthusiasm for cheese is genuine and infectious, makes a point of sourcing cheeses herself, direct from small farms and suppliers. Other Gallic edibles include exquisite walnut oil, delectable jams and superb Normany cider and wines, chosen to complement the cheeses on offer. A tasting room area offers a chance to sample charcuterie and cheeses as well as dishes made in the kitchen downstairs.

French Food Shops

French Bubbles

⊡ *22 Wellington Street, WC2E 7DD*
☎ *020 7240 1604*
🖱 *www.frenchbubbles.co.uk*
🚌 *Covent Garden LU*
🕐 *Tues-Sat 11am-11pm, Sun 11am-8pm*

This orignally-conceived fromagerie-cum-wine bar offers a chance to buy a range of over 40 carefully sourced, artisanal French cheeses and good quality French, regional charcuterie, from smoked saucisson to cured meats. As the name suggests, there is also a fine selection of French grower champagnes to tempt you, sourced from independent, family-owned vinyards. The staff are happy to offer advice and guidance.

Laduree

⊡ *71-72 Burlington Arcade, W1J 0QX*
☎ *020 7491 9155*
🖱 *www.laduree.fr*
🚌 *Green Park, Piccadilly LU*
🕐 *Mon-Sat 9am-6pm*

This petite, golden-coloured shop offers a chance to sample Laduree's famous macaroons. These are exquisitely colourful, dainty creations with flavours ranging from striking liquorice or coffee to delicate orange blossom or pistachio. The branch at Harrods in Knightsbridge also offers a splendidly opulent café.

Maison Bertaux

⊡ *28 Greek Street, W1D 5DQ*
☎ *020 7437 6007*
🖱 *www.maisonbertaux.com*
🚌 *Leicester Square LU*
🕐 *Mon-Sat 8.30am-11pm,*
  Sun 8.30am-9pm

Founded in 1871, this characterful patisserie is the area's last surviving food shop link to Soho's nineteenth-century French community. Tucked away down a side-street, it has a loyal clientele who enjoy the excellent pastries, good coffee and Bohemian atmosphere, lovingly sustained by Michelle, the manager. As one sits sipping coffee, trays of freshly made croissants or fruit tarts are brought out from the kitchen and regulars pause at the till for a few moment's gossip.

The Market Quarter

⊡ *36 Elizabeth Street, SW1W 9NZ*
☎ *020 7824 8470*
🖱 *www.marketquarter.com*
🚌 *Victoria LU/Rail*
🕐 *Tues-Wed 11am-7pm,*
  Thurs/Fri 11am-8pm, Sat 10am-6pm

A smart, Belgravia-based shop, showcasing fine French foods and wines, such as foie gras, cassoulet, truffle oil and wines sourced from small French wine producers, many of them organic or biodynamic.

Paul

🏠 29 Bedford Street, WC2E 9ED

☎ 020 7836 3304

✎ www.paul-uk.com

🚌 Covent Garden LU

🕐 Mon-Fri 7.30am-9pm
Sat-Sun 9am-9pm

The first London branch of an established French bakery chain, now widespread throughout the city. It combines a bakery with a salon de thé in which to indulge in a coffee éclair or sample a slice of freshly baked quiche Lorraine.

Pierre Hermé

🏠 13 Lowndes Street, SW1X 9EX

☎ 020 7245 0317

✎ www.pierreherme.com

🚌 Sloane Square LU

🕐 Mon-Sat 10am-6.30pm
Sun 12noon-5pm

A chic boutique, offering Herme's elegant, subtly-flavoured macaroons and his sophisticated chocolats, all made in France and transported to London. Other French treats to be found here include a range of cakes, nougat, calissons, hot chocolate powder, teas and jams such as pear and violet, blackcurrant and peach, apricot and saffron.

Poilâne

🏠 46 Elizabeth Street, SW1W 9PA

☎ 020 7808 4910

✎ www.poilane.com

🚌 Sloane Square LU, Victoria LU/Rail

🕐 Tues-Sat 7am-7pm, Sun 7am-6pm

This small, dainty shop was the first London branch of Lionel Poilâne's famous Parisian bakery. The shop's basement has a wood-fired brick oven where the master baker works through the night making the tangy sourdough loaves for which Poilâne is famous, as well as delicious croissants.

North

La Fromagerie

🏠 30 Highbury Park, N5 2AA

☎ 020 7359 7440

✎ www.lafromagerie.co.uk

🚌 Highbury & Islington LU/Rail

🕐 Mon 11am-7.30pm,
Tues-Sat 9.30am-7.30pm,
Sun 10am-4.30pm

Under a dark blue awning, a window filled with appetising tarts and pastries marks the presence of this attractive shop. Inside, the shelves are packed with carefully chosen delicacies. Pride of place goes to the cheese room at the back with its range of artisanal cheeses, many of which are French.

Spirit of Absinthe

- 🏠 41 Chalcot Road, NW1 8LS
- ☎ 020 7483 1971
- 🚌 Chalk Farm LU
- 🕐 Mon-Fri 8am-7pm, Sat & Sun 9am-5pm

An off-shoot of the popular French restaurant L'Absinthe next door, this small café-cum-traiteur offers a selection of French traiteur dishes and carries a small range of French foodstuffs including biscuits, jams and sweets.

West

Maison Blanc

- 🏠 102 Holland Park, W11 4UA
- ☎ 020 7221 2494
- 🖊 www.maisonblanc.co.uk
- 🚌 Holland Park LU
- 🕐 Mon-Wed 8am-7pm
  Thurs-Fri 8am-7.30pm,
  Sat 7.30am-7pm, Sun 8.30am-6pm

A striking display of elegant cakes draws customers into this attractive French patissierie shop and café, a Holland Park insitution. Baked goods on offer include rustic-style French breads and elegant cakes and pastries. Among the traditional French treats on offer are classic tarte au citron, Bûches de Noel (at Christmas) and Tarte Bonne Femme.

South-West

La Grande Bouchee

- 🏠 31 Bute Street, SW7 3EY
- ☎ 020 7589 8346
- 🚌 South Kensington LU
- 🕐 Mon-Fri 8am-7pm, Sat 8am-6pm
  Sun 12noon-4pm

This small, well-established shop-cum-café has served generations of Lycee students with coffees, pastries and sandwiches. Foodstuffs range from French cereals, compotes and dairy products to champagne and caviar.

Le Pascalou

- 🏠 359 Fulham Road, SW10 9TW
- ☎ 020 7352 1717
- 🚌 Fulham Broadway LU
- 🕐 Mon-Sat 8am-7.30pm, Sun 10am-6pm

This upmarket, handsome Gallic shop is aimed at an affluent clientele. It sells an impressive range of foodstuffs, from savoury saucisson, pâtés and condiments to French cereals, chocolates, biscuits and confectionary. In front of the shop there's an eye-catching display of fresh fruit and vegetables as well as fish and seafood.

South-East

Boulangerie Jade

- 🏠 *44 Tranquil Vale, SE3*
- ☎ *020 8318 1916*
- 🚆 *Blackheath Rail*
- 🖱 *www.boulangeriejade.com*
- 🕐 *Mon-Sat 8am-6pm, Sun 9am-5pm*

A tempting array of French breads are all freshly baked on the premises. Cakes and pastries are also very popular with the Blackheath regulars who often stay to enjoy a coffee. Seasonal specialities include Christmas treats such buche de Noel, available in different flavours.

East

Androuet

- 🏠 *Old Spitalfields Market*
  107b Commercial Street, E1 6BG
- ☎ *020 7375 3168*
- 🖱 *www.androuet.co.uk*
- 🚆 *Liverpool Street LU/Rail*
- 🕐 *Mon-Sun 10am-7pm*

Run with knowledgeable enthusiasm by Alexandre Guarneri, this London branch of the famous Parisian cheese shop sells a varied range of seasonal, high-quality French cheeses, sourced directly from their producers and sold at their peak of condition.

Eating Places

French eateries in London range from cafés serving delicious pastries to some seriously chic and elegant establishments.

Central

Club Gascon £££££-£££££

- 🏠 *57 West Smithfield, EC1A 9DS*
- ☎ *020 7796 0600*
- 🖱 *www.clubgascon.com*
- 🚆 *Farringdon LU/Rail*

A luxurious establishment specialising in the cuisine of south-west France.

French Bubbles ££-£££

- 🏠 *22 Wellington Street, WC2E 7DD*
- ☎ *020 7240 1604*
- 🖱 *www.frenchbubbles.co.uk*
- 🚆 *Covent Garden LU*

Intimate and rustic in style, this cosy wine bar-cum-bistro offers a chance to sip a flute of one of their many characterful 'grower champagnes', sourced from France's smaller independent, family-owned vinyards, and enjoy dishes showcasing the French cheeses and charcuterie on sale here, from tartines to desserts such as chocolate fondant with bleu des Basques cheese.

Galvin Bistrot de Luxe

££££-£££££

⌨ *66 Baker Street, W1U 7DJ*
☎ *020 7935 4007*
✐ *www.galvinrestaurants.com*
🚌 *Baker Street LU*

This handsome restaurant, evoking a Parisian brasserie, has a well-deserved reputation for its excellent French food and wines. The courteous, knowledgeable service adds to the appeal.

Maison Bertaux £

⌨ *28 Greek Street, W1D 5DQ*
☎ *020 7437 6007*
🚌 *Leicester Square LU*

A vintage Soho café in which to enjoy a café au lait or freshly squeezed orange juice and a freshly baked pastry. Their almond croissants are renowned.

Mon Plaisir £££-££££

⌨ *21 Monmouth Street, WC2H 5DD*
☎ *020 7836 7243*
✐ *www.monplaisir.co.uk*
🚌 *Covent Garden, Leicester Square LU*

London's oldest French restaurant is still going strong. Here one can enjoy well-prepared, classic dishes such as steak tartare or coq au vin in pleasantly old-fashioned, atmospheric surroundings.

Paul £

⌨ *29 Bedford Street, WC2E 9ED*
☎ *020 7836 3304*
✐ *www.paul-uk.com*
🚌 *Covent Garden LU*

The backroom café area offers a chance to sit and sample sweet pastries and a selection of light savoury snacks.

Poilâne Cuisine de Bar ££

⌨ *29 Bedford Street, SW3 2TB*
☎ *020 3263 6019*
✐ *www.poilane.com*
🚌 *Sloane Square LU*

A light and airy, casual dining offering from the acclaimed Parisian bakers, a select range of light dishes including tartines (open sandwiches), made from Poilâne's trademark sourdough.

Terroirs ££-£££

⌨ *5 William 1V Street, WC2*
☎ *020 7036 0660*
✐ *www.terroirswinebar.com*
🚌 *Charing Cross LU/ Rail*

Spread over a ground floor and basement areas, this pleasantly informal wine bar and restaurant has a following for its simple, immaculately executed seasonal food and extensive wine list.

Zedel ££-£££

- 20 Sherwood Street, W1F 7ED
- ☎ 020 7734 4888
- 🖋 www.brasseriezedel.com
- 🚌 Piccadilly Circus LU

A glorious, atmospheric brasserie offering in an Art Deco setting from experienced restaurateurs King and Corbyn, a retro French menu with excellent versions of brasserie classics such as steak with pepper sauce and duck confit at remarkably reasonable prices.

North

L'Absinthe ££-£££

- 40 Chalcot Road, NW1
- ☎ 020 7483 4848
- 🖋 www.labsinthe.co.uk
- 🚌 Chalk Farm LU

Run with panache by owner Jean-Christophe Slowik, this intimate French bistro hums with diners enjoying their meals. The reasonably-priced menu offers classic French fare, from chicken liver parfait to tasty steak frites. The set lunch is a bargain and the corkage added to the wines for sale is very reasonable.

Almeida ££££

- 30 Almeida Street, N1
- ☎ 020 7354 4777
- 🚌 Highbury & Islington LU/Rail

This stylish Islington restaurant focuses on classic French food. Dishes to be found on the menu include hand-carved jambon du Bayonne with celeriac remoulade, superior steak au poivre and a range of tarts, presented (tongue-in-cheek) on a trolley.

Le Crêperie de Hampstead £

- Corner of Hampstead High Street and Perrins Lane, NW3
- 🚌 Hampstead LU

This corner stall is something of a Hampstead institution, serving excellent take-away sweet and savoury crêpes, such as classic crêpes Suzette. Customers stand mesmerised watching thin pools of batter metamorphose into crêpes.

South-West

La Cigale £

- 44, Harrington Road, SW7 3ND
- ☎ 020 7581 1881
- 🖋 www.lacigalelondon.com
- 🚌 South Kensington LU

A French café much frequented by the local Gallic community.

Racine £££££-£££££

- 239 Brompton Road, SW3
- 020 7584 4472
- www.racine-restaurant.com
- Knightsbridge LU, South Kensington LU

Chef-Patron Henry Harris's love of French bourgeois cuisine, shines through the menu at this elegant, smooth-running restaurant, much frequented by South Ken's French community. Expect impeccably executed versions of classic French dishes such as Bayonne ham with remoulade, rabbit with mustard sauce or crème brulee.

Soif ££-£££

- 27 Batterseas Rise, SW11 1HG
- 020 7223 1112
- www.terroirswinebar.com
- Clapham Junction Rail

A sister-restaurant to Terroirs, this pleasantly informal restaurant offers an extensive range of interesting wines and a daily-changing menu showcasing good quality, seasonal ingredients with dishes ranging from a simple serving of excellent charcuterie to classic dishes such as tete de veau.

East

Androuet Restaurant ££

- Old Spitalfields Market
- 107b Commercial Street, E1 6BG
- 020 7375 3168
- www.androuet.co.uk
- Liverpool Street LU/Rail

One for cheese-lovers, this pretty, intimate restaurant with a patio dining area looking out over Spitalfields Market is linked to the cheesemongers next door and so offers a selection of seasonal, classic cheese-based dishes, such as raclette, and the chance to enjoy fine examples of cheeses such as burrata and Comte.

Brawn ££-£££

- 49 Colombia Road, E2 7RG
- 020 7729 5692
- www.brawn.co
- Hoxton Rail

This relaxed Hackney wine bar, part of the Terroirs stable, offers an extensive wine list, with the emphasis firmly on natural wines, and a daily-changing menu of well-executed dishes such as pigs trotters with sauce gribiche or onglet with mash.

Cookbooks

My personal recommendations of cookbooks for this cuisine, including new books and out-of-print classics:

Bistro Cooking
Patricia Wells
An appealing collection of recipes for classic French dishes garnered from bistros across France..

Charcuterie & French PorkCooking
Jane Grigson
A mixture of scholarly knowledge and practical food writing.

Larousse Gastronomique
A fascinating gastronomic encyclopaedia.

Cooking in Provence
Alex Mackay
An attractively illustrated cookbook by an accomplished chef offering an appealing taste of Provence.

French Country Cookery
Elizabeth David
An elegantly written, discriminating guide to traditional French cooking.

French Provincial Cookery
Elizabeth David
A classic cookbook by a master food writer.

Floyd on France
Keith Floyd
A jaunty, accessible collection of French recipes from the flamboyant Floyd.

I know How to Cook
Ginette Mathiot
An impressive tome. This is an authentic French cookbook, offering over 1.400 recipes for classic French dishes.

Mastering the Art of French Cookery (Vols 1 & 2)
Simone Beck, Louisette Bertholle & Julia Child
A well-respected, practical classic.

Simple French Food
Richard Olney
A wonderful, authoritative insight into French bourgeois cuisine, written with love and knowledge.

Greek London

Greenhill Grocers

The Greek community in London today is about 160,000 strong and largely made up of Greek Cypriots; its growth has been a purely twentieth-century phenomenon. Historically, however, there was a small mainland Greek presence in London dating back to the eighteenth century. Bishop Timotheus Catsiyannis, of the Cathedral of Aghia Sophia on Moscow Road, has traced back the histories of such prominent Greek families as the Rallis. Pandias Ralli (1793-1865), a prosperous merchant from Chios, came to Britain to expand the family business. He was a leading figure in the early Greek community in Britain, becoming Consul of Greece in 1835.

The Greek community used the Russian Chapel for their religious services and ceremonies until 1837 when a Greek Chapel of Our Saviour was established at 9 Finsbury Circus, where the Ralli brothers had their business. By 1843 Pandias felt this chapel to be inadequate and proposed building a new church. Seven years later the Greek Church of Our Saviour was opened at London Wall, followed by the completion of the Cathedral of Aghia Sophia in Moscow Road in 1878.

The real growth in London's Greek community came much later, as a result of Britain's relations with Cyprus. This Mediterranean island was leased to the British government in 1878 by the Ottomans, and annexed as a colony by Britain in 1914. During the period of British rule, the lack of opportunities in Cyprus drove many Cypriots to Britain. In the 1930s, the Christian Cypriot Brotherhood was founded in London to offer support to this expat community. The number of Cypriots coming to Britain increased appreciably after the Second World War Many found work as kitchen hands and waiters, and in the garment industry. Soho was an early focal point but there was a shift to Camden Town and in 1948 Greek Cypriots took over the Church of All Saints on Pratt Street. In 1960, Britain withdrew from Cyprus and as a result 25,000 Cypriots came to this country in 1961 seeking work. The Turkish invasion of Cyprus in 1974 caused the next major influx, with hundreds of refugees fleeing to Britain to seek refuge.

During the 1960s the Greek community moved out from Camden, many of them heading north to Turnpike Lane, Wood Green and Palmers Green. Green Lanes, a long road in Haringey, was a focal point for Greek Cypriots but today only a few veteran Greek Cypriot shops remain in the area. Green Lanes now houses a Turkish and Kurdish community while the Greek community has dispersed through London's north-eastern suburbs.

Greek Cuisine

The cuisine of ancient Greece, chronicled by the second-century writer Athenaeus, has now been overlayed by other influences. A history of occupation by the Romans, Venetians and Turks has left distinct traces: pasta dishes, kebabs, coffee and honey pastries. There is a clear overlap between Greek and Turkish cooking, especially apparent in Cypriot cooking, and the debate over who originated which dish still continues today. There are also differences: alcohol and pork, prohibited to the Turks under Islam, are used in Greek cooking in dishes like stifatho and afelia. Easter, the most important religious festival in the Greek calendar, is marked by a host of traditional Greek dishes such as mayeritsa: a soup made from lamb head, heart, liver, lungs and intestines; and tsourekia: a braided loaf decorated with a red-dyed, hard-boiled egg, evoking the colour of Christ's blood.

The physical geography of Greece has influenced its cuisine. The long coastline of the mainland and the islands, shared between three seas, means an abundance of fish and seafood dishes. Mediterranean fish soups, such as bouillabaisse, may be Greek in origin. The lack of grazing ground meant that traditionally, meat was scarce and had to be ingeniously spun out: minced and layered with aubergine in moussaka or with macaroni in pastitio, or cubed and skewered in kebabs. Goats and sheep, able to thrive on the rocky hills, were more popular than cattle, with their need for pasture.

From Arcadia onwards this pastoral tradition has continued, and dairy products such as yoghurt and cheese still play an important, nutritious part in Greek cookery. The pungent flavour of sheep's, and goat's, milk provides a characteristic sharp note. In agriculture the olive and vine, able to flourish on the rocky hill tops, continue to dominate as they have done for centuries. Their products are essential to Greek cooking: olives on the table, mellow-flavoured olive oil, wine for drinking and cooking and vine leaves for dolmathes. The host of nut trees that thrive in Greece, such as almond, pistachio, walnut and stone pine, play their part, adding flavour and texture to both sweet and savoury dishes.

The lemon, also grown plentifully,

sounds one of the keynotes of Greek cooking. Its fresh, sharp flavour characterises dishes such as avgolemono sauce and soup. The fragrant herbs that grow wild on the hill tops are another source of flavour. Athenaeus wrote of herbs being scattered on fish and grilled meat; rigani, or oregano, 'joy of the mountain' is especially popular. The hills are also the source of horta: wild green leaves such as dandelion, wild mustard and chicory, popularly eaten boiled with a dressing.

One Greek influence that has been embraced in kitchens all over the West stems from the Middle Ages. Cooks who entered the monasteries but continued their culinary vocation adopted tall white hats to distinguish themselves from the black-robed and hatted monks – hence the origin of the chef's white hat. The lavish feasts described by Athenaeus or Hesiod the Epicurean in one of the world's first cookbooks are no longer perceived as characteristic Greek cooking. Instead, Greek food is today valued for its flavourful simplicity.

Glossary

Bulgar (pourgori): parboiled, cracked wheat grains, available either coarse or finely ground.

Bulgar

Cheeses: *anari*, a soft cheese, similar to Italian ricotta; *feta*, a salty, crumbly white cheese made from cow's, sheep's or goat's milk, often stored in brine; *halloumi*, a firm white cheese with a rubbery texture, often flavoured with mint.

Colocassi: a large, brown, fibrous tuber with a distinctive white stump, which is a staple of Cypriot cookery.

Colocassi

Filo: paper-thin pastry, sometimes spelled 'phyllo', used in both sweet and savoury dishes. It's usually available frozen, but occasionally fresh filo can be found. When using filo, be careful not to let it dry out.

Glyko: preserved fresh fruit, such as quinces and cherries, in a sweet syrup.

Kataifi: a vermicelli-like pastry, formed by pouring batter through a fine sieve onto a hot surface; usually found frozen.

Loundza: smoked pork loin, a traditional Cypriot Christmas food.

Louvana: a type of vetch, recognisable by its curly tendrils, eaten as a salad leaf.

Mahlepi: the fragrant kernel of the blackcherry stone, sold in husked form and added to sweet yeast breads.

Mastic: the fragrant resin of an evergreen tree, sold in powdered form for use in sweet yeast breads.

Olive oil: in Greek mythology the olive tree was a gift from Athena (the goddess of wisdom and warfare). The rich, fruity oil adds a distinctive flavour.

Olives: *Kalamata,* named after the city, are the famous, large, purple-black olives. *Tiasis*, or cracked olives, are partially-crushed olives which have been marinaded, often with olive oil, lemon slices, garlic and cumin seeds.

Ouzo: clear, anise-flavoured liquor, distilled from grapes. When diluted, this potent aperitif becomes white and cloudy and is nicknamed 'lion's milk'.

Parsley: the flat-leafed, flavourful variety known as 'continental parsley' is a basic herb in Greek cookery.

Pasta: dried pasta is a legacy of the Italian influence on Greek cookery. Shapes include *macarona* (long thick tubes of pasta), *manestra* (pasta kernels), and *vermicelli*, often cooked with bulgar.

Purslane (glysterida): a green salad vegetable with rounded clover-shaped leaves, sometimes called 'Cypriot watercress'.

Retsina: wine with a distinctive resin flavour, traceable back to the days when wine was kept in goat skins sealed with pitch.

Rocket (rocca): a green salad leaf with a distinctive peppery flavour, which is now very fashionable.

Loukanika

Sausages: bastourma, dark, short, spiced sausages; loukanika, thin sausages popularly flavoured with allspice, savory and orange peel or coriander seeds.

Savory: a peppery-flavoured herb, which looks similar to thyme.

Tahini: a smooth paste made from pounded sesame seeds.

Tarama: smoked grey mullet roe or, more commonly, cod roe, used to make taramasalata.

Trahani: brown, stubby, crumbly tubes made from fermented cracked wheat and yogurt. They have a tangy flavour and should be soaked before using.

Vine leaves: large, distinctively-shaped leaves, used principally to make dolmathes. Occasionally found fresh but usually preserved in brine, when they need soaking to rinse off the excess salt.

Yoghurt: thick, creamy Greek yoghurt, made from sheep's or cow's milk.

Food Shops

A typical Greek or Greek Cypriot food shop is a greengrocer, proudly carrying a selection of Cypriot fruit and vegetables. In addition, stock usually includes loaves of freshly-baked village bread, olives, bottles of olive oil, feta cheese, sheep's yoghurt, pulses and grains – the essentials of a Mediterranean diet.

North

Clocktower Store

🖳 *52 The Broadway, N8 9TP*
☎ *020 8348 7845*
🚌 *Finsbury Park LU/Rail, then the W7 bus*
🕐 *Mon-Fri 8.30am-7pm,*
    Sat 8.30am-6pm, Sun 10am-5pm

This friendly, bustling Cypriot greengrocer, just by Crouch End's landmark Clock Tower, offers an excellent range of fruit and veg including fresh herbs to huge watermelons. Inside are staples such as village bread, feta and olive oil.

Greenhill Grocers

🖳 *24 Greenhill Parade, EN5 1EU*
☎ *020 8449 3879*
🚌 *High Barnet LU*
🕐 *Mon-Sat 9am-8pm, Sun 10am-3pm*

Christalla and George Vosku set up this greengrocers in 1989 and are still running it to this day with friendly courtesy. The front part of the shop offers an eye-catching display of fresh fruit and vegetables, from figs, pomegranates and quinces to colocassi, okra and bunches of fresh herbs. Other good things on offer range from frozen artichoke hearts and black-eye beans to olives, Greek pasta, feta and Christalla's own-made olive bread. They have a loyal local following, with one contented customer observing 'This is my little bit of heaven'.

Andreas Michli & Sons

🖳 *405-411 St Ann's Road, N15 3JL*
☎ *020 8802 0188*
🚌 *Harringay Green Lanes Rail*
🕐 *Mon-Thurs & Sat 9.30am-7.30pm,*
    Fri 9.30am-8.30pm, Sun 11am-3.30pm

Tucked away just off Green Lanes, Andreas's characterful row of shops sells everything from food to barbecue equipment. Andreas takes particular pride in the fresh produce, which includes delights such as bergamot lemons, myrtle berries, juicy un-waxed oranges and spanking fresh bunches of chard and spinach.

Tony's Continental Stores

⌖ *140 High Road, N2 9ED*
☎ *020 8444 5545*
🚌 *East Finchley LU*
🕐 *Mon-Fri 8am-7pm*
  Sat 8am-6.30pm, Sun 10am-1pm

From watermelons and figs in the summer to quinces and huge field mushrooms in the autumn, there is always a good range of produce at this self-service greengrocer. The place is run with friendly courtesy and efficiency by the Athanasiou family.

West

Athenian Grocery

⌖ *16a Moscow Road, W2 4BT*
☎ *020 7229 6280*
✐ *www.atheniangrocery.co.uk*
🚌 *Bayswater LU*
🕐 *Mon-Fri 8.30am-5.30pm,*
  Sat & Sun 8.30am-1.30pm

Down the road from St Sophia is this charming corner shop, Britain's oldest Greek deli, established in 1952. Its blue-painted exterior and boxes of vegetables strike an attractive Mediterranean note. Stock includes seasonal items such as green almonds and fresh vine leaves, as well as basic staples. Banter here includes genially exchanged insults with regular customers, but service is friendly and helpful.

Eating Places

Central

Vasis ££

⌖ *56 Maple Street, W1T 6HW*
☎ *020 7580 4819*
✐ *www.vasisrestaurant.co.uk*
🚌 *Warren Street*

Andy Stylianou has been running this veteran Greek taverna since 1979 and continues to do so with genial hospitality and an eye for detail. Customers can enjoy generous portions of freshly-made, home-cooked Greek food. Meze dishes include exemplary deep-fried kalamari and more robust mains such as charcoal-grilled meats and slow-cooked dishes including rabbit stifado or kleftico.

Konaki ££

⌖ *5 Coptic Street, WC1A 1NH*
☎ *020 7580 9730*
✐ *www.konaki.co.uk*
🚌 *Tottenham Court Road LU*

Hidden down a Bloomsbury side-street, this well-established, friendly Greek restaurant has a small courtyard for al-fresco dining. The food is traditional, so classic dishes such as moussaka, and service is friendly.

North

Café Corfu ££

🖼 *7 Pratt Street, NW1 0AE*
☎ *020 7267 8088*
🚌 *Camden Town LU*

A contemporary bar-cum-restaurant offering above average Greek cooking and an excellent Greek wine list.

Daphne ££

🖼 *83 Bayham Street, NW1 0AG*
☎ *020 7267 7322*
🚌 *Camden Town LU*

A convivial Greek restaurant offering decent Greek food in a traditional environment that has remained unchanged for years. It is popular for both romantic tête-à-têtes and parties of friends.

Lemonia ££-£££

🖼 *89 Regent's Park Road, NW1 8UY*
☎ *020 7586 7454*
✐ *www.lemonia.co.uk*
🚌 *Chalk Farm LU*

A Primrose Hill institution, this established, family-run restaurant continues to serve up its taste of the Mediterranean to a loyal local following.

Vrisiaki ££

🖼 *73 Myddleton Road, N22 8LZ*
☎ *020 8889 8760*
🚌 *Bounds Green LU*

Warmly recommended by Cypriot friends, at first sight this looks solely like a take-away kebab house. Venture in, however, past the busy charcoal grills and it opens into a large, popular restaurant. Those with gargantuan appetites should opt for mezedes, a seemingly never-ending array of dishes, starting with nibbles such as cracked olives and working up via seafood to a platter of grilled meats.

Cookbooks

My personal recommendations of cookbooks for this cuisine, including new books and out-of-print classics:

Vefa's Cookbook
Vefa Alexiadou
A magnificent, magisterial tome of traditional, regional Greek recipes. It offers a genuine and delicious insight into this ancient cuisine.

Flavours of Greece
Rosemary Barron
An evocative collection of over 250 recipes, ranging from olive bread to houmous.

A Book of Mediterranean Food
Elizabeth David
An informative book which, although not solely about Greek cookery, captures the flavours of the Mediterranean.

Mediterranean Seafood
Alan Davidson
A fascinating and authoritative guide to Mediterranean seafood.

Mediterranean Cookery
Claudia Roden
A well-written and attractive book, dealing with Mediterranean cuisine as a whole but with plenty of Greek recipies.

The Greek Cook
Rena Salaman
Attractively and clearly illustrated with mouth-watering photographs, this appetising cookbook offers a seasonal look at Greek cuisine.

Meze
Rena Salaman
A pretty cookbook offering recipes for meze dishes from Greece and Lebanon.

Italian London

Lina Stores

Italian links with London date back to the Roman invasion in AD 43 and the creation of a settlement named 'Londinium'. Over subsequent centuries Italians came to live in London, but particularly so in the first half of the nineteenth century when waves of political refugees arrived. The community continued to grow through the turbulent times of Italian Unification and war with Austria – by 1900 there were around 10,000 Italians in London.

The historical Italian quarter, founded in the mid-nineteenth century, was in Clerkenwell and Holborn, known to outsiders as 'Little Italy' and to its residents as 'The Hill'. The nickname 'The Hill' came from two important streets in the community: Back Hill and Eyre Street Hill. St Peter's Church was the community's focal point, erected in 1864 with money donated by Italian immigrants. Its importance to the Italian community continues to this day. Although the Italian population has now dispersed from Clerkenwell, the legacy of this period is still visible in the area around King's Cross and Holborn where red, white and green signs over barbers, cafés and shops patriotically signal Italy.

Every July the Feast Day of Our Lady of Mount Carmel is celebrated with a procession through Clerkenwell from St Peter's, followed by a 'sagra' or fête. One of the few religious processions to take place in London, it has been enacted since the 1880s and older Italians have fond memories of attending it as children. Even today, the procession draws Italians back to Clerkenwell from all over Britain. There is a great sense of community, with the different generations all present and participating. Stalls are set up on the streets selling delicious Italian snacks such as polenta e salsiccie (cornmeal and sausages), freshly-roasted porchetta (pork) and slices of savoury tarts – all washed down with wine.

The other traditional Italian area in London was Soho, which also saw an influx of Italians in the 1860s. Despite the internment of Italian residents as 'enemy aliens' during the Second World War and the tragic death in 1940 of 470 Italian internees being deported to Canada when the 'Arandora Star' was sunk by the Germans, the Italian community continued to maintain its links with Britain. In the 1950s and 1960s, during the espresso bar boom, a wave of immigrants, mostly from the south of Italy, came to London seeking work and settled in Soho as waiters and restaurateurs.

Italian Cuisine

Italian cuisine is very much a regional affair; the different parts of Italy, united only in the last century, have their own dishes and even their own ingredients. The historical divide between the prosperous, industrial north and the poor, rural south also extended to foodstuffs. Rice, cornmeal polenta, and fresh egg pasta were the staples of the north while in the south factory-made, dried durum wheat pasta was eaten. Cooking fats varied: the north used butter, middle-Italy pig fat, and the south, olive oil. With the post-war migration of labour from south to north and the growth of mass-production, regional eating patterns became less rigid. Today the Mediterranean diet, stemming from the south, is valued for its health-giving qualities. Dried pasta and olive oil, low in saturated fats, are now eaten throughout Italy.

Despite this blurring of the north-south divide, regional characteristics are still apparent. Tuscan cuisine comprises rustic, peasant food such as bean soup (the Tuscans are nick-named 'mangiafagioli', bean-eaters), bruschetta and charcoal-grilled meat such as bistecca fiorentina, as well as T-bone steak traditionally from the Val di Chiana. Rice dishes are still popular in the north, where rice was traditionally grown, and in Lombardy you find risotto alla Milanese, flavoured with saffron, wine and stock. Roman cuisine is that of the 'quinto quarto', the fifth quarter, with the poor eating what was left after the rich had eaten, hence strongly-flavoured offal dishes. Sicily has a rich, varied culinary inheritance due to a history of invasions by the Greeks, Romans, Arabs and Normans. The Arab legacy is particularly noticeable, with sultanas, aubergines, pistachio nuts and spices being popular ingredients in Sicily.

Italian cooking is noted for its emphasis on clear, simple flavours. Good ingredients are the key to Italian cooking and seasonality is valued. Foods continue to be associated with the regions, towns or villages that have traditionally produced that ingredient: the best radicchio from Treviso, with its annual radicchio festival; balsamic vinegar from Modena; prosciutto from Parma or San Daniele; fontina cheese from Val d'Aosta; and costly white truffles from Alba.

Glossary

Baccala: pungent salted, dried cod – needs soaking before cooking.

Balsamic vinegar: an aromatic brown vinegar made from wine must and historically from Modena. Traditionally-matured balsamic vinegar is very expensive while cheaper, commercially produced balsamic vinegar compresses the maturing process into a few years.

Ciabatta: a flavourful, distinctively-textured bread, named after a slipper because of its flattened, oval shape.

Balsamic Vinegar

Colomba: a dove-shaped cake similar to panettone, but traditionally eaten at Easter.

Farro: a staple of the early Romans, this ancient grain – a form of wheat – is enjoying a revival. Available either whole or cracked, it has a chewy texture and was traditionally used in hearty soups.

Foccacia: a flat, salty bread flavoured with olive oil and sometimes additionally with rosemary, onions or sage; known as schiacciata in Tuscany.

Fontina: semi-soft cow's milk cheese, traditionally from Val d'Aosta, and famously used to make fonduta, a fondue flavoured with white truffles.

Gorgonzola: Italy's most famous blue cheese, made in Piedmont and Lombardy, traditionally matured in caves. Production today ranges from industrial to artisanal.

Lardo di Colonnata: a traditional delicacy, consisting of cured pork fat, flavoured with salt, herbs and spices, and eaten sliced extremely finely as an antipasto.

Marscapone: an extremely rich cream cheese, an essential ingredient of the popular dessert tiramisu.

Mortadella: a large pink sausage, traditionally from Bologna, flavoured with peppercorns, garlic and pistachios. It can be eaten like a salami or used in cooking.

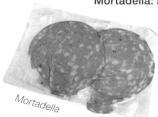

Mortadella

Mozzarella: a mild white cheese, famously used on pizzas. Buffalo's milk mozzarella, with its melting texture and rich flavour, is rarer and more expensive than the widely-available cow's milk version. Baby mozzarellas are called 'bocconcini'.

Olive oil: a key ingredient in Italian cooking, olive oil is labelled according to its acidity levels. Extra Virgin must have no more than 1% acidity. As with wine, different regions produce different-flavoured olive oils, with Tuscan olive oil being famously piquant.

Olive Oil

Pancetta: the Italian equivalent of bacon, this is made from the same cut of meat – pig belly.

Panettone: a light, brioche-style cake, containing sultanas, traditionally given at Christmas time, the season when London's Italian delis stock several versions.

Panettone

Parmesan

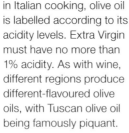

Parmesan: the best-known Italian cheese and also the largest and longest-matured cheese produced in Italy, this hard-grating cheese traditionally comes from around Parma. Grana padano is a similar cheese produced in Lombardy. Buy chunks of Parmesan and keep them refrigerated, wrapped in foil, to be used as required.

Pasta: this famous Italian staple comes both fresh and dried and in a multiplicity of forms. Fresh pasta, made with eggs, can be bought ready-made from delicatessens. Dried pasta is made from durum wheat, with reliable Italian brands including Barilla and Da Cecco.

Pecorino: a hard sheep's milk cheese, available in regional variations: Pecorino Romano, Pecorino Sardo, (from Sardinia) and Toscana, from Tuscany.

Pine nuts: small ivory-coloured kernels from the stone pine tree, with a distinctive flavour.

Polenta: a Northern Italian staple made from maize, polenta flour is available in fine or coarse versions. Pre-cooked polenta flour, scorned by purists, is also available.

Polenta

Porcini: wild Boletus mushrooms, prized for their flavour and priced accordingly. Dried porcini mushrooms, often in pieces, are easily found, while fresh porcini are much rarer.

Porcini

Prosciutto Crudo: the most famous of these salt-cured hams is Parma ham, cured for 14 months. San Daniele, cured for 12 months, is considered another fine prosciutto.

Ricotta: a light, bland sheep's whey cheese, drained in baskets which give it its distinctive woven markings. It is used in both sweet and savoury dishes.

Rocket: known as 'rucola', this peppery, jagged leaf is increasingly available as a chic salad leaf. Italians are fond of pointing out that in Italy it grows wild as a weed.

Salami: ready-to-eat, salt-cured sausages, available in a range of sizes and flavours, such as fine-textured Milano or finocchiona, flavoured with fennel.

Salsiccie: Italian sausages, usually made from pork. Luganega is a mild sausage from Lombardy, sold in long narrow coils, while in the South chilli is often added as a flavouring.

Sun-dried tomatoes: as their name suggests, these are dried tomatoes, available either in their dry state or preserved in olive oil.

Truffles: these rare tubers with their overwhelming and distinctive flavour are astronomically expensive, especially when sold fresh. White truffles from Alba are particularly prized. Tinned and bottled truffles are available as is truffle-flavoured olive oil.

Rocket

Food Shops

The older Italian delicatessens in London grew out of the community's needs, starting as everyday corner-shops supplying foods that had to be specially imported. In some cases the shop acted as an informal community centre, lending money, explaining English laws and providing advice. As the Italian community has become assimilated into British life this role has disappeared. In recent years, many of these traditional Italian groceries have now gone, often driven out by huge rent hikes. With Italian food now enjoying a huge wave of fashionable popularity, newer, more upmarket delicatessens have entered the market aimed primarily at the British.

Central

Gelupo

⌨ *7 Archer Street, W1D 7AU*
☎ *020 7287 5555*
🖱 *www.gelupo.com*
🚌 *Leicester Square/Piccadilly Circus LU*
🕐 *Mon-Thurs 12noon-11pm,*
   Fri-Sat 12noon-1am, Sun 12noon-10pm
   Sun 11am-4pm

In addition to its delectable gelati, Gelupo – set up by Bocca di Lupo restaurant – offers a select collection of high-quality Italian delicacies, such as truffle honey, Sabadi chocolates, fine olive oils, Italian wines and Mantovan Zacche risotto rice. In-house delicacies made by Bocca di Lupo's chefs include salamis, nduja (chilli-spiced pork paste), salsicce, pasta sauces such as pigeon ragu and fresh pasta. Frozen desserts such as Zuppa Inglese and Bonet are another draw.

I Camisa & Son

⌨ *61 Old Compton Street, W1D 6HS*
☎ *020 7437 7610/4686*
🖱 *www.icamisa.co.uk*
🚌 *Leicester Square LU,*
   Tottenham Court Road LU
🕐 *Mon-Sat 9am-6pm*

On this bustling Soho thoroughfare, this classic Italian deli is a local institution, used by chefs and Soho residents alike. Established in 1961, it has a seemingly perpetual queue of loyal regulars, attracted by the quality of the cheeses, meats and delicious home-marinated olives. Bags of fresh rocket, fragrant basil and sweet Sicilian cherry tomatoes are another draw. Fresh, own-made pasta includes pappardelle, parma ham tortellini and gnocchi and there are excellent home-made sauces such as pesto, pomodoro and porcini.

Gastronomeria Italia

🏠 *8 Upper Tachbrook Street, SW1V 1SH*
☎ *020 7834 2767*
🚇 *Pimlico LU, Victoria LU/Rail*
🕐 *Mon-Fri 9am-6pm, Sat 9am-5pm*

This homely delicatessen is well-used by Italians and Spaniards from the local community. As well as a good basic stock of Italian ingredients, they sell tasty Italian snacks to cater to the lunchtime market.

Gastronomica

🏠 *45 Tachbrook Street, SW1V 2LZ*
☎ *020 7233 6656*
🚇 *Pimlico LU,Victoria LU/Rail*
🕐 *Mon-Sat 8am-11pm, Sun 9am-10pm*

Run by an experienced team of Italian food importers, this café-cum-deli offers a select range of good quality Italian foodstuffs, notably cheeses, charcuterie and fine wines.

La Bottega

🏠 *25 Eccleston Street, SW1W 9NP*
☎ *020 7730 2730*
✎ *www.labottega65.co.uk*
🕐 *Mon-Fri 8am-7pm, Sat 9am-6pm, Sun 9am-5pm*

The flagshop establishment in Roberta and Bepi's mini-chain, this café-cum-deli stocks Italian cheeses and charcuterie, dried pasta and wines, while Christmas sees an abundant selection of good quality panettone.

Lina Stores

🏠 *18 Brewer Street, W1F 0SH*
☎ *020 7437 6482*
✎ *www.linastores.co.uk*
🚇 *Leicester Square LU, Oxford Circus LU, Piccadilly Circus LU*
🕐 *Mon-Fri 9am-6.30pm, Sat 9am-5.30pm*

With its pistachio-coloured façade and vintage lettering, Lina Stores is a much-loved Soho institution, which recently underwent a tastefully-executed revamp. Stock, in addition, to the famous fresh pasta, including signature pumpkin tortelloni, includes an upmarket selection of Italian charcuterie, cheeses and store-cupboard ingredients. Service is friendly and helpful.

Princi £-££

🏠 *135 Wardour Street, W1F 0UT*
☎ *020 7478 8889*
✎ *www.princi.co.uk*
🚇 *Leicester Square LU, Oxford Circus LU Piccadilly Circus LU,*
🕐 *Mon-Sat 7am-12midnight, Sun 9am-11pm*

At last! – a great Italian pasticceria in London, smartly housed in this pasticceria-meets-pizzeria-meets bar offering from restaurateur Alan Yau. On offer from the in-house bakery are freshly baked focaccia and a tempting array of sweet treats such as cannoncini, crostata and cannoli Siciliani. Seasonal treats include colombe and panettone.

Spianata £

- 3 Hay Hill, W1J 6AS
- ☏ 020 3632 8085
- 🖰 www.spianata.com
- 🚌 Green Park LU
- 🕐 Mon-Fri 7.30am-5.30pm

Stylish and contemporary, this Mayfair addition to the Spianata group, offers its trademark, freshly-made Roman style panini, made from own-baked thin, crisp pizza bianca Romana bread, with fillings such as mortadella, Parma ham and mozzarella and gorgonzola, speck and pear, as well as sweet treats including tiramisu and Italian cakes.
Branches: various, see website

North

Amici Delicatessen

- 78 High Road, N2 9PN
- ☏ 020 8444 2932
- 🚌 East Finchley LU

A down-to-earth Italian delicatessen-cum-café, offering snacks and coffees in addition to a range of Italian foodstuffs.

Angel Delicatessen

- 48 Cross Street, N1 2BA
- ☏ 020 7226 1951
- 🚌 Angel LU
- 🕐 Mon-Sat 8am-6pm, Sun 9am-4pm

This deli-cum-café makes a good cappuccino as well as offering a good stock of Italian foodstuffs.

Gallo Nero

- 75 Stoke Newington High Street, N16 8EL
- ☏ 020 7254 9770
- 🚌 Rectory Road or Stoke Newington Rail
- 🕐 Mon, Wed-Sat 8.30am-5.45pm, Tues 8.30am-1.45pm

Run with affable courtesy by owner Michele Mori, this classic Italian deli, established in 1988, is, as Michele puts it, 'full of food'. There is an extensive range of stock, including dried pastas (De Cecco, Agnesi and Garofalo), charctuerie 'from north to south Italy', 30 cheeses, antipasti, fresh pasta and wines and spirits.

Gallo Nero

- 45 Newington Green Road, N1 4QT
- ☏ 020 7226 2002
- 🚌 Canonbury Rail
- 🕐 Mon, Wed-Sat 8.30am-6pm, Tues 8.30am-2pm

Roberto Mori runs this branch of Gallo Nero, which offers an excellent range of Italian foodstuffs served with a friendly and knowledgeable courtesy.

The Gazzano's

167-9 Farringdon Road, EC1R 3AL

020 7837 1586

Farringdon LU

Tues-Fri 7.30am-5.30pm,
Sat 8am-5pm, Sun 10am-2pm

Founded in 1901, this veteran Italian delicatessen, still run by the Gazzano family, is still going strong – a legacy of the days when Clerkenwell was known as 'Little Italy'. Deli stock is comprehensive and there's also a café area in which customers can sit and enjoy an espresso and panini. Sundays sees the shop filled with Italians popping in to stock up with ingredients or grab a coffee following Mass at St Peter's church down the road.

Giacobazzi's Delicatessen

150 Fleet Road, NW3 2QX

020 7267 7222

Hampstead Heath Rail

www.giacobazzis.co.uk

Mon-Fri 9.30am-7pm, Sat 9am-6pm

A Hampstead institution, the Giacobazzis' well-established deli offers a tempting range of good things to eat, from classic Italian antipasti, charcuterie and groceries to treats such cannoli and Oddono's gelati. A particular highlight is the range of home-made fresh pasta including gorgonzola and walnut or artichoke and ricotta tortelloni, potato gnocchi and pappardelle.

Monte's

23 Canonbury Lane, N1 2AS

020 7354 4335

www.montesdeli.com

Highbury & Islington LU/Rail

Mon-Fri 10am-7pm,
Sat 10am-6pm, Sun 10am-4pm

A smart, contemporary Italian deli, with upmarket stock to match from Italian cheeses to charcuterie.

Olga Stores

30 Penton Street, N1 9PS

020 7837 5467

Angel LU

Mon-Fri 9am-8pm, Sat 9am-7pm,
Sun 10am-2pm

This attractive deli, established in 1988, caters to its Islington clientele with a wide selection of foodstuffs, from marinated olives to breads. Best-selling items include home-made lasagne and pasta sauces – from tomato-based arrabiata to pesto.

Parkway Delicatessen

30 Parkway, NW1 7AH

020 7267 0076

Camden Town LU

Mon-Sat 9.30am-6.30pm

This small, old-fashioned deli, run by Safia Hasan, offers a basic selection of Italian foodstuffs.

Italian Food Shops

Saponara

🏠 23 Prebend Street, N1 8PF
☎ 020 7226 2771
🚌 Angel LU
🕐 Mon-Thurs 8am-6pm, Fri 8am-10pm,
   Sat 9am-10pm

Run with friendly courtesy by brothers Marco and Vincenzo Saponara, this roomy deli and bar offers a classic Italian mixture of delicious things to eat and drink. The store has a very good selection of authentic antipasti, cold meats and organic Italian wines and now offers freshly made stone-baked pizza which is served into the evening on Fridays and Saturdays.

Salvino Ltd

🏠 47 Brecknock Road, N7 0BT
☎ 020 7267 5305
🚌 Buses 29, 253 or 10
🕐 Mon-Sat 9am-7pm

An agreeably down-to-earth shop run by the Salvino brothers. As importers of Italian food their range of stock is well above average, with good cured meats and wines.

Terroni's

🏠 138-140 Clerkenwell Road, EC1R 3DL
☎ 020 7837 1712
🚌 Farringdon LU
🕐 Mon-Fri 8am-6pm, Sat 9am-5pm,
   Sun 10am-2pm

This latest incarnation of Terroni's (which, having being established in 1878, had the proud title of England's oldest Italian deli) is now a café-cum-deli, selling a range of Italian ingredients.

North-West

L'Angolo

🏠 120 College Road, NW10 5HD
☎ 020 8969 5757
🚌 Kensal Green LU, Kensal Rise Rail
🕐 Mon-Fri 9am-6.30pm, Sat 9am-6pm,
   Sun 9.30am-1pm

Very much a local institution, Carmelo's attractive cornershop ('angolo' means corner in Italian, by the way) offers an appetising range of foodstuffs, from staples such as dried pasta, risotto rice and sauces to charcuterie, fresh pasta and fresh produce from chestnuts to porcini mushrooms. Lunchtimes see a patient queue waiting for made-to-order panini and coffees to go.

Gastronomia La Delizia

🏠 51-53 Fairfax Road, NW6 4EL
☎ 020 7624 4040
🚌 Swiss Cottage LU
🕐 Mon-Fri 8am-7pm, Sat 9am-6pm,
   Sun 9.30am-1pm

A classy addition to Swiss Cottage's food

scene. This spacious, chic Italian deli and bar, is run with pride by the Zairy family. A well-stocked deli counter offers both core staples and treats, such as smoked tuna, fresh pasta as well as a colourful range of antipasti dishes. The store-cupboard stock is equally impressive, from Italian stock cubes and bottled sauces to stone-ground polenta. A small freezer contains porcini, carciofi, fiori di zucca and frutti di mare and there is a range of Italian wines. The foodstuffs have been carefully chosen by Pnina Zairy; 'I'm very fussy about food,' she says simply.

West

Exeter Street Bakery

- 18 Argyll Road, W8 7DB
- 020 7937 8484
- High Street Kensington LU
- Mon-Sat 8am-7pm, Sun 9am-6pm

This small shop showcases the bakery's range of Italian breads, from pane Pugliese to ciabatta, offering also pizza, coffee and crostata.

Melograno Alimentari

- 4 Clarendon Road, W11 3AA
- 020 7727 3119
- www.melograno.co.uk
- Holland Park LU
- Mon-Fri 8.30am-8pm, Sat 8.30am-7pm, Sun 9am-6pm

This smart deli with jaunty bright red shelving, which opened in 2011, carries a select range of upmarket stock including Pastificio dei Campi pasta, River Café olive oil, genuine balsamic vinegars and high-quality charcuterie.

Negozio Classica

- 283 Westbourne Grove, W11 2QA
- 020 7034 0005
- www.negozioclassica.co.uk
- Notting Hill LU
- Tues-Fri 9.30am-8pm, Sat 9.30am-7pm, Sun 11am-4.30pm

This sleek operation is a contemporary take on the Italian 'enoteca' or wine shop. Here one can sit at the chrome bar sampling wines, eating antipasti platters or sipping on an expertly-made cappuccino made from Saint Eustachio coffee. A large range of fine Italian wines, including top-notch vin santo, are available by the glass, plus select artisanal foodstuffs including chestnut honey, trout cheeks in oil and Italian saffron.

Speck

⊞ *2 Holland Park Terrace, W11 4ND*
☎ *020 7229 7005*
🚌 *Holland Park LU*
🕐 *Mon-Fri 9am-8.30pm, Sat 8.30am-7pm*
This small, established delicatessen
shop carries an upmarket range of Italian
foodstuffs, with burrata cheese a speciality
while its range of home-made dishes are a
popular draw

Tavola

⊞ *155 Westbourne Grove, W11 2RS*
☎ *020 7229 0571*
🚌 *Notting Hill Gate LU*
🕐 *Mon-Fri 10am-7.30pm, Sat 10am-6pm*
Alistair and Sharon Little's attractive food
shop reflects their knowledgeable love
of Italian cuisine with a range of carefully
chosen products. Unusual Italian wines, fine
balsamic vinegars and olive oils and artisanal
dried Pugliese pasta are some of the Italian
foodstuffs on offer. Alistair's own-cooked
dishes include an exemplary pasta e fagioli
soup.

Valentina

⊞ *145 Notting Hill Gate, W11 3LB*
☎ *020 7702 1181*
✎ *www.valentinafinefoods.com*
🚌 *Notting Hill Gate LU*
🕐 *Mon-Fri 8am-10pm, Sat-Sun 8am-10.30pm*

This smart addition to the Valentina group of
delicatessens combines a ground floor deli
with an upstairs restaurant. The deli has an
impressive range of Italian foodstuffs, from
cheeses and charcuterie to store-cupboard
staples, while treats include Marine Ices
ice cream. There is a cluster of tables from
which to enjoy a cappuccino and nibble an
Italian pastry.

South-West

Italo

⊞ *13 Bonnington Square, SW8 1TE*
☎ *020 7450 3773*
🚌 *Vauxhall LU/Rail*
🕐 *Mon-Fri 9.30am-9.45pm,
Sat 9.30am-7pm*
Tucked away by leafy Bonnington Square
Gardens, this corner shop, founded by
Charlie Boxer and Luigi Lieto, offers a select
range of well-chosen foodstuffs, such as
stuffed fresh pasta, Italian salsicce and
bright yellow-yolked Macchiavelli eggs. It
does a roaring trade in food to go, from
baked lasagne to coffee and sandwiches.

Luigi's Delicatessen

⊞ *349 Fulham Road, SW10 9TW*
☎ *020 7352 7739*
🚌 *Fulham Broadway LU*
🕐 *Mon-Fri 9am-9.30pm, Sat 9am-7pm*

This long-established, roomy, cheerful delicatessen attracts a steady stream of loyal customers. The stock is extensive and high-quality; 40 olive oils, an ample stock of quality Italian dried pastas and over 300 Italian wines, spirits and aperitivos. There is an appetising display of homemade sauces and dishes.

La Picena

🔲 *5 Walton Street, SW3 2JD*
☎ *020 7584 6573*
🚇 *Knightsbridge LU*
🕐 *Mon-Fri 9am-7.30pm, Sat 9am-5.30pm*

Tucked away behind Harrods is this long-established, refreshingly down-to-earth delicatessen. It carries a basic range of Italian provisions and does a popular line in food to go, such as lasagne and homemade pasta sauces.

Valentina

🔲 *210 Upper Richmond Road West, SW14 8AH*
☎ *020 8392 9127*
🚇 *Mortlake Rail*
🕐 *Mon-Sun 8.30am-10pm*

This attractive, friendly delicatessen-cum-restaurant, the original Valentina, has a loyal local following. Stock covers classic Italian staples and a well-chosen range of treats.

Valentina

🔲 *75 Upper Richmond Road, SW15 2SR*
☎ *020 8877 9906*
✒ *www.valentinafinefoods.com*
🚇 *East Putney LU*
🕐 *Mon-Sat 8am-9pm, Sun 12noon-6pm*

Very much Valentina Fine Food's flagship, this family enterprise (jointly run by the Zoccola and Arcari families) combines a spacious, light and airy ground floor deli with a café area and an upstairs restaurant. The stock here is admirably comprehensive, from cheeses, charcuterie, Garofalo pastas, jarred sauces to cakes (such as torta della nonna), honeys and Marine Ices ice cream as well as Valentina's own olive oil, made from olives from their Italian family estate. Fabio, family member and manager here, is particularly proud of the extensive range of Italian wines.

Vallebona

🔲 *59 Weir Road, SW19 8UG*
☎ *020 8944 5665*
🚇 *Wimbledon Park LU*
🕐 *Sat 9.30am-4pm*

Saturdays see this Italian food wholesaler, specialising in gourmet Sardinian foodstuffs, open the doors of its warehouse for tasting and shopping, with good things on offer including artisanal cheeses, regional salami and a range of sweet and savoury delicacies.

South-East

La Gastronomeria

⌨ *135 Half Moon Lane, SE24 9JY*
☎ *020 7274 1034*
🚃 *Herne Hill Rail, North Dulwich Rail*
🕐 *Mon-Fri 9am-5.30pm, Sat 9am-5pm*

A friendly, well-stocked Italian deli offering customers a solid range of basic groceries, from Italian dried pastas to packets of biscotti. Popular items on the deli counter include home-made pasta and antipasti.

Fine Foods

⌨ *1218 Long Lane, SE1 4QB*
☎ *020 7403 7513*
🖋 *www.finefoodse1.co.uk*
🚃 *London Bridge LU/Rail*
🕐 *Mon-Thurs 7.30am-8pm,*
Fri 7.30am-6pm,
Sat 8.30am-6.30pm, Sun 10am-4pm

Run with jovial affability by its owner Melo, this small, picturesque Italian deli has a loyal following. The wooden shelves are lined with a tempting assortment of own-imported products including white truffle cream, jarred grilled artichokes in oil and condiments and there's a small deli counter with charcuterie and cheeses. Customers drop in for a take-away coffee and a chat or to tuck into a freshly-made panini at one of the tables at the back.

Gennaro Delicatessen

⌨ *123 Lewis Grove, SE13 6BG*
☎ *020 8852 1370*
🖋 *www.italianfoodexpress.co.uk*
🚃 *Lewisham Rail*
🕐 *Mon-Sat 9am-6.30pm*

This well-established, traditional Italian delicatessen, run by Antonio and Elena, has a loyal local following, attracted by both the shop's range of stock and the friendly, helpful service.

East

Gastronomica

⌨ *New Crane Wharf, 75 Garnet Street, E1*
☎ *020 7481 8669*
🚃 *Wapping LU*
🕐 *Mon-Wed 8am-8pm,*
Thurs-Sat 8am-10pm,
Sun 9.30am-6.30pm

Founded by the Italian food importers, this smart Italian deli and café offers an upmarket selection of Italian foods, including cheeses, charcuterie, cakes and fine wines.

Eating Places

The enormous popularity of Italian food in the UK has seen a huge range of Italian restaurants opening up, with chains such as Carluccio's and Jamie's Italian bringing Italian food to a wide audience. In London you can find a huge range of Italian eateries, from small cafés serving coffee and panini and pizzerias to elegant, expensive restaurants offering authentic, delicious and regional Italian cuisine.

Central

Bar Italia £

🖃 *22 Frith Street, W1*
☎ *020 7437 4520*
✎ *www.baritaliasoho.co.uk*
🚌 *Leicester Square LU*
    Tottenham Court Road LU

Despite its cult status as the place for a late night espresso, Bar Italia, opened in 1949 by Lou and Caterina Polledri, remains thankfully down-to-earth – coming complete with a giant video screen for Italian football and the photo of the heavyweight boxing legend Rocky Marciano glowering down from behind the bar.

Bocca di Lupo £££-££££

🖃 *12 Archer Street, W1D 7BB*
☎ *020 7734 2223*
✎ *www.boccadilupo.com*
🚌 *Leicester Square LU,*
    Piccadilly Circus LU

Discreetly positioned down a tiny Soho backstreet near Shaftesbury Avenue, this attractive restaurant is perpetually buzzing with contented diners enjoying a delicious taste of Italy. Chef Jacob Kennedy's kitchen serves up a frequently changing, seasonal menu of well-executed regional Italian dishes. Delectable desserts, especially the own-made gelati and sorbeti, are not to be missed.

Caffé Caldesi £££

🖃 *118 Marylebone Lane, W1U 2QF*
☎ *020 7935 1144*
✎ *www.caldesi.com*
🚌 *Baker Street LU*

Run with brio by husband-and-wife team Giancarlo and Katie Caldesi, this appealing Italian establishment offers an informal café area downstairs and a more formal restaurant upstairs.

Caffé Vergnano 1882 £

62 Charing Cross Road, WC2H 0BU

020 7240 3512

www.caffevergnano1882.co.uk

Leicester Square LU

A small, intimate café, known for its excellent coffee, from espresso to cappuccino.

La Bottega £

25 Eccleston Street, SW1W 9NP

020 7730 2730

www.labottega65.co.uk

London Victoria LU / Rail

The flagshop establishment in Roberta and Bepi's mini-chain, this café-cum-deli does a roaring lunchtime trade in panini, salads, pastries and coffees.

Locanda Locatelli ££££

8 Seymour Street, W1H 7JZ

020 7935 9088

www.locandalocatelli.com

Marble Arch LU

This sophisticated and elegant restaurant is a showcase for the considerable culinary talents of acclaimed Italian chef Giorgio Locatelli. A stylish seasonal menu offers diners to enjoy a wide range of accomplished dishes made from discernibly fine ingredients.

Machiavelli Kitchen & Dining Room ££-£££

69 Long Acre, WC2E 9JS

020 7240 2125

www.machiavellifood.co.uk

Covent Garden or Holborn LU

A pleasantly informal establishment in which to enjoy a coffee and pastry or eat more substantially.

Manicomio ££-£££

85 Duke of York Square, SW3

020 7730 3366

www.manicomio.co.uk

Sloane Square LU

Quality ingredients are at the heart of good Italian cooking and Manicomio's, set up by Italian fine food importers, has impeccable credentials on that front. The restaurant is smart in a pleasantly understated way and serves up decent Italian food complemented by a shrewdly chosen wine list.

Mele e Pere ££-£££

46 Brewer Street, W1F 9TF

020-7096 2096

www.meleepere.co.uk

Leicester Square, Piccadilly Circus LU

An attractive, contemporary take on a trattoria, serving a daily changing menu of tasty Italian food and offering an excellent value set lunch.

Pizzeria Malletti £

- 26 Noel Street, W1F 8GY
- ☎ 020 7439 4096
- www.pizzaeriamalletti.co.uk
- Oxford Circus LU

This diminutive pizzeria has a cult following, offering slices of freshly-made pizza, available to take away or eat in, perching on a stool.

Princi £-££

- 135 Wardour Street, W1F 0UT
- ☎ 020 7478 8889
- www.princi.co.uk
- Leicester Square or Piccadilly Circus LU

All-day Italian eating is on offer at this stylish establishment from brioche and cappuccino for breakfast, to freshly baked pizza slices, filled focaccia bread, salads and hearty pasta bakes at lunchtime and through the night. There is now a sit-down pizzeria area in which diners can enjoy Neapolitan-style pizzas.

Sardo £££

- 45 Grafton Way, W1T 5DQ
- ☎ 020 7387 2521
- www.sardo-restaurant.com
- Warren Street LU

As the name suggest, Sardinian specialities, including traditional pasta dishes such as spaghetti bottariga or malloreddus are on offer here in this well-established Italian restaurant.

Theo Randall at the Intercontinental ££££

- 1 Hamilton Place, Park Lane, W1J 7QY
- ☎ 020 7409 3131
- Hyde Park Corner LU

Theo Randall, formerly Head Chef at the River Café, has a keen following for his accomplished, seasonal Italian cooking, showcased here in smart surroundings.

Zafferano ££££

- 15 Lowndes Street, SW1X 9EY
- ☎ 020 7235 5800
- Knightsbridge LU

A pioneer of fine Italian food in London, this elegantly rustic restaurant continues to pull in the punters, drawn by the excellent Italian cooking and charming service.

North

Marine Ices ££

- 8 Haverstock Hill, NW3 2BL
- ☎ 020 7482 9003
- www.marineices.co.uk
- Chalk Farm LU

In addition to Marine Ices' famous ice cream parlour, there is also a relaxed family-friendly restaurant offering tasty pizzas and pasta.

West

Assaggi ££££

🏠 *The Chepstow, 39 Chepstow Place, W2 4TS*

☎ *020 7792 5501*

🚌 *Notting Hill Gate LU*

Located above a pub, this small restaurant is noted for its flavourful, authentic Italian food.

Franco Manca ££

🏠 *144, Chiswick High Road, W4 1PU*

☎ *020 8747 4822*

✍ *www.francomanca.co.uk*

🚌 *Turnham Green*

A spacious West London branch of the acclaimed Brixton Market pizzeria, serving up their trademark sourdough pizzas.

The River Café £££££

🏠 *Thames Wharf, Rainville Road, W6*

☎ *020 7381 8824*

✍ *rivercafe.co.uk*

🚌 *Hammersmith LU*

Founded by the late Rose Gray and Ruthie Rogers, this famous restaurant by the Thames was an early pioneer of authentic, seasonal Italian cookery and continues to work its magic. A number of best-selling 'River Café' cookbooks have helped establish this restaurant's fine reputation.

South-West

La Bottega £

🏠 *25, Lower Sloane Street, SW1W 8HD*

☎ *020 7730 8844*

✍ *www.labottega65.com*

🚌 *Sloane Square LU*

A small Italian café, always busy selling coffees, paninis and Italian pastries.

Donna Margherita ££-£££

🏠 *183 Lavender Hill, SW11 5TE*

☎ *020 7228 2660*

✍ *www.donna-margherita.co.uk*

🚌 *Clapham Junction Rail*

Pizzas freshly baked in a wood-fired oven are the draw at this lively Neapolitan restaurant.

Franco Manca ££

🏠 *4 Market Row SW9 8LD*

☎ *020 7738 3021*

✍ *www.francomanca.co.uk*

🚌 *Brixton LU/Rail*

In the heart of Brixton Market, this pleasantly casual pizzeria buzzes with appreciative diners. A short, to-the-point, seasonal menu offers a choice of six pizzas, all with the trademark thin sourdough base, with the emphasis on top-notch ingredients. Prices are remarkably reasonable given the quality.

Riva £££

🖥 *169 Church Road, SW13 9HR*
☎ *020 8748 0434*
🚌 *Barnes Bridge Rail*

A restaurant pioneer of regional Italian cooking, Riva continues to offer imaginative and tasty dishes in an elegant setting. The food, atmosphere and charming, professional service means it has a loyal clientele.

Valentina £-££

🖥 *75 Upper Richmond Road, SW15 2SR*
☎ *020 8877 9906*
✎ *www.valentinafinefoods.com*
🚌 *East Putney LU*
🕓 *Mon-Sat 8am-9pm, Sun 12noon-6pm*

Very much Valentina Fine Food's flagship, this light and airy family-run enterprise combines a spacious deli with a café area and a notably family-friendly upstairs restaurant, showcasing ingredients on sale in the deli. Dishes range from excellent antipasti to hearty dishes such as capella Romana, tagliatelle with nonna's meatballs wrapped in speck ham and baked in the oven.

Cookbooks

Secrets of an Italian Kitchen
Anna del Conte
Anna del Conte offers a genuine and appetising insight into Italian cuisine.

Italian Food
Elizabeth David
First published in 1954, this book is still as valid and useful as when it was first written – a classic.

The River Café Classic Italian Cook Book
Rose Gray and Ruth Rogers
An elegant cookbook, bringing together a delicious collection of classic Italian recipes.

The Classic Italian Cookbook, The Second Classic Italian Cookbook, Marcella's Kitchen
Marcella Hazan
Three wonderful cookbooks by a highly respected authority on Italian cuisine.

Made In Italy: Food & Stories
Giorgio Locatelli
Acclaimed Italian chef Giorgio Locatelli offers an inspiring collection of delicious recipes and evocative anecdotes.

Japanese London

Atari-Ya Foods

The Japanese presence in London is a comparatively recent phenomenon. Japan's deliberate cultural isolation for hundreds of years was broken down in the seventeenth century by Portuguese traders and missionaries, but contact with the West remained limited. It was during Japan's post-Second World War business boom, as the country restored and developed its economy, that a community developed in London. It is primarily a business community, consisting of families on postings for large companies and banks. The temporary nature of most of these postings has kept the community transitory and relatively rootless. Social life, as in Japan, is conducted largely round the golf course and at business lunches.

It used to be said that the Japanese lived on the Northern Line, which provided access to all their needs, from the City for work to the leafy suburbs of Finchley and Golders Green for housing, with much-valued golf courses nearby. The presence of the Oriental City shopping plaza at Colindale was prompted by the growth of this North London community. The shifting of the Japanese School to Acton, however, has opened up a new area of suburban London for the Japanese community and the Northern Line is no longer the sole axis. Acton's Japanese community are now catered for by two kindergartens and primary schools, as well as Japanese food shops, book shops, property letting agencies and restaurants. The past decade has also seen a growing Japanese presence in the West End, with shops opening specifically to cater for the influx of prosperous Japanese tourists.

Japanese Cuisine

This highly refined cuisine, which developed in isolation for hundreds of years, is both aesthetic and ascetic. In Japan's codified society, a meticulously disciplined approach governs food preparation as well as other aspects of life. Presentation is all-important: small portions of foods are carefully arranged, delighting both the eye and the palate. Nouvelle cuisine borrowed greatly from Japanese culinary aesthetics.

'Kisetsukan' is the Japanese term for a sympathy with nature, important in Japanese culture. Dishes are designed to echo nature, perhaps creating a miniature landscape or simply a natural gracefulness. A great value is placed on freshness and seasonality. Fish and vegetables, two key foodstuffs, are at their best fresh. Sashimi, raw fish served with a dipping sauce, epitomises this emphasis. Even though modern preserving techniques have robbed seasonality of its practical imperative, it continues to be valued. There is a whole range of dishes, such as cherry blossom rice or oden, eaten in appropriate months and seasons, with even preserved ingredients such as pickles and miso pastes changing according to the time of year. The flavour of individual ingredients is emphasised in the cooking rather than disguised. Even a Japanese stew retains the separate flavours of ingredients rather than blending them into a whole.

The range of seasonings in Japanese food is limited, falling into three broad categories: salty (provided by shoyu and dashi), sweet (from sugar, mirin and sake) and citrus (from yuzu and dai dai fruits). Shiso leaves and sansho provide an extra aromatic touch. These flavourings are used over and over again in different combinations. Pickles are carefully chosen to go with particular dishes. Fish and seafood, as befits a nation of islands, play a large part in the cuisine, from the basic soup stock to fishcakes and sausages. An extenstion of this love of seafood has been the use of seaweeds or sea-vegetables, a hallmark of Japanese cooking.

Many of the unique aspects of Japanese cuisine come from the fact that it developed to a great extent in isolation. However, over centuries, a number of foreign influences filtered through. China, between the sixth and eighth centuries, had an effect on many aspects of Japanese life including food – hence chopsticks, tea, the nutritious soya bean, rice and noodles. Zen Buddhism provided both the aesthetic criteria of Japanese cuisine and the emphasis on vegetables. It was only in the nineteenth century that the Japanese began eating red meat more widely. Certain dishes can be traced directly to outside sources, although most have been refined into something quintessentially Japanese. Portugese missionaries in the sixteenth century are said to have requested gambas fritta, fried prawns. From this developed the dish tempura: whole prawns and slices of vegetables cooked briefly in an exquisitely light batter so that the flavour and freshness of the ingredients are highlighted rather than disguised.

Glossary

Agar agar (kanten): a vegetarian setting agent obtained from seaweed, available either in powdered form or in translucent strands.

Azuki beans: small dark red beans. In a sweetened paste form (*an*), they form a principal ingredient in Japanese cakes.

Bean curd (tofu): an ivory-coloured soya bean product with a firm custard texture, available either fresh or vacuum-packed. *Kinu* or silk tofu has a more delicate texture than *momen* or cotton tofu. *Koyadofu* is freeze-dried tofu, dull brown with a spongy texture. *Aburage* are thin deep-fried sheets of bean curd.

Bonito: dried bonito fish flakes, together with kombu seaweed, are used to make dashi soup stock and also as a garnish. *Dashi-no-moto* is an instant granule form of dashi stock, available in packets.

Dashi-no-moto

Burdock (gobo): a long slender root vegetable, available fresh and canned.

Chrysanthemum leaves (shungiku): the leaves of the edible garland chrysanthemum (not to be confused with our ornamental inedible one), used as a garnish and a vegetable.

Daikon: a large, long, mild, white radish, also called mooli in greengrocers. Dried daikon strips, called *kiriboshi daikon*, need soaking before use.

Fish and Seafood: raw fish, either in sashimi or sushi, is one of the most famous elements of Japanese cuisine. Popular fish include mackerel (*saba*), salmon (*sake*) and tuna (*maguro*), with the latter graded according to its fattiness. Grilled eel (*unagi*) is a prized delicacy. Popular seafood includes abalone (*awabi*), horse clams (*mirugai*), scallops (*hotategai*), salmon roe (*ikura*), octopus (*tako*) and squid (*ika*).

Fishcakes and fish sausages: boiled, baked and deep-fried fishcakes and sausages come in various forms, and are often found in the deep freeze section. Popular varieties include: *naruto maki*, a fish sausage with a spiral pink or yellow pattern running through it; *satsuma-age*, oval-shaped fried fishcake; and *chukuwu*, a fish sausage.

Flours: rice flour (*joshinko*) is used for savoury doughs. Glutinous rice flour (*mochiko*) and soya bean flour (*kinako*) are used mainly for desserts.

Gingko nuts (ginnan): maidenhair tree kernels. Fresh gingko nuts (which need shelling) are ivory-cloured, while tinned, shelled gingko nuts are pale green.

Kabocha: Japanese pumpkin, often sold deep-frozen.

Kampyo: dried gourd or winter melon strips, used for tying food.

Kabocha

Kinome: prickly ash tree leaf, used as a garnish.

Konnyaku: a bland, glutinous substance made from the root of the devil's tongue plant, often labelled 'alimentary paste' and found in the chilled section or freezer. Konnyaku noodles, called *shirataki* (meaning white waterfall), are sold packaged in water.

Kuzu: a white starch made from the kuzu vine root, sometimes labelled 'kuzu arrowroot'.

Lotus root (renkon): a crunchy root with a decorative tracery of holes, available fresh, in sausage-like links, or tinned.

Mirin: a sweet Japanese rice wine, used as a glazing ingredient.

Miso: fermented soya bean paste, available in a variety of colours and flavours. In general, the light miso pastes have a more delicate flavour than the darker ones. It is usually found in the chilled or freezer section and should be stored in the fridge.

Mochi: cooked glutinous rice, pounded to a paste.

Mountain yam (yama no imo): a large, pale-skinned, sweet-flavoured tuber, which comes in different shapes.

Mushrooms: these include large, brown-capped *shitake* (available both fresh and dried), tiny white-capped clusters of *enokidake*, light brown *shimeji* and large, brown *matsutake*.

Natto: fermented soya beans with a pungent smell and sticky texture.

Noodles: *harusame*, fine cellophane noodles made from mung beans whose Japanese name means 'spring rain'; *soba*, brown buckwheat noodles; *somen*, fine wheatflour noodles, sometimes flavoured with green tea; *udon*, thick, white wheatflour noodles.

Soba noodles

Panko: Japanese dried breadcrumbs, coasely ground into large flakes, used to give a crisp texture to deep-fried dishes such as *tonkasu*.

Pickles: *sudori shoga*, pickled ginger, traditionally eaten with sushi; *takuan*, pickled daikon, often bright yellow in colour.

Ponzu: a citric vinegar.

Potato starch (kataturika): strongly binding sweet potato starch.

Rice: short grain, slightly glutinous rice is the staple. A very sticky glutinous 'sweet rice' is used to make desserts and cakes.

Rice vinegar (su): delicate rice vinegar, used in making sushi.

Sake: rice wine, both drunk and used as a flavouring in cooking.

Sansho: known as 'Japanese pepper' this is the seed of the prickly ash tree.

Seaweed

Seaweeds: *kombu*, a dark large-leafed seaweed used in making dashi stock; *nori*, thin green sheets of dried seaweed used for sushi, available untoasted or toasted; *wakame*, dried lobeleaf seaweed.

Shichimi togarashi: a piquant seven-spice mix containing chilli.

Shiso: the aromatic red or green leaves of the perilla or beefsteak plant, used to add both flavour and colour.

Soya beans: raw soya beans (*edamame*), available frozen, are a poplar snack food. Dried soya beans (*daizu*) need long cooking.

Soy sauce (shoyu): Naturally brewed Japanese soy sauce, available both dark and light, has a different, more subtle flavour than Chinese soy sauce. Kikkoman is a reputable shoyu manufacturer.

Shiso

Trefoil (mitsuba): a leaf herb, often found freeze-dried.

Umeboshi: small, deep red, pickled plums, with a tart flavour.

Warabi: young edible sprouts of bracken, picked before they have uncurled, available dried or vacuum-packed.

Wasabi: a pungent green rhizome, often compared to horseradish, usually sold in paste or powder form, but now being grown in the UK for the first time, so also available fresh.

Wasabi

Wheat Gluten (fu): wheat gluten forms, often coloured, used rather like croutons in soups and simmered dishes.

Yuzu: an aromatic citrus fruit with a distinctive aroma and taste, used to flavour oil.

Food Shops

Japanese food shops often demand high prices for their stock – something about which the Japanese expat community grumble. Many of the foodstuffs are imported from Japan and all of these are beautifully packaged, from rice-paper ribbon-wrapped noodles to wacky packets of sweets. Fish and meat counters are a beautiful sight, with finely-sliced meat and displays of seafood from coiled octopus to a mosaic of mackerel fillets.

In general Japanese food shops are well-ordered, with ingredients grouped together: flavourings, pickles, noodles. Often, the goods have small labels giving the English names.

Central

Arigato

- 48-50 Brewer Street, W1F 9TG
- 020 7287 1722
- Leicester Square, Piccadilly Circus LU
- Mon-Sat 10am-9pm, Sun 11am-8pm

This friendly, down-to-earth supermarket is a well-established Soho institution. The stock covers basics from miso paste to soba noodles while the take-away sushi is very popular with local office workers.

Centre Point Food Store

- 20-21 St Giles High Street, WC2H 8LN
- 020 7836 9860
- www.cpfs.co.uk
- Tottenham Court Road LU
- Mon-Sat 10am-11pm, Sun 12noon-11pm

In the shadow of the looming tower, the Centre Point Food Store is a large, well-stocked food shop, offering both Japanese and Korean foodstuffs. Stock is includes freezers containing Japanese cuts of meat and fish, fresh vegetables and fruit, noodles, miso pastes and flavourings as well as snacks and sweets. If the sight of all these Japanese ingredients gives you an appetite, simply head upstairs to the Sushi Café.

Japan Centre Food Shop

- 14-16 Regent Street, SW1Y 4PH
- 020 3405 1246
- www.japancentre.com
- Piccadilly Circus LU
- Mon-Sat 10am-9pm Sun 11am-7pm

This long-established food hall, now on Regent Street, is perpetually humming with shoppers and diners. The new food hall offers an extensive range of Japanese ingredients, from sliced fish and meat and natto to bonito stock powder and condiments. Ready-to-eat food ranges from bento boxes and sushi to Japanese desserts and there's a small dining area.

Minamoto Kitchoan

- *44 Piccadilly, W1J 0DS*
- *020 7437 3135*
- *www.kitchoan.com*
- *Piccadilly Circus LU*
- *Mon-Fri & Sun 10am-7pm,*
  Sat 10am-8pm

This dainty shop specialises in Japanese confectionery known as wagashi. These are exquisite-looking creations made from red bean paste, rice flour and fruit and bean jelly all of which are tastefully wrapped and packaged. Seasonal wagashi include melon and white peach jellies. Prices are high – reflecting the fact that these items are traditionally given as gifts. There is a small seating area where you can sit and enjoy green tea and a cake.

North

Atari-Ya Foods

- *15-16 Monkville Parade,*
- *Finchley Road, NW11 0AL*
- *020 8458 7626*
- *www.atariya.co.uk*
- *Golders Green LU, then bus 82, 102, 260*
- *Mon 12noon-7.30pm; Tues-Fri & Sun*
  10am-7.30pm; Sat 9am-7.30pm

This large, neatly arranged shop, run with helpful courtesy by Mr Togashi, stocks a good range of Japanese foodstuffs, from frozen seafood to store-cupboard items such as green tea, sushi rice, noodles and condiments. The freshly-made sushi, which can be taken away or eaten at a small counter, is a popular draw.

Atari-Ya Foods

- *595 High Road, N12 0DY*
- *020 8446 6669*
- *www.atariya.co.uk*
- *West Finchley LU; Bus 263*
- *Mon-Fri 9am-6.30pm,*
  Sat 9am-7pm, Sun 10am-7pm

A neat shop dominated by a long fish counter, with the staff behind it expertly preparing the fish. In addition, there is a limited selection of groceries and a small chilled cabinet containing essentials such as fresh tofu.

Fuji Foods

- *167 Priory Road, N8 8NB*
- *020 8347 91770*
- *www.fujifoods.co.uk*
- *Finsbury Park LU, then W7 bus*
- *Tues-Fri 11am-7.30pm*
  Sat 11am-7pm, Sun 11am-5pm

This small, immaculate shop offers an excellent range of Japanese foodstuffs, from frozen fish cakes to fresh tofu. Pride of place goes to the fresh fish and sushi counter. It is here that Mr Fuji deftly and expertly prepares his own sushi rolls, nigiri and sashimi.

Hello Kitchen

🏠 *10 North End Road, NW11 7PH*
☎ *020 8209 3487*
🖥 *www.hellokitchen.co.uk*
🚇 *Golders Green LU*
🕐 *Mon-Sat 10am-8pm, Sun 11am-7pm*

Opposite Golders Green tube station, a few doors down from the Japanese Homes letting agency, this friendly shop stocks a good and competitively-priced range of Japanese foodstuffs. The shop also does a brisk business with its take-away sushi which is freshly prepared at the back of the shop.

Wing Yip (London) Ltd

🏠 *395 Edgware Road, NW2 6LN*
☎ *020 8450 0422*
🖥 *www.wingyip.com*
🚇 *Colindale LU*
🕐 *Mon-Sat 9.30am-7pm,*
   Sun 11.30am-5.30pm

This massive Chinese supermarket, located just off Staples Corner, contains all the basics for the Japanese kitchen from noodles and dried seaweed to Japanese tea and sake.

North-West

Natural Natural

🏠 *1 Goldhurst Terrace, NW6 3HX*
☎ *020 7624 5734*
🖥 *www.natural-natural.co.uk*
🚇 *Finchley Road LU*
🕐 *Mon-Sat 9am-8pm, Sun 10am-7pm*

A small, friendly shop offering a range of foodstuffs from fresh produce to food to take away.

West

Atari-Ya Foods

🏠 *7 Station Parade, Noel Road, W3 0DS*
☎ *020 8896 1552*
🖥 *www.atariya.co.uk*
🚇 *West Acton LU*
🕐 *Tues 11am-6.30pm, Wed-Fri 10am-*
   6.30pm,Sat 9am-7pm, Sun 10am-7pm

In West Acton's leafy suburbs, this small corner food shop, is particularly strong on fresh seafood, with stock ranging from dressed crab to black cod and razor clams. Other foods in stock include store-cupboard basics and a selection of fresh fruit and vegetables, such as gobo or daikon.

Natural Natural

- 20 Station Parade, Uxbridge Road, W5 3LD
- 020 8992 0770
- Mon-Sun 9am-8pm

This friendly, down-to-earth shop caters comprehensively for West London's Japanese community, with stock ranging from fresh fruit and vegetables in boxes outside to shelves of sake, freezers filled with frozen vegetables such as burdock and huge sacks of sushi rice stacked on the floor inside. Take-away foods such as tonkatsu and Japanese cakes are a popular draw with Japanese commuters returning home.

Tetote Factory

- 12 South Ealing Road, W5 4QA
- 020 8579 8391
- www.tetotefactory.co.uk
- South Ealiing LU
- Tues 10am-5pm, Wed-Sat 8.30am-5pm, Sun 10am-4pm

This small, friendly bakery sells its own freshly baked Japanese breads, baguettes and buns, both sweet and savoury, to an appreciative local audience.

Japanese Tableware

Doki

- 207 High Road, HA3 5EE
- 020 8861 4277
- www.dokiltd.co.uk
- Harrow & Wealdstone LU
- Mon-Sat 9.30am-6.30pm, Sun 10am-6pm

This polite, friendly shop specialises in Japanese ceramic tableware and carries an extensive range of reasonably-priced bowls, plates, tea cups and sauce dishes in both traditional and contemporary styles.

Mail-Order

The Wasabi Company

- www.wasabigrowersuk.co.uk
- 01929 463824

This innovative British company has succeeded in growing fresh wasabi (often called Japanese horseradish) in the UK for the first time ever, selling it to both the restaurant trade and the general public.

Eating Places

Once Japanese restaurants in London were exclusive, expensive affairs. With sushi now stocked alongside sandwiches in British supermarkets, Japanese food has now become far more widely available, but the best sushi is still to be found in Japanese foodshops and restaurants. While London boasts a number of extremely elegant and luxurious Japanese restaurants, diners can nowadays also choose from casual noodle bars and the popular conveyor-belt sushi restaurants.

Central

Abeno Too ££

- 47 Museum Street, WC1A 1LY
- 020 7405 3211
- www.abeno.co.uk
- Holborn LU, Tottenham Court Road LU

This small, cosy restaurant offers a chance to sample 'okonomi-yaki' – tasty Japanese pancakes made from a thick batter containing shredded cabbage, and topped with ingredients ranging from meat to seafood. Each okonomi-yaki is freshly cooked to order on a table griddle in front of the diner by polite, friendly staff.
Branch: Abeno Too, 17-18 Great Newport Street, WC2 (020 7579 1160)

Atari-Ya £

- 20 James Street, W1U 3EH
- 020 7491 1178
- www.atariya.co.uk
- Bond Street LU

Known for their food shops. Atari-Ya also run a number of restaurants including this West End take-away sushi bar offering good-quality sushi and sashimi at competitive prices. Limited seating is available, but expect a lunchtime rush.

Chisou £££

- 4 Princes Street, W1B 2LE
- 020 7629 3931
- www.chisourestaurants.com
- Oxford Circus LU

A short stroll from Oxford Circus, this established restaurant is discreet, smart and perpetually buzzing with diners. Quality ingredients, an interesting and extensive menu offering dishes from chawan mushi to deep-fried oysters, a range of fine sakes and friendly attentive service make a winning combination.

Delicatessen Yoshino £

⊞ *59 Shaftesbury Avenue, W1D 6LF*
☎ *020 7434 3610*
🚌 *Piccadilly Circus*

In the heart of theatreland, this narrow shop offers Yoshino's excellent, freshly-made and reasonably-priced sushi to go, with toppings and fillings ranging from salmon or eel to avocado or cuumber,

Dinings £££-££££

⊞ *22 Harcourt Street, W1H 4HH*
☎ *020 7723 0666*
🖰 *www.dinings,co.uk*
🚌 *Marylebone LU/Rail*

Served in small, austere surroundings, this restaurant specialises in contemporary, imaginative 'Japanese tapas' dishes, all made from top-notch ingredients.

Go Chisou £-££

⊞ *3 Princes Street, W1B 2LE*
☎ *020 7629 0029*
🖰 *www.gochisou.co.uk*
🚌 *Oxford Circus LU*

Aimed at busy lunchtime diners, this branch of Chisou offers take-away sushi rolls, salads and a selection of hot dishes, with limited seating available.

Haru Sushi

⊞ *3 Melcombe Street, NW1 6AE*
☎ *020 7224 4311*
🚌 *Baker Street LU*

A small sushi shop, predominantly operating as a take-away but with a few seats at which to sit and sample.

Koya ££

⊞ *49 Frith Street, W1D 4SG*
☎ *020 7434 4463*
🖰 *www.koya.co.uk*
🚌 *Leicester Square/Piccadilly Circus LU*

Specialising in its own-made udon noodles, this simple yet stylish restaurant offers these thick noodles in a range of forms: hot udon in hot broth, cold udon with hot broth, cold udon with dipping sauce. Such is the restaurant's popularity, that a queue of would-be diners waiting patiently is a usual sight.

Nagomi ££

⊞ *4 Blenheim Street, W1S 1LB*
☎ *020 7165 9506*
🖰 *www.nagomi.co.uk*
🚌 *Bond Street LU*

Tucked away down a tiny West End side-street, this small, cosy Japanese restaurant offers tasty Japanese food, with the set lunches notably good value. Regular customers return for dishes such as the flavourful braised pork belly.

Nambu-tei ££-£££

🖃 *Berkeley Arcade,*
   209A Baker Street, NW1 6AB
☎ *020 7486 5026*
🖱 *www.nambu-tei.co.uk*
🚌 *Baker Street LU*

Tucked away in a small shopping arcade, with the restaurant discreetly hidden from public gaze, Nambu-tei is something of a hidden gem. The main dining room fills up quickly with regulars in the know tucking into assorted dishes from the extensive menu.

Sushi Tetsu £££

🖃 *12 Jerusalem Passage, EC1V 4JP*
☎ *020 3217 0090*
🖱 *www.sushitetsu.co.uk*
🚌 *Farringdon LU*

A tiny, austere, traditional sushi restaurant offering impeccable sushi and sashimi, skilfully prepared by chef-patron Toro Takahashi.

Tonkotsu ££

🖃 *63 Dean Street W1D 4QG*
☎ *020 7437 0071*
🖱 *www.tonkotsu.co.uk*
🚌 *Leicester Square LU, Piccadilly Circus LU*

Fresh ramen noodles are the speciality here at this pared-down, minimalist restaurant (a new offering from the Tsuru restaurant group) served in a tasty pork stock soup with an assortment of toppings.

Yoshino ££-£££

🖃 *3 Piccadilly Place, W1J 0DB*
☎ *020 7287 6622*
🖱 *www.yoshino.net*
🚌 *Piccadilly Circus LU*

Discreetly located in a side-street off Piccadilly, this restaurant is noted for the quality of its fresh fish, which can be enjoyed in dishes such as sashimi and sushi platters. The set menus are excellent value and beautifully presented.

North

Asakusa ££-£££

🖃 *265 Eversholt Street, NW1 1BA*
☎ *020 7388 8533*
🚌 *Mornington Crescent*

Warmly recommended by Japanese friends, this shabby-looking restaurant offers evening diners some superb Japanese food at bargain prices. Such is its popularity that booking a table is strongly recommended.

Café Japan ££-£££

🖃 *626 Finchley Road, NW11 7RR*
☎ *020 8455 6854*
🚌 *Golders Green LU*

Small and down-to-earth, this Japanese restaurant has a loyal local following for its reasonably-priced sushi.

Jin Kichi £££
🖃 *73 Heath Street, NW3 6UG*
☎ *020 7794 6158*
🖰 *www.jinkichi.com*
🚇 *Hampstead LU*

A friendly, informal, long-established restaurant; specialising in yakitori dishes and so offering a large range of tasty salty-sweet skewered foods including chicken and prawns.

Shimo Gamo £££
🖃 *108 Parkway, NW1 7AN*
☎ *020 7424 9560*
🖰 *www.shimogamoaz.com*
🚇 *Camden Town LU*

A wide-ranging menu, especially during the evening when specialities such as the beef hobayaki are offered, discreet, calm interior and polite, helpful service make this Japanese restaurant well worth sampling. Set lunches are a notable bargain, offering generous portions of high quality food.

Sushi-Say £££-££££
🖃 *33B Walm Lane, NW2 5SH*
☎ *020 8459 2971*
🚇 *Willesden Green LU*

In deepest Willesden, this well-established restaurant, with its pretty, rustic décor, is something of an oasis. It has a considerable regular clientele, drawn back by the delicious, freshly prepared Japanese food and the pleasantly relaxed and convivial atmosphere.

Tosa £££
🖃 *152 High Road, N2*
☎ *020 8883 8850*
🖰 *www.tosauk.com*
🚇 *East Finchley*

This small, cosy restaurant, a branch of the Hammersmith restaurant (see below) serves up an appetising range of Japanese dishes, specialising in skewers of ingredients such as chicken liver, quail's eggs and shiitake mushrooms, freshly grilled to order over charcoal.

North-West

Atari-Ya £-££
🖃 *75 Fairfax Road, NW6 4EE*
☎ *020 7328 5338*
🖰 *www.atariya.co.uk*
🚇 *Swiss Cottage LU*

A sushi bar outlet from an established chain of Japanese food shops, this simply-styled sushi bar offers a chance to sample good-quality sushi and sashimi at reasonable prices.

West

Atari-Ya £££

⬚ *1 Station Parade,*
Uxbridge Road, W5 3LD
☎ *020 8896 3175*
🖱 *www.atariya.co.uk*
🚌 *Ealing Common LU*

Owned by the well-established chain of
Japanese food shops, this straightforward
restaurant specialises in excellent value
sushi, with the specials well worth
investigating.

Tosa

⬚ *332 King Street W6 0RR*
☎ *020 8748 0002*
🖱 *www.tosauk.com*
🚌 *Ravenscourt Park LU*

A small, friendly restaurant offering sushi,
sashimi and noodles, but particularly noted
for its extensive range of tasty, freshly grilled
skewers of ingredients from offal to fish.

East

Moshi Moshi Sushi ££-£££

⬚ *Unit 24 (above Platform 1,*
behind M & S) Liverpool Street Station,
EC2M 7QH
☎ *020 7347 3227 / 3237*
🖱 *www.moshimoshisushi.co.uk*

Founded by Caroline Bennett in 1994,
Britain's first conveyor belt sushi restaurant
offers an excellent range of freshly prepared
sushi and sashimi in light, airy surroundings,
with the emphasis admirably on sustainably
sourced fish and seafood.

Cookbooks

My personal recommendations of cookbooks for this cuisine, including new books and out-of-print classics:

Food of Japan
Shirley Booth
An illuminating look at Japanese cuisine with recipes and detailed ingredient information.

Step-by-Step Japanese Cooking
Leslie Downer and Minoru Yoneda
A clear and well written introduction to Japanese cuisine.

Easy Sushi
Emi Kazuko
An illustrated, accessible guide to the joys of home-made sushi.

Harumi's Japanese Cooking
Harumi Kurihara
Aimed at demystifying Japanese cuisine, this is an attractive, appetising introduction to Japanese cuisine.

The Heart of Zen Cookery
Soei Yoneda
A guide to the centuries-old vegetarian cuisine of the Zen temples.

Jewish London

Daniel's Bagel Bakery

The Jewish presence in England dates back to the eleventh century when French Jews followed William the Conqueror and settled here. They were legally restricted to certain trades and professions but moneylending, forbidden to Christians, was allowed, indeed encouraged, and became the basis for a prosperous and established community. Persecution of the Jews grew, however, and in 1290 all Jews were expelled from England by Edward I.

Following the expulsion of Jews from Spain in 1492, some Sephardi Jews (Mediterranean Jews) accepted the Christian faith but continued to practise Judaism in secret. They became known as Marranos and a small community of them settled in London. In 1655 Rabbi Menassah ben Israel, resident in Holland, appealed to Oliver Cromwell to permit Jewish resettlement. In June of the following year Cromwell declared that Judaism would again be permitted in England and a small community of Sephardi merchants, bankers, bullion dealers and gem importers settled in London. The Sephardi community's first synagogue was in a house at Creechurch Lane in the East End. In 1701, when this became too small, the Bevis Marks synagogue was built – and continues in use to this day.

The Jewish community was also expanded by the immigration of Ashkenazi Jews from Eastern Europe, who followed a different liturgy. In general they were artisans, peasants, tailors and shoemakers. By 1690, they had established their own synagogue in Dukes Place. George I encouraged German Jews to come to England and by the middle of the eighteenth century the Ashkenazi community outnumbered the Sephardi.

Aldgate and Houndsditch were popular Jewish areas, although in the first half of the nineteenth century a move took place among the established and prosperous Jewish families, such as the Rothschilds and Montefiores, who left St Swithins Lane for the fashionable West End. In 1858, a special parliamentary resolution enabled Lionel de Rothschild to take his seat in the House of Commons, which marked a watershed in Jewish emancipation in Britain. During the late nineteenth century middle-class Jews moved into the new suburbs and by 1882, the St John's Wood synagogue was in operation.

For the poorer Jewish immigrants, however, the East End remained the focus. As Stephen Brook puts it in his fascinating book, *The Club,* 'Jews tend to live in enclaves not out of natural gregariousness but because they want to be close to institutions vital to the life of the community. Religious Jews will not ride or drive on the Sabbath so they wish to live within easy walking distance of a synagogue. They also needed convenient access to Jewish schools (there were seven in existence in 1851) and kosher butchers. Naturally new arrivals tended to join fellow Jews in the areas favoured by those who had arrived before them.'

Following the assassination of the liberal Russian Tsar Alexander II in 1881, a series of pogroms was unleashed in Russia and Poland, which continued into the early twentieth century. Thousands of Jews fled westwards, many aiming for and reaching America, but some staying in Britain instead of continuing their journey. Between 1881 and 1914 the Jewish population of the East End swelled by well over 100,000 people. These were Orthodox, Yiddish-speaking, semi-skilled or unskilled Jews; and the already established Anglo-Jews felt ambivalent about the influx, fearing an anti-Semitic backlash.

The Ashkenazi immigrants moved into the East End, especially around Whitechapel. Food shops sold the herrings and pickles of their homelands and the number of chevras

(small synagogues) grew. The United Synagogues established dispersal committees to encourage Jewish immigrants to move out of the East End into the expanding suburbs of Dalston, Stoke Newington and Hackney. In the 1920s there was a move northwards from the East End into Stamford Hill and then into the newly established suburbs of Golders Green, Edgware and Ilford.

The rise of anti-Semitism in the 1930s brought in around 70,000 Jews from Central Europe, with the influx increasing sharply after the 1938 Anschluss (unification) with Austria and the Kristallnacht pogrom. These were prosperous middle-class refugees who settled in north-west London in areas such as Hampstead, St John's Wood and Swiss Cottage. The decline of the Jewish East End community was hastened by the war, bombing destroying both families and property. Instead of returning after service or evacuation, many East End Jews opted for the suburbs with their by now well-established Jewish communities. By the 1970s the population of the East End Jewish community had shrunk to less than 5,000; today, around a third of Britain's Jewish population lives in north-west London.

Jewish Cuisine

Jewish cuisine reflects the widely dispersed Jewish community by containing a range of dishes and styles of cooking from around the world. Two broad and diverse strands stem from the culinary traditions of the Ashkenazi and the Sephardi. The former, influenced by long, cold winters, features preserved and pickled dishes such as rollmop herrings and smoked salmon; while the latter delights in aromatic spices and Mediterranean produce such as aubergines, peppers and olive oil. Common to all Jewish food, however, are the Kashrut, the strict dietary laws governing the preparation and consumption of food, which stem from biblical injunctions. They have been adhered to over the centuries.

Leviticus permits certain fish and meat: 'Any animal that has true hoofs, with clefts through the hoofs, and that chews the cud such you may eat' and 'Anything in water, whether in the seas or in the streams, that has fins and scales these you may eat'.

Cattle, sheep and most fish, therefore, are permitted, but pigs, rabbits and shellfish are not, neither certain birds nor anything that crawls or swarms. Permitted animals and birds must be ritually slaughtered in a way that allows as much blood as possible to drain from the carcass. As the consumption of blood is forbidden, raw meat must be 'koshered' by being soaked in water, treated with salt, drained and then rinsed.

The injunction 'Thou shalt not boil a kid in its mother's milk' has been interpreted to mean that meat and dairy products may not be consumed together. Food containing dairy products may not be eaten after meat until at least three hours have passed. This extends to separating kitchen equipment used for meat products from that for dairy products. 'Pareve' means neutral and refers to foods that may be eaten with either meat or dairy products.

The commandment that 'On the seventh day thou shalt do no

work, neither thy maidservant nor thy manservant' has produced a range of characteristically Jewish dishes that are prepared the day before they are eaten. Cholent is one of the most famous of these dishes: a Sabbath stew traditionally cooked slowly overnight. Harry Blacker, in his book of East End reminiscences Just Like It Was, writes of the cholent being 'carried to the nearest bakehouse, where for a small consideration (about 2 pence), the baker would put the pan in the oven to cook until the following midday'.

Religious festivals also influence Jewish cuisine. At Pesach (Passover), when wheat flour is banned, dishes are made with ground nuts, matzo meal or potato flour. Certain symbolic foods and dishes are eaten both during the weekly Shabbat (Sabbath) and the festivals. During Pesach, which celebrates the Jewish delivery from slavery to the Egyptians, a 'Seder' plate is assembled made up of symbolic ingredients such as haroset, a sweet fruit paste representing the mortar used by Jewish slaves when they worked

on the Pharoah's cities, and a bitter herb, such as endive, representing the bitterness endured during slavery. Matzos, the unleavened bread used during Pesach, represents the bread which didn't have time to rise as the Jews fled.

Another element common to Jewish cookery across the continents is its ingenuity, born out of the poverty and lack of ingredients which Jewish communities often suffered. Meat, in particular, was eked out in resouceful dishes such as helzel, stuffed chicken neck skin, and koureven, stewed chicken gizzards.

Glossary

Bagels: circular bread rolls with a distinctive, chewy texture which comes from being first boiled then baked. Increasingly available both plain and flavoured.

Bagels

Bulka: the 'everyday' cholla loaf, made from the same dough as bagels but shaped differently.

Cholla: a symbolic plaited loaf made from an egg-rich dough, and with a brown glaze. It plays a prominent part in most Jewish festivals and is especially associated with Shabbat, the weekly Sabbath.

Chopped liver: a tasty mixture of finely chopped liver, onion and hard-boiled egg.

Falafel: small, savoury chickpea croquettes, now regarded as an Israeli national dish.

Herring

Gefilte fish: minced fish balls, either poached or fried.

Herrings: a staple fish, preserved by salting or pickling. *Chopped herring*, a sweet-sour mixture of herrings, onions, apple, sugar and vinegar; *rollmops* or *Bismarcks*, pickled herrings rolled around onion rings; *schmaltz herrings* or *matjes*, smoked young herrings, often ready-filleted.

Kreplach: triangular dumplings with a meat or cheese filling. The three corners symbolise the three patriarchs: Abraham, Isaac and Jacob. These can be found ready-made in freezer sections.

Latkes: shredded potato fritters associated with Chanucah.

Latkes

Lokshen: egg noodles, used in soups and also to make lokshen kugel, a rich baked pudding, traditionally baked overnight for Shabbat.

Mandlen: from Yiddish for 'almonds', these are fried or baked dough 'soup nuts', used like croutons as a garnish.

Matzos: a flat unleavened bread, similar in texture and taste to a water biscuit. It is the main element in Passover cookery, which forbids the use of leavened grain. The entire process of matzo-making must take no longer than 18 minutes, otherwise fermentation may start.

Matzos

Matzo balls (knaidlach): walnut-sized, matzo-meal dumplings.

Matzo meal: a binding element made from finely ground matzos.

Rye bread: bread made from rye, with a distinctively rich flavour.

Salt beef: boiled and pickled beef, usually brisket. Available freshly-made or in packets.

Smoked salmon (lox): smoked salmon has its origins in London's nineteenth-century Jewish community, who brought the tradition of smoking fish to preserve it with them from Poland and Russia. Until the 1970s and the advent of salmon farming, wild Scottish salmon was used, with this luxurious food finding an appreciative audience both within and outside London's Jewish community. Today, smoked salmon continues to be popular within the Jewish community, with smoked salmon bagels a bakery bestseller.

Food Shops

The food shop has always been important in Jewish life, both to satisfy religious dietary needs and as a focus of identity. The food that we find in Jewish shops in Britain is predominantly Ashkenazi rather than Sephardi. In *'East End Story'*, A. B. Levy remembers the aromas that 'wafted through the open fronts of delicatessen shops, from smoked salmon and roe, barrelled cucumbers and sauerkraut, and herrings in various guises, kippered, schmaltz, chopped and pickled.' These items continue to be familiar Jewish deli fare but nearly all the East End shops have gone and the delicatessens are now found in the North London suburbs.

Perhaps what is most baffling for a non-Jew are the varying degrees of kosherness. The Kashrut are strict dietary laws which govern the preparation and consumption of foods. Certain food shops display certificates to show that they are supervised or licensed by authorities such as the Kedassia, the Joint Kashrus Committee of the Union of Orthodox Hebrew Congregations, the Adam Yisroel Synagogue and the Golders Green Beth Hamedrash Congregation. These are the shops and eating places that I have called 'kosher' in my guide, but readers should satisfy themselves as to the standards of Kashrut observed. Some shops have a large range of kosher foodstuffs without being supervised while others carry a range of non-kosher Jewish foods. Kosher food, nowadays, is an increasingly sophisticated business and the range of kosher items available has increased enormously, from tandoori chicken to champagne.

North

Adafina

- 67 Abbey Road, NW8 9QV
- 020 7624 2013
- www.adafina.co.uk
- St John's Wood LU
- Mon-Thurs 8.30am-6pm,
  Fri 8.30am-3 hours before Shabbat

A pleasantly light and airy, contemporary kosher food shop. It does a popular range of smartly-packaged in-house traiteur dishes, including the eponymous adafina (a Sephardi stew of slow-cooked beef and potatoes) and fish tagine. There is also an extensive stock of good quality deli items and groceries.

La Boucherie (Kosher) Ltd

- 4 Cat Hill, East Barnet, EN4 8JB
- 020 8449 9215
- New Barnet Rail
- Mon 8.30am-2.30pm, Tues-Thurs
  8.30am-5pm, Fri 8am-1pm, Sun
  8.30am-1.30pm and 3.30pm-7.30pm

This vast, scrupulously clean shop is one of London's leading kosher butchers and always bustles with customers. It's a large and efficient operation, with chefs working behind the scenes to produce the popular ready-made dishes such as Beef Wellington and the kofte kebabs for which La Boucherie is known.

Carmelli Bakeries

- 128 Golders Green Road, NW11 8HB
- 020 8455 3063
- www.carmelli.co.uk
- Golders Green LU
- Mon-Wed 7am-1am, Thurs 7am-Fri
  5.30pm (open throughout Thurs night),
  Sat 11pm through to Mon morning

Founded in 1987, this well-established kosher bakery continues to attract crowds of customers, particularly buzzing in the early hours of Sunday morning with people dropping in to buy freshly baked bagels. Noted for its bagels, it also offers a host of breads, cakes, pastries, quiches and biscuits. It is divided into a Pareve or 'non-milky' counter and a 'milky' counter.

J. A. Corney Ltd

- 9 Hallswelle Parade
  Finchley Road, NW11 0AA
- 020 8455 9588
- Golders Green LU then bus 82, 102, 260
- Tues-Thurs 7am-5pm, Fri 7.30am-4pm,
  Sat-Sun 7.30am-1pm

This well-established fishmonger's has been in the Corney family for decades. It stocks a large range of fish, such as St Peter's fish and carp and Jewish specialities such as minced fish (a mix of haddock, whiting and bream). They will also mince more expensive fish on request. Staff are friendly and knowledgeable.

Daniel's Bagel Bakery

- 13 Halleswelle Parade, Finchley Rd, NW11
- 020 8455 5826
- www.danielscatering.co.uk
- Golders Green LU then bus 82, 102, 260
- Sun-Wed 7am-9pm, Thurs 7am-10pm, Fri 7am-11 (2 hours before Shabbat)

A busy kosher bakery noted for its top-notch bagels as well as its good range of cholla, rye bread, pitta breads and pastries.

The Grapevine

- 94 Brent Street, NW4 2AD
- 020 8202 2631
- Hendon Central LU
- Mon-Wed 9am-6pm, Thurs 9am-8pm, Fri 9am-4pm, Sun 10am-2pm

This well-stocked kosher off-licence sells kosher wines from all over the world. They stock Kiddush, the sweet red wine used for sacramental purposes and Israeli wines.

Greenspans

- 9-11 Lyttelton Road, N2 ODW
- 020 8455 7709
- East Finchley LU
- Mon-Thurs & Sun 8.30am-5.15pm, Fri 8.30am-1pm

This roomy kosher butchers offers a fresh meat counter and a range of frozen ready meals. It's particularly noted for its own-cooked meats, including salt beef.

Hendon Bagel Bakery

- 55-57 Church Road, NW4 4DU
- 020 8203 6919
- Hendon Central LU
- Mon-Thurs 7am-11pm, Fri 8am-3pm Sat 7pm until Sun 11pm

A well-established and popular kosher bakery, selling bulka, rye breads, pretzels and a wide choice of bagels.

Panzer's

- 13-19 Circus Road, NW8 6PB
- 020 7722 8162 / 8596
- www.panzers.co.uk
- St John's Wood LU
- Mon-Fri 8am-7pm, Sat 8am-6pm, Sun 8am-2pm

Established in 1955, Peter Vogel now carries on the family tradition. In its range and depth of stock, Panzer's is more like a supermarket than a deli, stocking everything from Swiss Miss chocolate mallows to Israeli wine. The large deli-counter offers six types of herring and four grades of smoked salmon.

Platters

- 10 Halleswelle Parade Finchley Road, NW11 ODL
- 020 8455 7345
- Golders Green LU. then bus 82, 102, 260
- Mon-Sat 8.30am-4.30pm, Sun 8.30am-2pm

This friendly, well-established shop is run by the eponymous Platters family. It offers an extensive range of fresh, own-made, classic Jewish deli fare, from moreish fried gefilte fish to chopped liver.

North-West

Ivor Silverman

- 4-5 Canons Corner, HA8 8AE
  London Road, Stanmore, Middlesex
- 020 8958 8682 / 2692
- Stanmore LU
- Mon 8am-3pm, Tues-Wed 7.30am-6pm,
  Thurs 7.30am-7pm, Fri 8am-1pm,
  Sun 8am-3pm.

An elegant and upmarket kosher butcher-cum-deli. The butcher part of the shop offers freshly-cut meat and poultry and a large range of prepared meat dishes. Next door at the deli is a range of Jewish specialities such as chopped liver, latkes and delicious salt beef

East

Brick Lane Beigel Bake

- 159 Brick Lane, E1 6SB
- 020 7729 0616
- Liverpool Street LU/Rail
- Daily 24 hours

This small, down-to-earth bakery is a reminder of the East End's Jewish history. Piled high with freshly baked bagels and chollas, it remains hugely popular, attracting East End clubbers, Brick Lane market shoppers and London cabbies alike.

Grodzinski

- 170 Clapton Common, E5 9AG
- 020 8211 8108
- www.grodzinski.co.uk
- Stamford Hill Rail
- Sun-Thurs 7am-1am,
  Fri 7am-30mins before Shabbatt

Founded by the Grodzinski family in 1888, this veteran Jewish bakery offers an extensive range of bagels, breads, biscuits, pastries and cakes.

Mail Order

Forman & Field

- Stour Road, Fish Island, E3 2NT
- 020 8525 2352
- www.formanandfield.com

Founded in 1905, H. Forman is the last surviving East End smokery. Very much an artisanal business, the fish is still hand-filleted. Forman's is noted for the quality and freshness of its smoked salmon which can be acquired via their mail order service.

Eating Places

Central

Bevis Marks Restaurant £££-££££

⌖ *4 Heneage Lane, EC3*

☎ *020 7283 2220*

✐ *www.bevismarkstherestaurant.com*

🚇 *Aldgate, Liverpool Street LU*

An elegant kosher establishment, next to the historic Bevis Marks synagogue. It offers a stylish modern take on classic Jewish foods such as salt beef and chicken soup.

Nosh Bar £

⌖ *39 Great Windmill Street, W1*

☎ *020 7734 5638*

🚇 *Piccadilly Circus LU*

In the heart of theatreland, on the site of Phil Rabin's original, much-loved Nosh Bar, this retro-style bar has revived the tradition, serving hot salt beef sandwiches.

North

Aviv £££

⌖ *87 High Street, HA8*

☎ *020 8952 2484*

🚇 *Edgware LU*

A well-established kosher restaurant that specialises in Israeli food. For this reason there is a definite Middle Eastern flavour to the menu which offers mezze (including excellent houmous) and grilled meats.

Blooms £££

⌖ *30 Golders Green Road, NW11*

☎ *020 8455 1338*

🚇 *Golders Green LU*

Opened in 1965, this Golders Green institution has survived its better-known Whitechapel counterpart and continues to serve traditional kosher Jewish food. The salt beef is famous and the portions are generous. A great place to enjoy the comfort of homely Jewish food.

Dizengoff £££

⌖ *118 Golders Green Road, NW11*

☎ *020 8458 7003*

🚇 *Golders Green LU*

This popular eatery offers Sephardi food, such as Israeli grills and fresh salads.

Harry Morgan's £££

⌖ *31 St John's Wood High Street, NW8*

☎ *020 7722 1869*

🚇 *St John's Wood LU*

Dapper, well-established restaurant offering all the classics including chicken noodle soup with dumplings, salt beef and latkes.

Cookbooks

My personal recommendations of cookbooks for this cuisine, including new books and out-of-print classics:

The Book of Jewish Food
Claudia Roden
A characteristically fascinating and absorbing study of Jewish food around the world, taking in both Sephardi and Ashkenazi traditions.

The Complete International Jewish Cookbook
Evelyn Rose
An excellent basic and reliable cookbook by a doyenne of Jewish cookery.

Jerusalem
Yotam Ottolenghi and Sami Tamimi
A wonderfully appetising collection of recipes by two acclaimed Israeli chefs, exploring the rich and diverse culinary heritage of Jerusalem and offering recipes from the city's many, diverse communities.

Jewish Cooking from Around the World
Josephine Bacon
A lively and accessible cookbook exploring both Sephardi and Ashkenazi cooking.

The Jewish Heritage Cookbook
Marlena Spieler
A well-illustrated cookbook filled with appetising recipes, including classics like gefilte fish, hamantashen and chopped eggs and onion.

New Jewish Cuisine
Evelyn Rose
A straightforward book of Jewish recipes.

Warm Bagels & Apple Strudel
Ruth Joseph and Simon Round
An appetising collection of both Ashkenazi and Sephardi recipes, from falafel to lokshen pudding.

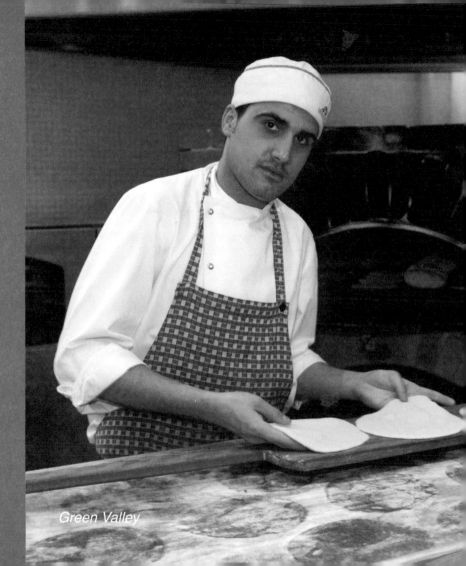

Middle Eastern London

Green Valley

The Middle Eastern community in London comprises several nationalities, drawn here at different times and for varying reasons.. The Egyptians came to Britain in the 1940s and 1950s, both for education and work. The oil boom in the 1970s and the discovery by Arab countries of new sources of wealth and power resulted in an increasingly wealthy Arab presence in London, mainly focused around Mayfair and Kensington. A series of political disturbances has also contributed considerably to the Middle Eastern presence here. The overthrow of the Shah and the Iranian revolution brought in an influx of wealthy Iranian families who were able to use their money and connections to escape, many to America but some to London. They were followed by political opponents of the Ayatollah, seeking refuge. The civil war in Lebanon resulted in a substantial Lebanese presence in London. Edgware Road, Bayswater, Mayfair, Knightsbridge and Kensington together form the heartland of the Middle Eastern community, served by a splendid assortment of restaurants, fruit juice bars, cafés, banks, shops and clubs.

The Turkish community (which is included in this chapter because of the Ottoman Empire's culinary influence on Middle Eastern cuisine) is predominantly Turkish-Cypriot; many came to Britain because they were displaced following the Turkish invasion of Cyprus in 1974. For some time the community was largely based in Islington, Hackney and Haringey, with the Stoke Newington end of Green Lanes being a particular focal point. Many of the cafés and kebab houses remain male preserves, with the sound of backgammon being played behind the scenes.

Middle Eastern Cuisine

This is an ancient cuisine, whose recipes can be traced back many hundreds of years. An Egyptian recipe for melokhia soup, for example, dates from the time of the Pharoahs. The former spice routes which passed through the Middle East have left a fragrant legacy in the region's cooking.

Claudia Roden, an authoritative and knowledgeable writer on Middle Eastern cookery, identifies four main strands: Iranian or Persian, Arab, Ottoman Turkish and North African and I've followed her approach in the shops included in this chapter. Iranian cuisine is subtle and refined, a product of ancient Persia. Rice forms the heart of the cuisine and is carefully cooked and exquisitely garnished. The combination of meat with fruit or nuts is a hallmark of the Persian kitchen, shown in dishes such as koresh-e-fesenjan, chicken in walnut and pomegranate sauce. Arab cuisine is very flavourful, using strong-tasting herbs such as mint

and coriander and fragrant spices such as cardamom, cinnamon and allspice. Grilled meats are popular, served with rice, burghul or flat breads

During the Ottoman Empire, Turkish cuisine reached luxurious heights. Cooking at the Topkapi Palace in Istanbul followed rules, still followed by chefs today. Ottoman food was spread through the Empire by the army, with shish kebab said to date back to when Turkish soldiers cooked over their camp fires. This culinary legacy includes stuffed vegetables, such as imam bayaldi (an aubergine dish named after a priest who swooned with delight upon trying it); and layered nutty pastries in sweet syrups, beloved throughout the Middle East. North African cooking, in contrast, has a fiery element, produced by hot sauces such as harissa. It is also a cuisine of subtle and delicate spicing.

The influence of Islam means that certain dietary laws are observed

WITH PARSLEY &

£5.00/KG

CUCUMBER PICKLED

£5.00/KG

GREEN OLIVES WITH

throughout the Middle East. Pork is forbidden and meat must be ritually slaughtered. Lamb is the most highly-prized meat throughout the region. Yoghurt is widely used: as a refreshing drink, in hot and cold soups, and in salads and marinades.

Glossary

Allspice: round berry, similar to peppercorns, with a flavour of nutmeg, cinnamon and cloves.

Apricot paste sheets (amretin): translucent orange sheets made from apricots which, when diluted with water, make a refreshing drink. Especially popular during the fasting month of Ramadan.

Apricot paste sheets

Arab bread (khoubz): flat round bread

Barberries (zerezhk): small, tart, red berries, used dried in Iranian cooking to add colour and flavour.

Burghul (bulgar): parboiled, cracked grains of wheat, available both coarse or finely ground.

Barberries

Coriander: a flat-leafed green herb, similar in appearance to flat-leafed parsley but with a distinctive sharp taste.

Couscous: fine yellow cereal made from semolina.

Dibbis: thick, dark brown syrup made from dates.

Dill: a caraway-scented herb with fine, feathery green fronds.

Dried limes (limoo): hard, brown, dried limes, used to add a distinctive flavour to Iranian and Iraqi soups and stews.

Dried mulberries: mulberries are prized in Iranian cuisine, with sweet-tasting, honey-coloured dried mulberries sold loose or packaged.

Dried limes

Filo: paper-thin fine pastry usually found frozen but occasionally available fresh.

Freekeh: roasted green wheat.

Golpar: Persian hogwart, available in seed form or ground. Valued for its anti-flatulence properties, the seeds are used in pickling while golpar powder is sprinkled over pulses.

Harissa: a fiery, red pimento paste.

Kashk: stony lumps of pungent dried buttermilk, used in soups and stews. Also available in powdered form.

Dried mulberries

Konafa (kadaif): a vermicelli-like dough, white in its raw state but resembling shredded wheat once cooked.

Labne (lebne): thick, strained concentrated yoghurt (usually sold bottled) which has been shaped into balls, and floats in oil.

Mahlab: small, pale brown seeds which are the kernels of blackcherry stones, with a spicy fragrance.

Melokhia: a green, leafy vegetable, similar in appearance to mallow, used in making a famous eponymous Egyptian soup. Fresh melokhia is sometimes found, while dried is readily available.

Merguez: a spicy sausage from North Africa.

Okra: tapering, ridged green pods, available fresh, dried, tinned or frozen.

Onion seeds (sharmar): small, black teardrop-shaped seeds, not related to onions!

Orange–flower water: a fragrant flavouring made from orange flower essence, used in sweets, drinks and desserts.

Orange peel: fine strips of dried orange peel, traditionally from sour (Seville) oranges.

Pine nuts: small, ivory-coloured kernels, with the fine, long Lebanese pine nuts being particularly prized.

Nibbed pistachios

Pistachio: a small, green-coloured nut, indigenous to Iran.

Pomegranate syrup (pomegranate molasses): made from the concentrated juice of sour pomegranates and used in Iranian cooking.

Pomegranate

Pulses: black-eyed beans, with characteristic black markings; chickpeas, rounded yellow peas; Egyptian brown beans (ful), small brown broad beans.

Quince: a hard yellow-skinned fruit, resembling a large, craggy pear. Usually cooked, whereupon its flesh turns pink.

Quince

Rice: long-grain rice is a Middle Eastern staple. Fine quality Iranian rice is hard to get over here, with Basmati rice being the closest substitute.

Rose water: an essential scented flavouring made from rose essence and used in sweets and desserts.

Saffron: a costly spice made from the stigmas of a variety of crocus, sold in thread or powdered form.

Salep: a thickening agent made from dried, crushed orchid roots, used in Iran to thicken ice cream.

Sumac: a dark red powdery spice, made from crushed berries, with a tangy flavour. Sometimes diluted and used as a lemon juice equivalent.

Tahini: sesame seed paste.

Tamarind: a brown pod with sour, dark brown, pulpy flesh and seeds. Available in de-seeded pulp form or as a paste. Also used to make a syrup, which is then diluted into a refreshing drink.

Turmeric: an orange-fleshed root, usually sold in its ground form as a yellow-orange powder. It has a harsh, flat taste and is used to add flavour and a distinctive yellow colour to dishes.

Vine leaves: large, distinctively shaped leaves of the vine. Occasionally found fresh, but more usually sold in packets, preserved in brine, when they require soaking in water.

Yoghurt: tangy sheep's and goat's yoghurt as well as cow's yoghurt is widely used in Middle Eastern cooking.

Zahtar: a spice mix made from thyme, salt, sumac and sometimes roasted sesame seeds, often baked on the top of breads.

Food Shops

Spacious and comprehensive food shops, selling everything from fresh herbs to pretty pastries, as well as bakers and halal butchers, all serve the Middle Eastern community in London. Bustling Edgware Road is lined with Middle Eastern grocers, cafés and restaurants and is well worth exploring. Drive along the road late at night and you'll observe a lively, metropolitan scene with people sitting on pavement tables watching the world go by.

Central

Assal Patisserie

- 🏠 14 Connaught Street, W2 2AF
- ☎ 020 7706 2905
- 🚌 Marble Arch LU
- 🕐 Daily 9.30am-9pm

Run with charm and knowledgeable enthusiasm by Safa, this small shop sells a tempting range of own-made Iranian pastries, cakes and desserts such as lemon sorbet with falooda. In addition, stock includes dried fruits and nuts and spices such as Iranian saffron, with Safa very happy to offer advice.

Branch: 1076 Harrow Road, NW10 5NW (020 8969 2800)

Bateel

- 🏠 76 New Bond Street, W1S 1RX
- ☎ 020 7493 3199
- 🖊 www.bateel.co.uk
- 🚌 Bond Street LU
- 🕐 Mon-Fri 8.30am-8pm, Sat 10am-8pm, Sun 11am-6.30pm

This elegant shop with cool marble floors and dark wood counters and courteous staff offers a chance to sample 22 varieties of high-quality dates, ranging from hard, mildly sweet sokari to the esteemed, succulent, sweet khidri. As well as natural dates, there is a range of stuffed and chocolate-coated dates, with the shop living up amply to its claim to offer a 'gourmet date experience'.

Comptoir Libanais

- 🏠 66 Wigmore Street, W1U 1PZ
- ☎ 020 7935 1110
- 🖊 www.lecomptoir.co.uk
- 🚌 Marble Arch LU
- 🕐 Mon-Fri 8am-8pm, Sat-Sun 10am-8pm

This attractive, funky café comes complete with a deli section. On offer are a mouthwatering range of Middle Eastern goodies such as rose syrup, pomegranate molasses and harissa. The café counter also offers freshly baked breads, such as green and black olive bread and a delectable range of pastries.

Green Valley

🏠 *36 Upper Berkeley Street, W1H 5QF*

☎ *020 7402 7385*

🖇 *www.greenvalley.co*

🚌 *Marble Arch LU*

🕐 *Daily 8am-midnight*

Warmly recommended by cookery writer Claudia Roden, this spacious Lebanese shop, just off the Edgware Road, first catches the eye with its tempting window display of dainty Middle Eastern pastries. Stock is impressively comprehensive: fresh produce, groceries, a halal meat counter notably strong on offal and an in-house bakery with a baker industriously producing freshly-baked flatbreads and a traiteur counter offering superb mezze to take away. Customers with a sweet tooth are well-catered for by the ice-cream counter, pastry counter and a huge assortment of sweet meats.

Greenfields

🏠 *25 Crawford Street, W1H 1PL*

☎ *020 7723 2520*

🖇 *www.greenfieldsuk.co.uk*

🚌 *Edgware Road LU*

🕐 *Mon-Fri 8am-10pm, Sat & Sun 9am-10pm*

A friendly shop offering a range of Middle Eastern foodstuffs, from fresh produce to store-cupboard basics and including an impressive range of in-house spices such as zahtar. There is also a halal butcher's counter.

Maroush Deli

🏠 *45-49 Edgware Road, W2 2HZ*

☎ *020 7723 3666*

🖇 *www.maroush.com*

🚌 *Marble Arch LU*

🕐 *Daily 8am-12midnight*

Part of the established Maroush restaurant group, this smart, spacious establishment offers a selection of upmarket Lebanese traiteur dishes, baked flatbreads and sweet pastries.

Noura

🏠 *12 William Street, SW1X 9HL*

☎ *020 7235 5900*

🖇 *www.noura.co.uk*

🚌 *Knightsbridge LU*

🕐 *Daily 7.30am-c*

This smart branch of Noura, the Lebanese restaurant chain, also carries a deli section with a range of Lebanese foodstuffs and a tempting selection of pastries.

North

Antepliler

🗔 *47 Grand Parade, Green Lanes, N4 1AG*
☎ *020 8809 1004*
🚌 *Manor House LU*
🕐 *Daily 8am-10pm*

Bright and cheery, this bakery and café is
famous for its high quality Turkish pastries.
Truly luxurious nut-filled, syrup-laden
concoctions, delicious with coffee or mint tea.
Branch: 33A Newington Green, N16
(020 7226 9409)

Hormuz

🗔 *5 Ashbourne Parade, Temple Fortune,*
Finchley Road, NW11 0AD
☎ *020 8455 8184*
🚌 *Golders Green LU, then bus 82, 102, 260*
🕐 *Daily 9am-9pm*

Next door to an Iranian bookshop of the
same name, this neatly arranged Iranian
grocery is recommended by Claudia Roden
as having 'a lot of good things'. Inside
there is a pleasing cross-section of Iranian
foodstuffs: jams (including barberry), teas,
pulses, flower waters and syrups, pastries,
pickles and dairy products.

Phoenicia

186-188 Kentish Town Road, NW5 2AE

020 7267 1267

www.phoeniciafoodhall.co.uk

Kentish Town LU/Rail

Mon-Sat 9am-8pm, Sun 11am-4pm

This large, bright, halal food hall was deliberately named Phoenicia by its owner Ghassan to reflect its Mediterranean stock. Foodstuffs here range across the Mediterranean, so Italian pasta can be found beside couscous and Bulghur wheat, assorted Lebanese and Iraqi flatbreads nestle alongside ciabatta. One side of Phoenicia is a café, with a counter laden with Lebanese pastries, a nut counter and Italian ice creams as well as a sandwich bar.

Sahand

219 Regent's Park Road, N3 3LD

020 8343 4042

Finchley Central LU

Mon-Sat 8am-10.30pm, Sun 9am-9pm

An Iranian food shop offering a useful cross-section of Iranian ingredients.

Super Persia

621 Holloway Road, N19 5SS

020 7272 2665

Mon-Sat 7am-11pm, Sun 10am-4pm

Adding a touch of colour to Holloway Road, this bright shop is cheerfully decked out with plastic fruits and Astroturf by the fresh fruit and veg outside. Inside the shop is full of Iranian foodstuffs, from fresh cakes and pastries to frozen vegetables.

Turkish Food Centre

363 Fore Street, N9 0NR

020 8807 6766

Edmonton Green Rail

542-544 Lordship Lane, N22 5BY

020 8365 8846

Wood Green LU

Branches of the Turkish supermarket chain, see p.271 for main entry.

Yasar Halim

493-495 Green Lanes, N4 1AL

020 8340 8090

Manor House LU

Mon 8am-9.30pm, Tues-Sun 8am-10pm

This bustling Turkish food store usefully combines a bakery, greengrocer's, deli and halal meat counter. Here one can find anything from fresh green almonds and spanking fresh flat-leafed parsley to tubs of sheep's yoghurt. The bakery here remains a bustling focal point, with customers queueing for the freshly baked, round loaves of village bread. The sweet and savoury pastries such as guzleme, sold still warm from the oven, are also very popular.

Yasar Halim

2A Hedge Lane, N13 5SH

020 8882 3100

Palmers Green Rail

Mon-Sat 8am-10pm, Sun 10am-4pm

This Palmers Green branch of the established Green Lanes store offers an extensive range of stock, from keenly-priced fresh fruit and vegetables to an impressive array of olives.

West

Al Abbas

258-262 Uxbridge Road, W12 7JA

020 8740 1932

Shepherd's Bush LU

Daily 7am-12midnight

An admirably extensive range of stock at competitive prices ensure that this Middle Eastern food shop has a loyal local following, with shoppers stocking up on ingredients from flat breads to pomegranates.

Bahar Patisserie

349 Kensington High Street, W8 6NW

020 7603 5083

High Street Kensington LU

Daily 8.30am-9pm

A bright, cheery Iranian food shop, with stock ranging from fresh fruit and vegetables to sweet pastries.

Damas Gate

81 Uxbridge Road, W12 8NR

020 8743 5116

Shepherd's Bush

Daily 9am-9.30pm

This bustling, roomy, down-to-earth, Middle Eastern store offers an impressive range of ingredients. Outside is an eye-catching display of fruit and vegetables, from apricots and peaches to aubergines and peppers. Inside stock includes halal meat, grains, pulses, nuts and sweetmeats and an extensive range of breads – including flatbreads and injeera.

Lebanese Food Centre

153 The Vale, W3 7RH

020 8740 7365

Acton Central Rail

Daily 8am-10pm

A large friendly shop resembling a small supermarket, complete with a halal meat counter and an adjoining kebab restaurant. The stock is strong on basics such as pulses, spices and dried herbs with a small selection of fresh fruit and vegetables outside on the pavement.

Le Marrakech

⌂ *64 Golborne Road, W10 5PS*

☎ *020 8964 8307*

🚇 *Ladbroke Grove LU*

🕐 *Mon-Sat 8.30am-7.30pm,*
    Sun 10am-4pm

An attractive front-of-shop display of earthenware tagines indicates this food shop's Moroccan roots. Inside, there are delights such as olives with kumquats, pomegranate molasses and pickled lemons.

Middle East Food Market

⌂ *383-385 Uxbridge Road, W3 9SA*

☎ *020 8752 0678*

🚇 *Ealing Common LU*

🕐 *Daily 9am-10pm*

In effect a mini-supermarket, this large shop offers a butcher's counter, fresh produce, a bakery section and a large range of Middle Eastern foodstuffs.

Reza Patisserie

⌂ *345 Kensington High Street, W8 6NW*

☎ *020 7602 3674*

🚇 *Kensington High Street LU*

🕐 *Daily 8.30am-9pm*

This long-established shop, reputedly the first Iranian food shop in London, is still going strong. On offer are fresh fruits and vegetables, an assortment of freshly-baked pastries and Iranian ingredients.

Sara Super Market

⌂ *7 Hereford Road, W2 4AB*

☎ *020 7229 2243*

🚇 *Bayswater LU, Notting Hill Gate LU,*
    Queensway LU

🕐 *Daily 8am-11pm*

Tucked away down a side-street, this small, neat, friendly shop offers fresh fruit and vegetables such as pomegranates and sour cherries and a selection of Iranian basics. In addition, the shop is well known within Britain's Iranian community for its stock of Iranian music (both classical and popular) and films.

Zaman

⌂ *347-349 High Street Kensington,*
    W8 6NW

☎ *020 7603 8909*

🚇 *Kensington High Street LU*

🕐 *Daily 9am-10pm*

'Iranian Caviar' says the awning on this attractive shop, signalling one of the many delicacies to be found within. A colourful fresh fruit and vegetable display in front of the shop, includes seasonal treats such as hand-picked pomegranate kernels, mild-flavoured, fresh pistachios and sweet lemons. Stock includes an eye-catching self-service counter of nuts, seeds and dried fruit such as mulberries and figs, a chilled cabinet with labne and yoghurt drinks and an assortment of pickles with their characteristic sour scent. Non-edible items on sale include inlaid backgammon boards, splendid Iranian teapots and tea-glasses and a basement room of CDs and tapes. Popular Iranian music is played in the store adding to the atmosphere of the place.

Super Masoud

🏠 *9A Hammersmith Road, W14 8XJ*
☎ *020 7602 1090*
🚌 *Olympia LU*
🕐 *Daily 10am-10pm*

This down-to-earth Iranian food shop offers fresh produce at the front and a range of basic foodstuffs inside.

South

Tas EV

🏠 *97-99 Isabella Street, SE1*
☎ *020 7620 6191*
🚌 *Waterloo LU/Rail*
🕐 *Mon-Fri 7.30am-10pm,*
    Sat 8.30am-10pm, Sun 8.30am-8.30pm

Spectacularly housed in a railway arch, this stylish delicatessen and café stocks a huge range of Turkish foodstuffs. The in-house bakery produces a range of breads, including traditional 'pide' – a flatbread.

South-East

Oli Centre

🏠 *332-334 Walworth Road, SE17 2NA*
☎ *020 7703 9765*
🚌 *Elephant and Castle LU*
🕐 *Daily 24 hours*

An impressive range of stock, from fresh produce to a butcher's counter, is on offer at this huge, fantastically useful Turkish food shop, which has a loyal local following.

Persepolis

🏠 *28-30 Peckham High Street. SE15*
☎ *020 7639 8007*
✉ *www.foratasteofpersia.co.uk*
🚌 *Peckham Rye Rail*
🕐 *Mon-Sun 10.35am-9pm*

This Iranian delicatessen is run with panache by Sally Butcher, who, together with her Iranian husband Jamshid, also runs a business importing Iranian food. The stock here is impressive, from Iranian pastries, flavoured with rosewater, and smoked sturgeon to pomegranate molasses and dried soured cherries. This is a wonderfully personal shop, with Sally's humorous handwritten notes about ingredients, Persian customs and advice adorning the shelves. In addition to the food stock, there's a tempting display of Persian homewares, films and music.

Sally herself is the author of two great Middle Eastern cookbooks, *Persia in Persepolis* , on Iranian food, and *Veggiestan*, 'a vegetable lover's tour of the Middle East', and is happy to answer questions and give advice.

Turkish Food Centre

- 163-165 Bromley Road, SE6
- 020 8698 9880
- www.tfcsupermarkets.com
- Catford Bridge Rail
- Daily 8am-10pm

A spacious branch of the well-established Turkish supermarket.

South-West

Del' Aziz

- 24-28 Vanston Place, SW6 1AX
- 020 7386 0086
- www.delaziz.co.uk
- Fulham Broadway Rail
- Mon-Sat 7am-8pm, Sun 8am-6pm

Dominating a Fulham side-street, Del'Aziz is an eye-catching operation with colourful displays of Moroccan ceramic tableware and an appetising range of patisserie and sweets. Inside, Del'Aziz operates as a deli and café, with a central dining area and a long counter, offering own-cooked dishes.

Mediterranean Food Centre

- 45A & B Streatham Hill, SW2 4TS
- ☎ 020 8678 1385
- 🚆 Streatham Hill Rail
- 🕐 Daily 6am-1am

This large corner store serves the local community by offering, as its sign declares, 'English, Turkish, Greek, West Indian Food'. Fresh fruit and vegetables include quinces and pumpkins alongside chow-chows and yams. The comprehensive stock also features pulses, dairy products, dried fruit, nuts and spices. Next door is the bakery, selling freshly baked pide and they also have a halal butcher's counter.

Nour Cash & Carry

- 23 Market Row, Brixton SW9 8LB
- ☎ 020 7274 4600
- 🚆 Brixton LU/Rail
- 🕐 Mon-Sat 7am-7pm, Sun 8am-7pm

This Iranian-run family shop – a much-loved Brixton Market institution – is a cavernous affair, carrying an extensive range of competitively-priced Middle Eastern foodstuffs; a great place for rootling around among the shelves to see what interesting ingredients you can discover.

East

Turkish Food Centre

- 89 Ridley Road, E8
- ☎ 020 7254 6754
- ✎ www.tfcsupermarkets.com
- 🚆 Dalston Junction Rail
- 🕐 Daily 8am-10pm Summer; 8am-9pm Winter

A large, down-to-earth, competitively-priced Turkish supermarket. Stock ranges from an ample selection of fresh fruit and vegetables to an impressive assortment of nuts.

Turkish Food Centre

- 647-66 High Road, E11
- ☎ 020 8558 8149
- ✎ www.tfcsupermarkets.com
- 🚆 Leytonstone LU
- 🕐 Daily 8am-10pm Summer; 8am-9pm Winter

A large branch of the Turkish supermarket chain, which carries an extensive, keenly-priced range of foodstuffs.

Middle Eastern Food Shops

Eating Places

London's thriving Middle Eastern restaurants cater very much for the ex-pat community and therefore standards are generally high. The range is such that you can enjoy simple but good street food, such as a tasty lamb kebab washed down with freshly squeezed fruit juice, or a leisurely meal of sophisticated Lebanese mezze in elegant surroundings.

Central

Al-Hamra ££££
- 31-33 Shepherd Market, W1J 7PT
- ☎ 020 7493 1954
- www.alhamrarestaurant.co.uk
- Green Park LU

Established in 1984, this well-established Lebanese restaurant offers a classic, formal Lebanese dining experience, with food from assorted mezze to charcoal-grilled meats and prices reflecting the affluent location.

Al Sultan ££££
- 51-52 Hertford Street, W1J 7ST
- ☎ 020 7408 1155
- www.alsultan.co.uk
- Green Park LU

This intimate, upmarket Lebanese restaurant is an excellent place in which to sample quality mezze, such as smooth-as-silk hummus shawarma, topped with pine nuts and tender pieces of lamb.

Ali Baba ££
- 32 Ivor Place, NW1 6DA
- ☎ 020 7723 5805
- Baker Street LU

This modest café, with its bargain-priced food, is recommended by Claudia Roden for its 'real Egyptian' food. The melokhia and falafel are particular recommended.

Colbeh ££-£££
- 6 Porchester Place, W2 2BS
- ☎ 020 7706 4888
- www.colbeh.co.uk
- Marble Arch LU

This small, pretty, long-established Iranian restaurant has a loyal following for its traditional Iranian dishes.

Comptoir Libanais £-££
- 66 Wigmore Street, W1U IJT
- ☎ 020 7935 1110
- www.lecomptoir.co.uk
- Marble Arch LU

In the heart of the West End, this wittily stylish café, adorned with striking murals, offers both sweet and savoury treats including prawn falafel wraps and rosewater-flavoured macaroons.

Honey & Co £-££

25a Warren Street, London W1T 5LZ

020 7388 6175

www.honeyandco.co.uk

Warren Street LU

This small, simple space belies its somewhat austere surroundings with both its friendly service and its vividly colourful, flavourful Middle Eastern food, ranging from mezze to substantial mains. The carefully-cooked pulses are a particular forte.

Levant £££-££££

Jason Court, 76 Wigmore Street, W1U 2SJ

020 7224 1111

www.levant.co.uk

Bond Street LU

Discreetly located in a basement, this glamorous Lebanese bar and restaurant, with its over-the-top décor, is a great place to enjoy decent mezze and drinks.

Original Tagines ££

7A Dorset Street, W1U 6QN

020 7935 1545

www.original-tagines.com

Baker Street LU

A small, charming Moroccan restaurant, serving dishes such as harira and grilled merguez in addition to its trademark assorted tagines.

Patogh ££

8 Crawford Place, W1H 5NE

020 7262 4015

Edgware Road LU

A down-to-earth Iranian restaurant, perennially busy with diners, noted for its kebabs.

Ranoush Juice Bar £-££

43 Edgware Road, W2 2JE

020 7723 5929

www.maroush.com

Marble Arch LU

Established in 1981, this smart juice bar was among the first establishments opened by the successful Maroush restaurant chain and continues to do a roaring trade with its tasty Lebanese snacks, including trademark lamb shawarma, and fresh fruit juices. Pay at the till first, then order your food.

Sofra ££

36 Tavistock Street, WC2E 7PB36

020 7240 3773

www.sofra.co.uk

Covent Garden LU

This spacious Turkish restaurant, part of the Sofra chain, offers an informal atmosphere in which to sample reasonably-priced, simple Turkish food.

Tas ££

- 33 The Cut, SE1 8LF
- 020 7928 2111
- www.tasrestaurants.co.uk
- Waterloo LU/Rail

This large, contemporary Turkish restaurant, one of a chain, offers reasonably-priced, tasty Turkish food.

Yalla Yalla £-££

- 1 Green Court, W1F 0HA
- 020 7287 7663
- www.yalla-yalla.co.uk
- Piccadilly Circus LU

Hidden down a Soho alleyway, this small, pretty Lebanese café offers mezze such as fried chicken livers with pomegranate molasses as well as grilled meats and filled wraps to take away.

North

Antepliler £-££

- 48 Grand Parade, Green Lanes, N4 1AG
- 020 8802 5588
- Manor House LU

A veteran Green Lanes Turkish restaurant, famous for its kebabs and pide.

Antepliler Ciger Kebap Salonu £-££

- 47 Grand Parade, Green Lanes, N4 1AG
- 020 8802 5588
- Manor House LU

Warmly recommended, this unassuming place specialises in offal dishes, with prices remarkably reasonable.

Mangal II £-££

- 4 Stoke Newington Road, N16 8BH
- 020 7254 7888
- www.mangal2.com
- Stoke Newington Rail

This popular Turkish restaurant has a loyal following for its great value grilled food.

Yayla £

- 429 Green Lanes, N4 1HA
- 020 8348 9515
- Manor House LU

Small, cheery corner café serving tasty Turkish food, from kebabs to pide.

West

Abu Zaad ££

- 29 Uxbridge Road, W12 8LH
- 020 8749 5107
- www.abuzaad.co.uk
- Shepherds Bush LU

A friendly, relaxed Syrian restaurant, offering generous portions of homely food.

Adams Café ££-£££

🏠 *77 Askew Road, W12 9AH*
☎ *020 8743 0572*
🖥 *www.adamscafe.co.uk*
🚇 *Hammersmith LU, then bus 266*

Abdel and Francis Boukra's long-established eatery operates as a café during the day, then as a pleasantly informal Tunisian restaurant at night serving good-value, tasty Tunisian food such as freshly fried brik and couscous dishes.

Alounak ££

🏠 *44 Westbourne Grove, W2 5SH*
☎ *020 7229 0416*
🚇 *Kensington Olympia LU/Rail*

Originally housed in a portacabin in an Olympia car park, Alounak has expanded into more conventional premises. Still on offer, however, is gutsy Persian food – excellent lamb kebabs and flavourful stews.

Behesht ££-£££

🏠 *1082-1086 Harrow Road, NW10 5NL*
☎ *020 8964 7222*
🖥 *www.behesht.co.uk*
🚇 *Kensal Green LU*

With its eye-catching lavish décor and buzzy atmosphere, this huge Iranian restaurant is enormously popular among London's Iranian community. Dishes include all the classics, from grilled lamb kebabs to koresht fesanjan.

Fresco £

🏠 *25 Westbourne Grove, W2 4UA*
☎ *020 7221 2355*
🚇 *Bayswater LU*

A colourful Lebanese café serving freshly-made fruit juices and a range of Lebanese-inspired snacks including wraps.

Hafez ££

🏠 *5 Hereford Road, W2 AB*
☎ *020 7221 3167 or 020 7229 9398*
🖥 *www.hafezrestaurant.co.uk*
🚇 *Bayswater or Notting Hill Gate or Queensway LU*

A pleasant, long-established Iranian restaurant offering classic dishes such as lavash bread with dips, grilled kebabs and Persian stews.

Maroush ££££

🏠 *21 Edgware Road, W2 2JE*
☎ *020 7723 0773 or 020 7262 1090*
🖥 *www.maroush.com*
🚇 *Marble Arch LU*

Very much an Edgware Road institution, this smart Lebanese restaurant serves high-quality food, complete with live entertainment at weekends.

Mahdi ££-£££

- 217 King Street, W6 9JT
- 020 8563 7007
- Hammersmith/Ravenscourt Park LU

Warmly recommended by Iranian friends, this large restaurant offers an extensive range of Iranian dishes.

Mohsen ££

- 152 Warwick Road, W14 8PS
- 020 7602 9888
- Earls Court LU
  Kensington Olympia LU/Rail

Despite an unprepossessing location, this small Iranian restaurant, with its outside courtyard area, was warmly recommended to me by the late food writer Margaret Shaida, author of *The Legendary Cuisine of Persia*. Diners here can enjoy dishes such as kebabs and stews, at their flavourful best.

Moroccan Food Stall £

- Golborne Road, W10
- Ladbroke Grove LU

A chance to sample authentic, tasty Moroccan street food at bargain prices.

Mr Falafel £

- Units T4-T5 New Shepherd's Bush Market, 11-13 Uxbridge Road, W12 8LH
- www.mrfalafel.co.uk
- Shepherds Bush LU

'The Best Palestinian falafel' proclaims the sign above the doorway of Ahmed Yassine's small, jaunty green-and-yellow café. It does a roaring trade in take-away falafel-filled wraps, with customers choosing from extras such as ful medames, avocado or pickled baby aubergines.

Yas ££-£££

- 7 Hammersmith Road, W14 8XJ
- 020 7603 9148
- www.yasrestaurants.com
- Kensington Olympia LU/Rail

Bright and cheerful, this friendly, well-established Iranian restaurant serves freshly baked Iranian breads, dips, kebabs and Persian stews. Business is brisk, especially late at night and early in the morning.

East

Mangal Ocakbasi £-££

- 10 Arcola Street E8 2DJ
- 020 7275 8981
- Dalston Kingsland Rail

A hugely popular Hackney institution, this down-to-earth Turkish restaurant noted for its flavourful grilled meat, freshly cooked on a huge charcoal grill, and gutsy mezze.

Cookbooks

My personal recommendations of cookbooks for this cuisine, including new books and out-of-print classics:

Persia in Peckham
Sally Butcher
A lively and engaging cookbook, written with zest by Sally Butcher, who runs Persepolis, a Persian delicatessen in Peckham.

Veggiestan
Sally Butcher
Sub-titled, 'A vegetable lover's tour of the Middle East', this personal exploration of the Middle East's rich, vegetable heritage is an appealing and characterful recipe book,

The Lebanese Cookbook
Hussein Dekmak
Classic Lebanese recipes from an acclaimed Lebanese chef.

A Season in Morocco
Meera Freeman
A gorgeously-illustrated taste of Morocco, written with affection and knowledge.

Lebanese Cuisine
Anissa Helou
An appetising cookbook offering an insight into the glories of Lebanese cuisine.

A New Book of Middle Eastern Food
Claudia Roden
A groundbreaking and seminal book when it was published in 1968, this classic bookcook remains an invaluable guide to Middle Eastern cookery. It is evocatively and authoritatively written, with tempting recipes.

The Legendary Cuisine of Persia
Margaret Shaida
An elegant and well-written book charting the history of Persian cuisine and filled with excellent recipes.

Moroccan Cuisine
Paula Wolfert
A seminal and delicious collection of Moroccan recipes.

Polish London

Polsmak

From the eighteenth century onwards, Poland's history of partition, invasion and resistance, created a Polish presence in London – a self-contained, close-knit community, with a military bias. Following the collapse of communism in Poland, however, business opportunities for British-born Poles have increased, and the former sense of exile which marked the expat Polish community has gone. London's Polish community, however, retains and cherishes a very strong awareness of its Polish roots.

In 1765, Poland was divided up between Austria, Prussia and Russia. Many Polish émigrés fled to France and a few to England, so starting a pattern of political exile. A succession of failed insurrections in 1830-31, 1848 and 1863-64 brought more exiles to Britain. In Highgate Cemetery, White Eagle Hill is the resting place of the leaders of the failed 1863-64 uprising. The author Joseph Conrad emigrated first to France and then to Britain after his father's arrest in the period prior to that rebellion. Some Poles came to Britain for purely economic reasons, taking on jobs as artisans or labourers. By the late nineteenth century, a Polish Christian community in London was centred around the Polish Catholic church on Devonia Road in Islington, Our Lady of Czestochowa. Large numbers of Polish Jews entered Britain during this period but they became assimilated into the Jewish community.

A real increase in Britain's Polish community – swelling its numbers from 5,000 to tens of thousands – came with the Second World War. Following the German invasion in September 1939, over 30,000 Poles from the government and the military came to Britain and a Polish Government-in-Exile under Prime Minister Sikorski was declared. Operational headquarters were set up around South Kensington and the Polish Air Force fought alongside the RAF. Their contribution was extensive: during the Battle of Britain one in seven of the German planes shot down was dispatched by Polish airmen. A memorial to the 1,241 Polish airmen who died stands on the edge of Northolt Airport.

The Soviet occupation of Poland and the Treaty of Yalta dispossessed thousands of Poles by handing over Eastern Poland to the Soviet Union, so many Poles who had come to Britain to fight in the war stayed on. The British government offered free domicile to the 250,000 Poles (and their families) who

had fought under British command, and over 150,000 accepted. Offers of British nationality were usually refused by Poles on patriotic grounds, in an effort to keep the political situation in Poland a 'live' issue.

Pos-World War II, high property prices created a move west from Kensington to Earls Court, with Cromwell Road becoming known as the 'Polish Corridor'. Polish clubs founded during the war, such as the magnificent White Eagle Club in Knightsbridge and the aristocratic Ognisko on Exhibition Road, had provided community focal points, but again rising costs edged the Polish community out into Balham, Chiswick and Ealing. Many of the upper and middle-class Poles (who constituted the majority of the community) had to adapt to difficult circumstances following the war.

The completion in 1982 of POSK, the Polish Social and Cultural Centre, at considerable expense, was a source of pride to London's expat Polish community. The Catholic Church, too, played an important part in London's Polish community, with around 12 Polish Catholic centres and churches in London. Following the collapse of Communism and the opening up of borders in 2004, London's Polish community has grown substantially. One estimate numbers London's current Polish community as being at least 120,000 people.

Polish Cuisine

The bitter Polish winters mean that many of the essential ingredients are those that can be stored or preserved: grains, root vegetables, sauerkraut, dried mushrooms, and salted and pickled herrings. Stews and soups are popular, with krupnik (barley soup) and yellow-pea soup dating back to the Middle Ages.

Polish food is often described as Russian-influenced and the cuisines do share many dishes and ingredients. Other influences on Polish food, include Italian cuisine (traceable back to the 1518 marriage of King Sigismund to Bona Sforza) and French cuisine, with one of the earliest Polish cookbooks translated from the French.

Meat has always been highly valued in Polish cookery. Every bit is used, producing the famous sausages, hams, black puddings, tongues and brawn. The Poles also enjoy game. Bigos, or huntsman's stew, is made from game, sauerkraut and sausages. When Bona Sforza and her Italian retinue came to live in Poland, they introduced salads and certain vegetables. Even today 'wloscyzna', the word for basic green vegetables, means 'things Italian'.

Grains and cereals have always been important crops for the Poles, and rye bread is a staple. In her fascinating book *Old Polish Traditions in the Kitchen and at the Table*, Maria Lemnis writes, 'The popularity of bread in Poland is manifested in the numerous old sayings, e.g. "bread unites the strongest"... or, sharper in tone, "whomever bread harms, a stick can cure"'. Cereals such as millet and buckwheat are used widely in dishes from soups to kasha, a purée of cooked grains.

The Catholic Church has had a marked influence on Polish cooking. Catholic festivals are celebrated with a host of special dishes and cakes. Catholic fasts are also an influence, with fish and mushroom dishes replacing meat at certain times of the year. Christmas Eve, for example, is traditionally celebrated with a feast including carp or pike.

Polish cookery remained frozen in time after the Second World War but following the collapse of Communism with increased travel and trading opportunities, Polish cuisine is developing and changing.

Glossary

Buckwheat

Buckwheat: a triangular brown-green grain. Buckwheat flour is used in blinis.

Cakes: Cakes and pastries are an important feature of Polish life, and a huge variety are made, with some traditionally eaten at Christmas and Easter. *Babka*, a famous Easter yeast cake with a distinctive fluted shape; *cheesecake*, traditionally baked and not oversweet; *makowiec*, poppy-seed roll; *mazurek*, flat, traditionally rectangular cakes eaten at Easter; and *paczki*, Polish doughnuts, often filled with plum jam.

Caraway seeds: tiny, ridged brown seeds, with an aniseed flavour.

Kohlrabi

Curd cheese: a slightly tangy soft cheese made from curds, used in *pierogi* (dumplings) and cheesecake.

Dill: a caraway flavoured herb with delicate, feathery fronds.

Dried mushrooms: hunting for wild mushrooms is a national pastime in Poland. Fresh wild mushrooms are rarely found in the shops, but both dried and pickled mushrooms are widely available.

Juniper berries: aromatic, blue-black berries, used with game.

Kohlrabi: a plump, rounded vegetable, either pale green or deep purple, called a 'cabbage-turnip' by Jane Grigson.

Pierogi: filled pasta pouches, often called Polish ravioli.

Pinhead barley: fine-grained barley.

Polish pure spirit: a powerful spirit – 168 proof – used to make vodka.

Poppy seeds: tiny white or purple-blue seeds, used in vast quantities in Polish baking.

Rye bread: a Polish fundamental. Rich-flavoured, dark brown Ukranian rye is distinctive.

Sauerkraut: pickled, shredded cabbage with a sharp flavour, available fresh or bottled.

Sausages: *boiling ring*, loops of spicy sausages; *kabanos*, long, thin pork sausages; *kielbasa*, pork and beef sausage flavoured with garlic; *krakowska*, garlic sausage, eaten as a salami.

Polish Sausage

Vodka: flavoured vodkas in Poland include: honey, lemon, *sliwowica* (prune), *winiak* (matured in wine barrels), *wisniak* (cherry), and *zubrowska* (bison-grass, easily identifiable because of the blades of long grass in the bottle).

Food Shops

Twenty years ago there were just a handful of Polish food shops in London, playing an important part as a meeting place for London's small, self-contained Polish community. Today, with a far larger Polish community in London, the phrase 'Polski sklep' (Polish Shop) crops up all over the capital and the original food shops have been joined by many new businesses.

Central

Topolski

🏠 *Borough Market, SE1 1TL*
🌐 *www.topolski.co.uk*
🚇 *London Bridge LU/Rail*

This small market stall offers a discriminatingly sourced, select range of artisanal Polish foodstuffs, including superior sausages and cured meats and an addictive horseradish paste.

North

Beetroot

🏠 *92 Fleet Road, NW3*
☎ *020 7424 8544*
🌐 *www.beetrootdeli.co.uk*
🚉 *Hampstead Heath Rail*
🕐 *Mon-Fri 7.30am-6pm, Sat 9am-5pm*

Bartek Fabianski's friendly deli-cum-café offers North Londoners a taste of Poland, from home-made pierogi or Polish pastries and cakes, either to take away or to sit and sample. Strategically positioned near St Dominic's church with its Polish congregation, Bartek has built up a loyal local following among Poles and British alike.

Eva Polish Deli

🏠 *36 High Road, N2 9PJ*
☎ *07738 732911*
🚇 *East Finchley LU*
🕐 *Mon-Fri 7am-7pm, Sat 8am-5pm*

This small, neat shop sells a range of Polish groceries, from sausages to sweets and also includes a small café area in which to drink coffee and sample cakes and pastries, such as Polish cheesecake.

Fortune Foods

387-389 Hendon Way, NW4 3LP

020 8203 9325

Hendon Central LU

Daily 10am-10pm

This roomy shop stocks an extensive range of East European foodstuffs from Lithuania, Poland, Russia and Slovakia.

West

Malgosa

118 Heath Road, Twickenham, TW1 4BW

020 8891 2670

Twickenham Rail

Mon-Sat 8am-6pm

Small, friendly, homely deli-cum-café offering a range of reasonably-priced Polish ingredients, from sausages to jams, and a range of daily-changing Polish dishes to eat in the backroom café area.

Polanka

258 King Street, W6 0SP

020 8741 8268

www.polanka-rest.com

Ravenscourt Park LU

Mon-Sat 10am-10pm, Sun 11am-8pm

This deli and restaurant is a firm favourite among London's Polish community. Stock includes Polish sausages and cured meats, sweets, cakes, Krakus jams and pickles.

Enca Foods

2 Salisbury Pavement
Dawes Road, SW6 7HT

020 7385 5762

Fulham Broadway LU

Mon-Fri 7am-6pm, Sat 8am-5pm

Hidden away among Fulham's backstreets is this well-established, family-run Polish food supplier. It is famous for the 30 types of sausages and cooked and cured meats made on the premises – an appetising, savoury smell permeates the shop. Raw carcasses are delivered to the back door to be transformed into specialities such as pork brawn or roasted pork poledwica. There is also a basic grocery stock of Central European foodstuffs.

Parade Delicatessen

8 Central Buildings, The Broadway, W5 2NT

020 8567 9066

Ealing Broadway LU/Rail

Mon-Fri 9.15am-6pm, Sat 9.15am-5pm

There's been a Polish food shop on these premises for well over 50 years now. This popular delicatessen, its windows plastered with Polish cards and posters, carries an excellent range of Polish foods from sausages and cured meats to curd cheese and pierogi. Also on offer is a good choice of groceries.

Polish Specialities

- 226-8 King Street, W6 0RF
- 020 8741 8686
- www.polish specialities.com
- Mon-Sat 9.30am-7.30am,
  Sun 11am-6pm
- Hammersmith LU

One of a chain of retail shops from a Polish food importer carrying an extensive range of Polish foodstuffs.

Polish Specialities

- 55 New Broadway, W5 5AH
- 020 8840 8016
- www.polish specialities.com
- Mon-Sun 8am-9pm
- Ealing Broadway LU, Rail

A branch of a chain of retail shops it carries an extensive range of Polish foodstuffs.

Prima Delicatessen

- 192 North End Road, W14 8NX
- 020 7385 2070
- West Kensington LU
- Mon-Thurs and Sat 9.30am-6pm,
  Fri 9.30am-7pm

Founded in 1948, this old-fashioned corner shop is warmly recommended by Polish friends. It has an excellent stock of Polish ingredients including sausages and smoked meats, rye breads, cakes and pastries as well as dried goods and chilled delicacies

South-West

Korona Delicatessen

- 30 Streatham High Road, SW16 1DB
- 020 8769 6647
- Streatham Hill Rail;
  Bus 159, 109 or 133
- Mon-Sat 9.30am-7pm,
  Sun 10.30am-3.30pm

This established food shop offers a fine, neatly-arranged selection of Polish and continental foodstuffs. The long chilled counter offers an extensive range of Polish, German, Hungarian and Italian sausages, salamis and cured meats and deli items such as fresh sauerkraut and cheeses. Fresh carp are stocked at Christmas.

Panadam Delicatessen

- 2 Marius Road, SW17 7QQ
- 020 8673 4062
- Balham LU/Rail
- Mon 9.30am-6pm, Tues-Fri 9.30am-
  6.30pm, Sat 9.30am-6pm,
  Sun 9am-1.30pm

This veteran delicatessen has been serving Balham's large Polish community for many years. The deli-counter offers a good selection of Polish meats and herrings, and there is a range of rye breads and cakes. The nearby Polish church explains the Sunday opening.

BOOKS FOR COOKS

This Notting Hill bookshop, crammed with cookbooks from floor to ceiling, is a goldmine for anyone interested in food and cookery. Appetising cooking smells waft out from the small café, where recipes from books stocked in the shop are tested daily while cookery classes take place in the demonstration kitchen upstairs.

4 Blenheim Crescent, W11 • T: 020 7221 1992 • www.booksforcooks.com • Tues-Sat 10am-6pm

Polish Specialities

- *73 Stockwell Road, SW9 9PY*
- *020 7733 3526*
- *www.polish specialities.com*
- *Stockwell LU*
- *Mon-Sat 10am-8pm,*
  Sun 10am-6pm

A branch of a large chain, this store carries a wide range of Polish foodstuffs.

Polish Specialities

- *258 Streatham High Road, SW16 1HT*
- *020 8696 7660*
- *www.polish specialities.com*
- *Streatham Raill*
- *Mon-Sat 10am-8pm,*
  Sun 10am-5pm

This store, one of a chain of Polish food specialists, carries an extensive range of Polish foodstuffs.

East

Polsmak

- *39 Balls Pond Road, N1 4BW*
- *020 7275 7045*
- *Dalston Kingsland Rail*
- *Mon-Fri 9am-8pm,*
  Sat-Sun 9am-6pm

A cheerful, friendly shop, Polsmak has an extensive array of Polish and East European foods. There is a fine assortment of sausages and cured meats such as boczek (Polish bacon), kielbasa Polska and baked pate, chilled goods such as large cartons of buttermilk, sieved cottage cheese and ready-made pierogi and Polish beers. Seasonal specialities include Easter cakes and pre-ordered Christmas carps. A steady stream of customers visit for coffee and tasty sandwiches – all freshly made to order.

Eating Places

Some of London's best-known Polish eating places continue to be housed in veteran clubs or institutions, characteristic of the close-knit Polish community.

Central

Gessler at Daquise £-£££

🏠 *20 Thurloe Street, SW7*

☎ *020 7589 6117*

🖱 *www.gessleratdaquise.co.uk*

🚇 *South Kensington LU*

This pleasantly old-fashioned restaurant was founded in 1947. Now run by the Gesslers (restaurateurs from Poland) the menu offers freshly cooked Polish dishes such as pierogi or bigos at reasonable prices.

West

Café Grove £

🏠 *65 The Grove, W5 5LL*

☎ *020 8810 0364*

🚇 *Ealing Broadway LU/Rail*

A pretty café serving Ealing's Polish community and offering a tempting range of savoury dishes and classic Polish cakes.

Ognisko Polskie £££

🏠 *Polish Hearth Club,*
  55 Princes Gate,
  Exhibition Road, SW7 7PN

☎ *020 7589 4635*

🖱 *www.ognisko.com*

🚇 *South Kensington LU*

Housed in the old-fashioned setting of the Polish Hearth Club, the restaurant here serves up traditional, classic Polish fare and offers a wide range of flavoured vodkas. Summertime sees diners enjoying alfresco meals on the terrace.

Patio ££-£££

🏠 *5 Goldhawk Road, W12 8QQ*

☎ *020 8743 5194*

🖱 *www.patiolondon.com*

🚇 *Goldhawk Road LU*
  Shepherd's Bush LU

Founded in 1986, Ewa Michalik's appealing, intimate restaurant attracts a loyal following for its generous helpings of tasty Polish food and convivial atmosphere.

Polanka £-££

258 King Street, W6 0SP

020 8741 8268

www.polanka-rest.com

Ravenscourt Park LU

This homely restaurant offers a chance to sample a range of Polish foods, from poppy seed cake to more substantial dishes such as golabki (stuffed cabbage leaves).

South

Baltic ££££-£££££

74 Blackfriars Road, SE1 8AH

020 7928 1111

Southwark LU/Rail

A smart, contemporary East European restaurant and vodka bar, serving elegant food and a spectacular range of vodkas.

South-West

Polish White Eagle Club ££-£££

211 Balham High Road, SW17 7BQ

020 8672 1723

www.whiteeagleclub.co.uk

Balham LU/Rail

Housed in a veteran Polish club, the restaurant here serves huge portions of reasonably-priced, traditional Polish food.

Cookbooks

My personal selection of cookbooks for this cuisine, including both new titles and out-of-print classics:

The Food & Cooking of Eastern Europe

Lesley Chamberlain

A clearly written, overall look at East European cookery.

Old Polish Traditions in the Kitchen and at the Table

Maria Lemnis and Henryk Vitry

A fascinating and evocative account of traditional Polish cuisine, studded with recipes.

The Food & Cooking of Poland

Ewa Michalik

Written by the owner of the Patio restaurant, this is an appealing insight into Polish cuisine with accessible recipes.

The Polish Kitchen

Mary Pininska

A well-written, knowledgeable book on Polish cookery, with appetising recipes.

South-East Asian

Longdan

The South-East Asian community in London is widespread and diverse, reflecting the variety of its national origins. The term 'South-East Asia' encompasses Indonesia, Malaysia, the Philippines, Singapore, Thailand and Vietnam.

There is no obvious centre for London's South-East Asian community, no equivalent, for example, to Gerrard Street for the Chinese community, but Peckham and Dalston are focal points for the Vietnamese, while Earls Court is a centre for the Filipino community.

Wat Buddhapadipa in Wimbledon, the UK's first Buddhist temple, is an important focal point for the Thai community. April sees Thai New Year celebrations at the temple, a characteristically friendly affair offering a chance to sample street-style Thai food from assorted stalls.

South-East Asian Cuisine

The term 'South-East Asian cuisine' is the blanket term used to describe the cuisines of Indonesia, Malaysia, the Philippines, Singapore, Thailand and Vietnam – a simple way to describe a complex set of overlapping national cuisines. Seemingly no dish has a single recipe in South-East Asia: variations abound from country to country, region to region and family to family. Satay in Thailand may be served with toast and a sweet chilli-based dipping sauce, whereas the Malaysian version comes with a spicy peanut sauce, cucumber and cubes of compressed rice. Differences stem from race and religion with, for example, pork avoided by the Muslim Malays but enjoyed by the Chinese. These variations help create a rich and diverse set of cuisines, but there are certain shared characteristics across the region.

Both Chinese and Indian cuisines have influenced South-East Asian food in cooking techniques and ingredients. From China comes the balancing of five flavours: sweet, sour, hot, salty and bitter, and from India, the use of spices and curry pastes. Like both Chinese and Indian cuisine, South-East Asian cuisine is mainly rice-based.

Certain ingredients provide unique flavours that distinguish South-East Asian cooking. Coconut milk, extracted from the flesh of the versatile coconut, is a key ingredient. It is widely used in both savoury and sweet dishes as a marinade, a stock, a curry base and a dairy equivalent. Fragrant aromatics have a citrus quality: lemongrass, lime juice, kaffir lime leaves and rind. To the Asian trinity of onion, garlic and ginger are added the more subtle rhizomes: galangal and krachai. Chillies, introduced by the Portuguese and Spanish in the sixteenth century, provide a chracteristic South-East Asian 'hot' kick.

Seafood is important in South-East Asian cooking and found in abundance. In its dried and fermented forms, seafood is used to add saltiness to food. Fish sauce often replaces soy sauce in Thailand, the Philippines and Vietnam, while pungent dried paste is used throughout South-East Asia.

Indonesian and Malay cooking are often grouped together, as the dominant religion in both countries is Islam.

Singapore is distinguished culinarily by Nonya or Straits Chinese cuisine, a unique blend of heavily spiced dishes combining Chinese and Malay ingredients and techniques. Thai cooking, with its emphasis on aesthetic presentation, is marked by its use of aromatic herbs such as coriander, Thai mint and several varieties of basil.

Filipino cuisine stands out from the rest of South-East Asia, as it was influenced by the Spanish colonisation of the country from 1521 to 1898 and subsequent American occupation until 1946. The Spanish influence is apparent in Filipino dishes such as adobo and paella while American influences crop up in a predeliction for condensed milk and apple pie. Brightly coloured rice cakes and desserts are also popular in the Philippines, made with ingredients such as makapuno, soft-fleshed coconut.

Vietnamese cuisine, influenced by Chinese and French cuisines, is noted for its subtlety and characterised by the generous use of fresh herbs, including basil, coriander and mint.

Glossary

Agar agar: a vegetarian setting agent obtained from seaweed which does not require refrigeration to set. Available in either powdered form or translucent strands. Filipino agar agar (*gulaman*) comes in bright pink and yellow to add colour to desserts.

Annatto (achuete): small red seeds which impart an orange colour.

Banana leaves: used to wrap foods in the way that kitchen foil is used, with the added virtue of also adding flavour to whatever is cooked within.

Basil: a herb used in Indonesian, Thai and Vietnamese cuisines. In Thailand one finds *bai horapa* (similar to European sweet basil), *bai mangluk*, and *bai garapo* or holy basil.

Thai Basil

Bean curd (tahu, tokua): a nutritious soya-bean product. Fresh ivory-coloured bean curd has a firm, custard texture and bland flavour and is sold packed in water. Deep-fried bean curd has a golden colour and spongy texture. Both are found in the chilled section.

Betel leaves (La lot): the large, heart-shaped, dark green leaves of a climbing pepper plant. With a distinctive flavour, these are used as an edible packaging in South-East Asian cooking. Wipe the leaves with a damp cloth before using them.

Candlenuts (kemiri, buah keras): large, white, waxy nuts, used to thicken curry pastes, sold unshelled. Raw macadamia nuts are the closest substitute.

Chilli paste (nam prik pow): a thick sauce made from chillies, onions and sugar.

Chillies (prik, cabe, sili labuyo): introduced from South America by the Portuguese and Spanish in the sixteenth century, chillies are an essential ingredient in South-East Asian cookery. Generally the smallest are the hottest, for instance, the tiny Thai bird's eye chillies.

Coconut milk (santen): this thick white 'milk' is made from the grated flesh of the coconut. Tinned coconut milk is the best option. Creamed coconut and coconut milk powder, both of which need mixing with hot water, are alternatives.

Coconut Milk

Galangal

Coriander (cilantro, Chinese parsley, daun ketumbar, pak chee): this green flat-leafed herb, similar in appearance to continental parsley, has a distinctive sharp flavour. Both the seeds and the leaves are used throughout South-East Asia.

Custard apple (sweet-sop): an apple-shaped, green-skinned fruit with creamy flesh and plentiful small seeds.

Duku (llangsat, ong kong): a fawn-skinned tropical fruit, related to the lychee, with a delicate, pomelo-like flavour.

Duku

Durian: a large, spiky, green-skinned fruit, prized as a delicacy throughout South-East Asia. It is notable for its pungent smell.

Fish sauce (nam pla, nuoc mam, patis): a thin, brown salty liquid, produced from compressed shrimps or small fish, and used similarly to soy sauce as a salty flavouring.

Galangal (Siamese ginger, kenguas, languas, ka): a fleshy rhizome, resembling a creamy-coloured root ginger with pink nodules, and a sharp, medicinal aroma. Available fresh, dried, or in powder form (Laos powder).

Ginger: a brown-skinned rhizome, noted for its aromatic flavour and digestive qualities. Lesser ginger (krachai in Thai) is a milder relation and, while similarly-coloured, comes in clusters of small 'fingers'.

Jackfruit: football-sized fruit with a thick prickly green skin, similar in appearance to durian. Jackfruit flesh is available tinned.

Kaffir lime (jeruk purut, makrut): large limes with a bumpy, dark-green skin. The glossy lime leaves, sold in bunches or packets of loose leaves, are widely used in South-East Asian cooking.

Kaffir Lime

Kalamansi: small, round, green citrus fruits used in the Philippines to make a refreshing drink.

Kangkong: water-convolvulus leaves, eaten as a green vegetable.

Lemongrass (serai, sereh, takrai): a fibrous grey-green grass with a white bulbous base and subtle citrus flavour.

Long coriander (ngo gai, saw leaf herb): a herb with a fragrance similar to that of coriander, used particularly in Vietnamese cookery.

Macapuno: a type of coconut with soft, slightly sticky flesh, used in Filipino desserts.

Mango: an orange fleshed, fragrant fruit, eaten fresh and used in desserts. Pale orange Thai mangoes are particularly prized for their delicate flavour and scoopable flesh.

Mangosteen: an apple-sized fruit with thick purple skin which, despite its name, is no relation to the mango. Inside, it contains white pulpy segments with a perfumed flavour.

Mangosteen

Milkfish (bangus): a bony, white-fleshed fish, cultivated and eaten extensively in the Philippines.

Mooli (daikon): a large, long white radish with crisp flesh.

Noodles: *cellophane noodles* (also known as beanthread, glass or transparent noodles) are fine threadlike noodles made from mung beans, which need soaking before they can be easily cut; *yellow egg noodles* (available fresh and dried); *dried white rice noodles* and *vermicelli*; *river rice* or *sarhor noodles*, made from ground rice and water. Fresh river rice noodles are sold in clear packets, usually stored near the chilled section.

Palm sugar (gula melaka): a caramel-flavoured, dark brown sugar made from the coconut palm flower, sold in small, hard cylinderical blocks.

Pandan leaves: long, thin, dark green screwpine leaves, sold fresh in bunches. They add a slightly nutty flavour to desserts.

Pawpaw (papaya): a gourd-like fruit, which comes in varying sizes and colours from deep green to orange. Green pawpaw is used in salads by the Thais.

Pea aubergine: tiny pea-sized aubergines with a sharp, bitter taste, used especially in Thai cooking.

Pea Aubergine

Pomelo (shaddock): the largest of the citrus fruits, resembling a huge grapefruit with a flattened end; used in Thai salads.

Prawn crackers (krupuk): flat wafers which puff up when fried. Emping are a slightly bitter Indonesian version, made with melinjo nuts, and used to garnish gado gado salad.

Rambutan: a fruit resembling a hairy, red egg – the name comes from 'rambut', Malay for 'hair'. Inside is a translucent, juicy egg-shaped fruit, prized for its refreshing qualities.

Rice: long-grain rice is commonly used, with the best coming from Thailand. The phrase 'perfumed rice' is an indicator of quality. Short-grained white and black glutinous rice is also used.

Rice paper wrappers: round, triangular or square rice flour wrappers, sold dried. Dip in hot water for just a few seconds before using.

Shrimps, dried: small, shelled, dried pink shrimps, with a strong salty flavour.

Shrimp paste (blachan, terasi, bagoong, kapee, mam tan): a paste made from fermented shrimps, available in many forms, from solid blocks to bottled pink-grey liquid.

Soy sauce: a dark brown, salty liquid made from fermented soya beans, available as thin, salty Light Soy Sauce or as thicker, sweeter Dark Soy Sauce. *Kecap manis* is a thick, sweet Indonesian soy sauce.

Starfruit (carambola): a ridged, fleshy fruit which produces star-shaped slices.

Straw mushrooms: cone-shaped mushrooms, usually available canned.

Tamarind (asam, mak kum): a bean-like fruit from the tamarind tree, available as a pulp, and used to add tartness to dishes. Tamarind sauce, although slightly salty, is a convenient version. 'Tamarind slices' comes from a different fruit with similar qualities.

Tempe: a pressed fermented soya bean product, with a nutty taste.

Turmeric: a slender, brown-skinned rhizome, with a deep orange flesh. Widely available in dried powdered form.

Ube: a bright purple, sweet yam used in Filipino cookery.

Yam bean   **Yam bean:** a brown-skinned, tuber, with dense white, slightly sweet, crunchy flesh. It is traditionally used in rojak salads.

Yard-long beans: as the name implies, these are long green beans, commonly cut into short lengths before cooking.

Food Shops

While British supermarkets increasingly carry some South-East Asian store cupboard-basics such as coconut milk or rice noodles, many of the more specialist ingredients can only be found at South-East Asian food shops. Traditionally, too, the more established Chinese supermarkets have acted as umbrella suppliers, carrying a range of South-East Asian ingredients.

Central

New Loon Moon Supermarket
⌑ *9a Gerrard Street, W1D 5PL*
☏ *020 7734 9940*
⌕ *www.newloonmoon.com*
🚇 *Leicester Square LU*
🕐 *Daily 10.30am-8pm*

This busy Chinese food shop is well known for the range and quality of its Thai ingredients. When in season, fresh fruits on display outside range from durians to mangosteens. A separate room inside the shop stocks a striking range of fresh Thai produce, including pandan leaves, petai beans, and green mangoes for Thai salads. The grocery section, spread out over a number of rooms, includes a good range of South-East Asian ingredients, including gula melaka, curry pastes and tapioca pearls.

See Woo

- ⊞ *19 Lisle Street, WC2H 7BE*
- ☎ *020 7439 8325*
- ⌕ *www.seewoo.com*
- 🚌 *Leicester Square LU*
- 🕐 *Daily 10am-8pm*

This veteran Chinese supermarket is also a reliable stockist of many South-East Asian ingredients, especially strong on fresh produce, including herbs and aromatics such as kaffir lime leaves, pandan leaves and galangal.

North

Kmart

- ⊞ *869 Finchley Road, NW11 8RR*
- ☎ *020 8209 0760*
- 🚌 *Golders Green LU*
- 🕐 *Mon-Sat 9am-9pm; Sun 11am-9pm*

Korean, Japanese and Filipino ingredients are on offer here. The stock consists primarily of dried, frozen, tinned or bottled ingredients, including an eye-catching range of tinned tropical fruits.

Taste of Siam

- ⊞ *45-47 Camden High Street, NW1 7JH*
- ☎ *020 7383 5002*
- ⌕ *www.taste-of-siam.co.uk*
- 🚌 *Camden Town / Mornington Crescent LU*
- 🕐 *Mon-Sun 10am-10pm*

This small, neat shop is run by the same people as the Thai restaurant next door. It has a good range of South-East Asian foodstuff from very reasonably priced fresh Thai herbs to store-cupboard staples such as rice noodles and sauces.

Wing Yip (London) Ltd

- ⊞ *395 Edgware Road, NW2 6LN*
- ☎ *020 8450 0422*
- ⌕ *www.wingyip.com*
- 🚌 *Colindale LU*
- 🕐 *Mon-Sat 9.30am-8pm, Sun 11am-5pm*

This huge Chinese supermarket, located just off Staples Corner, contains an impressive range of South-East Asian ingredients. It is particularly strong on bottled, tinned, dried and frozen foods. Fresh food includes seafood and a reasonable range of produce from lemon grass to mangoes.

West

Costcutter Oriental Supermarket

- ⊞ *28 Queensway, W2 3RX*
- ☎ *020 7243 2618*
- 🚌 *Bayswater/Queensway LU*
- 🕐 *Open daily 8.30am-9pm*

This roomy supermarket offers a selection of Chinese and Oriental ingredients, from fresh produce to frozen, dried, canned and bottled foodstuffs and beverages.

Manila Supermarket

🏠 *11-12 Hogarth Place, SW5 0QT*
☎ *020 7373 8305*
🚌 *Earls Court LU*
🕐 *Daily 9am-9pm*

As the name and the stacks of *The Filipino* newspaper near the door suggest, this friendly store specialises in Filipino foodstuffs such as purple yam jam, coconut spread and pork sausages. However, it also stocks an excellent range of general South-East Asian ingredients. One room contains freezers of grated cassava, fresh coconut milk, sweet potato leaves and a variety of fish and seafood.

Muay

🏠 *8A Hogarth Place, SW5 0PT*
☎ *020 7341 3599*
🚌 *Earls Court LU*
🕐 *Daily 8am-8pm*

This long, narrow Thai food shop (above a basement hairdressers) offers a cross-section of Thai ingredients, from green mangoes for Thai salads to bundles of lemon grass. Store-cupboard stock includes tubs of curry pastes, rice noodles and wrappers.

Sri Thai

🏠 *56 Shepherd's Bush Road, W6 7PH*
☎ *020 7602 0621*
🚌 *Shepherd's Bush LU*
🕐 *Daily 9am-7pm*

This veteran Thai shop, run with friendly courtesy by Mr and Mrs Threpprasits, has a great stock of Thai ingredients, with the excellent selection of fresh Thai produce, such as Thai basils, galangal and water mimosa, being a particular forte.

Tawana Oriental Supermarket

🏠 *16-20 Chepstow Road, W2*
☎ *020 7221 6316*
🖊 *www.tawana.co.uk*
🚌 *Bayswater LU*
🕐 *Daily 9.30am-8pm*

Given a cheery bright yellow makeover, this veteran Thai food shop is well stocked with a neatly-arranged selection of Thai staples, from curry pastes, coconut milk and galangal and, for those wanting a quick Thai fix, there is a popular take-away counter offering savoury and sweet Thai dishes and snacks.
Branch: 243-245 Plaistow Road, E15

South-East Asian Food Shops

South-East

Hiep Phat

- 233 Walworth Road, SE17 1RL
- 020 7703 3230
- Elephant and Castle LU
- Mon-Sat 10am-7pm, Sun 10am-5pm

A small, friendly shop offering a range of Vietnamese foodstuffs, such as noodles, curry pastes and condiments, tofu, as well as a small range of fresh produce.

See Woo Cash and Carry

- Furlong House, Horn Lane, SE10 0RT
- 020 8293 9393
- www.seewoo.com
- Westcombe Park Rail
- Mon-Sun 9.30am-7pm

This huge, cavernous cash-and-carry store carries an extensive range of Thai and Vietnamese foodstuffs.

Wing Thai Supermarket

- Unit 11A The Aylsham Centre, Rye Lane, SE15
- 020 7635 0714
- Peckham Rye Rail
- Mon-Fri 9am-9pm, Sat-Sun 10am-8pm

A friendly down-to-earth shop with stock ranging from fresh fish to noodles and Thai fragrant rice.

South-West

Amaranth

- 527 Garrett Lane, SW18 4SR
- 020 8871 3466 / 8874 9036
- Earlsfield Rail
- Mon-Sat 11.30am-10pm

An extension of the popular Thai restaurant this small food shop stocks basic Thai ingredients, including home-made curry pastes. Deliveries from Thailand arrive on Monday evening, so Tuesday is the best day for fresh Thai produce, such as holy basil or lime leaves. The shop's particular forte is its home-made, frozen ready-to-cook savouries, such as dainty spring rolls or red duck curry. Staff are friendly and happy to offer cooking advice.

Longdan

- 17 Wood Street, KT1 1TY
- 020 8546 1911
- www.longdan.co.uk
- Kingston Rail
- Mon-Sat 10am-9pm, Sun 11am-8pm

This spacious store, the flagship branch of the Longdan chain, billed as offering 'a new taste of the Orient' is an impressive operation. The wide-ranging stock, focused on Vietnamese foodstuffs, is neatly arranged and clearly labelled and staff are helpful.

Talad Thai

320 Upper Richmond Road, SW15 6TL

020 8789 8084

Putney Rail

Daily 9am-8pm

Upstairs is a Thai take-away while downstairs is a basement supermarket with fresh vegetables, herbs and fruits. The large freezer section contains meat and seafood with plenty of dried and tinned foodstuffs.

Paya Thai

101-103 Kew Road, TW9 2PN

020 8332 2959

Richmond LU/Rail

Daily 10am-7pm

This large store has an excellent and comprehensive stock of Thai ingredients, from fresh pea aubergines and fragrant Thai basil to bottles of fish sauce and tins of coconut milk.

Wing Thai Supermarket

13 Electric Avenue, SW9

020 7738 5898

Brixton LU/Rail

Mon-Sat 10am-7pm

Tucked away behind the bustling fruit and veg market stalls outside, this roomy store has a small fresh produce section. It is particularly strong on bottled, tinned and frozen Vietnamese goods.

East

Hoang-Nam

185 Mare Street, E8 3RH

020 8985 9050

London Fields Rail

Daily 9am-9pm

A large, well-established Vietnamese supermarket, particularly noted for its range of Vietnamese herbs and vegetables. Stock ranges from store-cupboard staples (rice, noodles, condiments) to frozen seafood.

Longdan

25 Hackney Street, E2 7NX

020 3222 0118

www.longdan.co.uk

Old Street LU

Mon-Sat 10am-10pm, Sun 11am-8pm

This Hackney outlet of the Longdan chain is a bright and airy establishment and comes complete with a popular bubble tea bar. Stock is impressively wide-ranging and comprehensively stocked, from fresh produce including an excellent range of fresh Vietnamese herbs, frozen meat and seafood, noodles, rice paper wrappers, condiments, curry pastes, teas, snacks and beverages and kitchenware. 'I like this shop becauses you can find things here that no-one else stocks,' explains one Vietnamese customer doing her weekly shop.

South-East Asian Food Shops

Longdan

🏠 *4 Estate Way, E10 7JN*
☎ *020 8556 8828*
🖱 *www.longdan.co.uk*
🚌 *Leyton LU, then bus 58 or 158*
🕐 *Mon-Fri 9am-7pm, Sat 9am-6pm,*
Sun 10am-6.30pm

One of the Longdan chain, noted for its range of Vietnamese ingredients, from rice noodles to bottled sauces.

Tawana Oriental Supermarket

🏠 *243-245 Plaistow Road, E15 3EU*
☎ *020 8503 1609*
🖱 *www.tawana.co.uk*
🚌 *Plaistow LU*
🕐 *Daily 9.30am-7pm*

A branch of the established Thai food shop, stocking a range of South East Asian ingredients.

Eating Places

London's South-East Asian eating out scene is a mixed affair. While Thai food continues to be popular and Vietnamese restaurants are on the roll, good Malaysian, Indonesian or Singaporean food is hard to find, lacking the depth and flavour found in the real thing. The places listed below are some of the best places to find authentic South-East Asian food from simple, reasonably-priced cafés to sophisticated, elegant restaurants.

Central

Banhmibay £-££

🏠 *4-6 Theobald's Road, WC1X 8PN*
☎ *020 7831 4079*
🖱 *www.banhmibay.co.uk*
🚌 *Chancery Lane LU*

Bringing an authentic taste of Vietnam to Bloomsbury, this pleasant, informal café serves up affordable, classic Vietnamese dishes with its signature dish being a range of banh mi, baguettes with fillings from shredded caramel pork to chargrilled prawns.

Bonda Café £-££

190 Sussex Gardens, W2 1PU

020 7402 5111

Paddington LU

Tucked away in a basement, this small unassuming restaurant offers a taste of Malaysia. It serves classic dishes such as nasi lemak and roti canai and is popular with homesick Malaysian expats. Reasonable prices add to the appeal.

C & R Café £-££

4-5 Rupert Court, W1D 6DY

020 7434 1128

Leicester Square LU

This bustling, down-to-earth café, hidden down a Soho back-alley, does a roaring business in bargain Singaporean and Malaysian dishes, including Hainanese chicken rice, laksa and ice kacang.

Cay Tre Soho £-£££

42-45 Dean Street, W1D 4PZ

020-7317 9118

Leicester Square LU

Appealingly styled, with its tiled floor and simple black tables, this Soho restaurant, part of the Cay Tre group, offers an informal chance to sample excellent Vietnamese cooking. As well as classic dishes – summer rolls and, of course, pho – are less familiar offerings such as clams with lemon grass and chilli.

Jom Makan £-££

5-7 Pall Mall East, SW1Y 5BA

020 7925 2402

Charing Cross LU

Just off Trafalgar Square, this spacious restaurant offers a chance to sample Malay dishes, from stir-fried noodles to rich, slow-simmered curries.

Kopi Tiam £-££

67 Charing Cross Road, WC2H 0NE

020 7287 1113

Leicester Square LU

Tucked away in an arcade, this down-to-earth restaurant offers a range of savoury and sweet Malaysian and Singaporean street food dishes and beverages. A particular highlight is the excellent, layered roti canai, expertly flicked out and cooked fresh to order at his corner counter by the Roti King, and served, as is traditional with a tasty curry sauce for dipping the flatbread into.

Malaysia Kopi Tiam £-££

67 Charing Cross Road, WC2H 0NE

020 7287 1113

Leicester Square LU

This down-to-earth café serves up generous portions of tasty Malay food such as char kway teow at bargain prices.

Nahm ££££

🖼 *The Halkin, Halkin Street, SW1X 7DJ*
☎ *020 7333 1234*
🚌 *Hyde Park Corner LU*

Showcasing the culinary talents of acclaimed Australian chef David Thompson, famed for his knowledge of Thai cuisine, this discreetly elegant restaurant offers a gourmet glimpse into this richly varied cuisine.

Pho £-££

🖼 *3 Great Titchfield Street, W1W 8AX*
☎ *020 7436 0111*
✉ *www.phocafe.co.uk*
🚌 *Oxford Circus LU*

A bright, airy café – one of a mini-chain – offering reasonably-priced Vietnamese food. The eponymous pho (noodles in broth), arrive accompanied by fragrant Vietnamese herbs.

Thai Square £££-££££

🖼 *21-24 Cockspur Street, SW1Y 5BL*
☎ *020 7836 7600*
✉ *www.thaisquare.net*
🚌 *Charing Cross LU*

Handsomely housed in the former Norwegian Embassy, this is the flagship branch of this Thai restaurant chain offering a range of classic Thai dishes, from fragrant curries to well-executed salads.

North

Khoai Cafe ££

🖼 *6 Topsfield Parade, Middle Lane, N8 8PR*
☎ *020 8341 2120*
🚌 *Finsbury Park LU/Rail, then the W7 bus*

Simple surroundings, combined with polite, friendly service, make this Crouch End restaurant a pleasantly unpretentious place to sample traditional Vietnamese dishes. Special favourites include betel leaf-wrapped beef and pho, in flavourful stock.
Branch: 362 Ballards Lane, N12 0EE (020 8445 2039)

O's Thai Café ££

🖼 *10 Topsfield Parade, N8 8PR*
☎ *020 8348 6898*
✉ *www.osbarsandcafe.com*
🚌 *Finsbury Park LU/Rail, then the W7 bus*

This bright, cosy café offers the chance to try tasty Thai dishes (such as green chicken curry) at very reasonable prices and has a loyal following among Crouch End diners.

Singapore Garden £££

🖼 *83-83a Fairfax Road, NW6 4DY*
☎ *020 7328 5314*
✉ *www. singoregarden.co.uk*
🚌 *Swiss Cottage LU*

A loyal multi-cultural clientele testifies to this smart, family-run, restaurant's commitment to admirably authentic Singaporean food. The menu offers predominantly Chinese food, but includes a selection of Singaporean delicacies such as mouth-watering and gloriously messy chilli crab, excellent satay and oyster omelette. This place also serves the best chendol (a coconut milk concoction) in town.

West

Satay House £££

- 🏠 *13 Sale Place, W2 1PX*
- ☎ *020 7723 6763*
- 🖱 *www.satay-house.co.uk*
- 🚌 *Edgware Road LU, Paddington LU/Rail*

Tucked away in a quiet side-street, this established restaurant has a following for its tasty Malaysian dishes such as murtabak (mince-stuffed flat bread) and nasi lemak (coconut rice). Desserts include such treats as pulot hitam (black rice in coconut milk).

Tawana ££

- 🏠 *3 Westbourne Grove, W2 4UA*
- ☎ *020 7229 3785*
- 🖱 *www.tawana.co.uk*
- 🚌 *Bayswater LU*

Run by the owners of Tawana Supermarket, this friendly, unpretentious Thai restaurant has built up a loyal local following.

Tukdin £-££

- 🏠 *41 Craven Road, W2 3BX.*
- ☎ *020 7723 6955*
- 🖱 *www.tukdin.co.uk*
- 🚌 *Paddington LU/Rail*

A relaxed, friendly Malaysian restaurant, warmly recommended by Malaysian friends. It offers an excellent assortment of traditional Malaysian dishes such as bandung noodles.

South

Champor-Champor £££-££££

- 🏠 *62-64 Weston Street, SE1 3QJ*
- ☎ *020 7403 4600*
- 🖱 *www. champor-champor.com*
- 🚌 *London Bridge LU/Rail*

With its vibrant décor, Champor-Champor stands out from the crowd. The menu, too, is similarly creative, offering beautifully-presented, Asian-inspired fusion food.

Kaosarn £-££

- 🏠 *Units 2 & 96, Granville Arcade, Brixton Market, SW9 8LD*
- ☎ *020 7095 8922*
- 🖱 *www. champor-champor.com*
- 🚌 *Brixton LU/Rail*

Part of the 'Brixton Village' phenomenon, this small, polite Thai restaurant serves flavourful renditions of Thai dishes such as larb (minced meat salad) or grilled, marinated half chicken.

Yum-D £

⌨ *14 Market Row, Brixton Market, SW9 8LD*
🚇 *Brixton LU/Rail*

A small, pretty, unpretentious Thai café offering a chance to sample home-style Thai cooking at very reasonable prices.

South-West

Blue Elephant £££-££££

⌨ *4-6 Fulham Broadway, SW6 2UB*
☎ *020 7385 6595*
🖱 *www.blueelephant.com*
🚇 *Fulham Broadway LU*

A veteran Thai restaurant, the Blue Elephant comes complete with lavish tropical-inspired décor and attentive staff. The cooking is above average, with the set-price Sunday buffet lunch a popular family occasion.

East

Cay Tre £-£££

⌨ *301 Old Street, EC1V 9LA*
☎ *020 7729 8662*
🖱 *www.vietnamesekitchen.co.uk*
🚇 *Old Street LU*

Excellent Vietnamese food, including both traditional and innovative dishes, served in simple, informal surroundings.

Rosa's Thai Café £-£££

⌨ *12 Hanbury Street, E1 6QR*
🖱 *www.rosaslondon.com*
🚇 *Liverpool Street*

This cheery, intimate café serves up a tasty selection of Thai classics.

Saigon Street Café £

⌨ *Broadway Market E8 4PH*
🖱 *www.caphevn.co.uk*
🚇 *London Fields Rail*

Saturdays on Broadway Market see a queue at the Saigon Street Café for cups of classic Vietnamese coffee. They also serve crisp Vietnamese-style baguettes filled.

Sedap

⌨ *102 Old Street, EC1V 9AY*
☎ *020 7490 0200*
🖱 *www.sedap.co.uk*
🚇 *Old Street LU*

Recommended by Singaporean friends, this attractive restaurant, with its simple, clean décor, offers an extensive menu of Malaysian dishes, with char kway teow a speciality.

Song Que Café £

⌨ *134 Kingsland Road E2 8DY*
☎ *020 76133 222*
🚇 *Old Street LU/Rail*

Highly recommended by pho-loving friends, this café serves great value, Vietnamese food.

Cookbooks

My personal recommendations of cookbooks for this cuisine, including new books and out-of-print classics:

Bill's Everyday Asian
Bill Granger
Popular Australian chef Bill Granger offers his own take on Asian-inspired cuisine with a collection of simple yet effective recipes for dishes from Vietnamese rice noodles with sticky prawns to Chinese custard tarts, in this attractive accessible cookbook.

The Complete Asian Cookbook
Charmaine Solomon
A comprehensive cookbook offering a useful insight into the diversity of Asian cuisine.

Far Eastern Cookery
Madhur Jaffrey
An appetising regional journey, with clear, useable recipes.

The Flavours of Vietnam
Meera Freeman
A clearly written, appetising Vietnamese cookbook.

Food and Travels Asia
Alastair Hendy
A spectacular book combining recipe's with Hendy's own evocative photographs.

Indonesian Food & Cookery
Sri Owen
An authoritative and in-depth book about Indonesian food, from the doyenne of Indonesian food.

South-East Asian Food
Rosemary Brissenden
An absolutely indispensable book on the cuisine of South-East Asia. The lovingly researched and written book is a mine of delicious recipes from throughout the region.

Thai Cooking
Jennifer Brennan
A classic book on Thai cuisine, lovingly and authoritatively written.

Spanish & Portuguese

Garlic Stuffed
90p/100g

Almond Stuffed
90p/100g

Pimento Stuffed
90p/100g

Mammouth
80p/100g

...n & Sundried
...o stuffed

...lossal

A & C Continental Grocers

Although a Spanish presence in London can be traced back to the Middle Ages, the real growth in the capital's Spanish and Portuguese communities came in the twentieth century. Following the Spanish Civil War (1936-39), many Spanish refugees and political exiles came to Britain. Republican exiles set up El Hogar Español (The Spanish House) in Bayswater: a cultural, social and political focal point. In addition to political reasons for coming to Britain, economic ones also played their part.

During the 1950s and 1960s, millions of working-class Spaniards were forced to leave Spain and look for work abroad because of the lack of opportunities at home. The area around Ladbroke Grove was a focal point for the Spanish community. Many of the Spanish in Britain were traditonally from Galicia, the north-west coastal region of Spain which has a seafaring and travelling tradition and which suffered in the post-war depression.

Despite the fact that Portugal is Britain's oldest ally (a tie dating back to the Treaty of Windsor in 1386) the Portuguese community in London is small. It was the decades after the Second World War which saw an influx of Portuguese arriving in London, largely as a result of a lack of economic opportunities in Portugal.

One traditional focal point for the city's Iberian community was the area around Golborne Road and Portobello. On these roads, the community is served by a Spanish school, Spanish and Portuguese delicatessens, and assorted cafés, bars and restaurants. Camden Town, Stockwell and Vauxhall, too, are home to a number of Portuguese food shops, cafés and restaurants.

Spanish & Portuguese Cuisine

Both Spanish and Portuguese cookery share many characteristic ingredients: salted cod, paprika sausages, rice, beans, garlic and olive oil. The Moorish occupation of the Iberian Peninsula from AD 711 has left its mark on the sweets of both countries, with ground almonds and egg yolks used in desserts and cakes such as the Portuguese touchino de ceu or Spanish tarta de naranja.

Seafood is important in both cuisines, with an extensive range fished on the countries' long coastlines. Many of the famous regional dishes are seafood-based, such as zarzuela (Catalan seafood stew), marmitako (Basque bonito soup) and Northern-Portuguese caldeirada. There is no squeamishness when it comes to seafood. Lampreys are eaten in Northern Portugal in a famous dish, lapreia a moda do Minho; while Spanish calamares en su tinta, calls for squid to be cooked in its own black ink. Absolute freshness is demanded and one traditional Spanish fish dish is nicknamed mato mulo (mule killer) because the fish used in it had to be rushed by mule from the coast to Madrid.

There are some obvious differences between the cuisines and national dishes. From Portugal's former colonies come spices and flavourings such as spicy piri piri sauce – used in both Brazil and East Africa. Tapas, however, are quintessentially Spanish. The term means 'little lid' and is thought to come from the bar tradition of covering glasses with a saucer of olives or nuts. Bars vie with each other to offer good tapas and the discerning Spanish, who both enjoy their food and take it seriously, hunt out their favourites with a passion.

Both Spain and Portugal retain a strong sense of regionalism, with traditional dishes still cherished. Many recipes feature a place name, such as de salmao a Lisboeta, or fabada Asturiana. As in Italian cuisine, certain areas or towns are known for the quality of their food, with the best Spanish seafood coming from Cadiz or Galicia and the best Portugese caldo verde from the Minho.

Glossary

Aguardiente (orujo): a potent Spanish spirit, distilled from the left-over grapes and pips after wine has been made.

Anchovies (boquerones, biqueiros): tiny cured fish with a strong, salty flavour.

Anchovies

Capers (alcaparras): the unopened buds of a Mediterranean shrub, sold and used in their pickled form. Spain is the world's largest producer of capers.

Cava: sparkling Spanish wine made using the champagne method, with Cordoniu and Frexenet among the best producers.

Charcuterie: *butifarra*, a white Spanish sausage, spiced with cinnamon, cloves and nutmeg; *chorizo* or *chourico*, pork sausages, flavoured with pimenton (Spanish paprika) and, when semi-cured, used in cooked dishes, to which they add a distinctive orange-reddish colour and flavour, or, when fully cured, eaten as a salami; *jamon de Serrano*, an air-dried Spanish ham, usually cured for around 9 months; *jamon Iberico* (pata negra) air-cured ham made from black Iberian pigs, the best of which is known as *jamon Iberico de bellota* made from Iberico pigs that roam in oak forests (dehesa) and eat an acorn-rich diet which gives a particular nutty flavour to the ham; *lomo*, cured pork loin from Spain; *presunto*, a fine salt-cured ham from Portugal, traditionally made from acorn-fed pigs from Tras-os-Montes; *sobrassada* a soft, spreadable, pimenton-spiced pork paste, a speciality from Majorca.

Cheese: *azeitaio*, small Portuguese sheep's milk cream cheeses; *cabrales*, a famous Spanish blue-veined cheese, made from cow's milk but sometimes with sheep's or goat's milk added; *evora*, a creamy, strong, salty sheep's milk cheese from Portugal; *idiazabal*, a much-prized, semi-soft cheese with a dark rind made from sheep's milk in the Basque region of Spain; *ilha*, a Portuguese Cheddar-like cheese made from cow's milk; *mahon*, a flavourful Spanish semi-soft cow's milk cheese; *manchego*, one of Spain's best-known cheeses, made with sheep's milk and sold in three grades depending on age; *roncal*, a hard, Spanish, sheep's milk cheese; *serra*, a soft, Portuguese, sheep's milk cheese.

Chickpeas (garbanzos, grado): hazelnut-shaped, yellow peas.

Coriander (coentros): a sharp-flavoured green herb, similar in appearance to continental parsley, widely used in Portuguese cookery.

Madeira: a famous Portuguese fortified wine, from the island of Madeira.

Madelenas: small, sweet, golden-brown cakes, eaten for breakfast in Spain.

Muscatel raisins: dried muscatel grapes, with a distinctive flavour.

Muscatel raisins

Olive oil: olive oil is produced in both Spain and Portugal and is the main cooking oil in both countries. Carbonell, with its elegant Art Nouveau labels, is one of Spain's famous brands.

Pimenton

Olives: green olives stuffed with anchovies are particularly popular in Spain.

Paprika: a bright red powder, made from ground sweet or spicy peppers and used as a spice.

Pimenton: Spanish paprika, made from ground Spanish paprika peppers, has a distinctive flavour and is available sweet, medium hot or hot. It is a popular Spanish spice, adding, for example, flavour and colour to chorizo sausages.

Pimientos de padron: slightly piquant, small peppers, delicious pan-fried and sprinkled with sea salt.

Pine kernels (pinon, pinhao): small, ivory-coloured stone pine kernels, used in both sweet and savoury dishes.

Piri piri: a hot Portuguese sauce made from chillies, a culinary legacy from Portugal's colonial past.

Piri- piri

Port: a fortified wine from the Douro valley in North-West Portugal. Its creation can be traced back to the early seventeenth century when, due to Anglo-French hostilities, Portuguese wine rather than French claret was exported to England.

Quince paste (membrillo, marmelo): a thick, golden, jelly-like paste made from quinces, eaten as a sweetmeat or as a classic accompaniment to cheese.

Rice: introduced by the Moors to Spain and Portugal in AD 711. Short-grain rice is used for Spanish paella.

Saffron

Saffron: a costly spice made from the stigmas of a type of crocus, sold in either thread or powdered form.

Salt cod (bacalao, bacalhau): dried, salted cod traditionally eaten on Fridays for religious reasons. In Portugal it is regarded as a national delicacy and there is said to be a different bacalhau recipe for every day of the year. It should be soaked for 24–36 hours before cooking to remove excess salt.

Sherry: a classic Spanish wine named after the town of Jerez and imported by the British since the fifteenth century.

Tiger nut (chufa): a small, wrinkled rhizome from which horchata, a refreshing almond-flavoured drink thought to have been introduced by the Moors, is made.

Turron: Spanish nougat, available in two forms: alicante, crisp and textured with chopped nuts, or jijona, soft and crumbly, made from ground nuts. Traditionally this is a Christmas treat but it is now available all the year round.

Vinho verde: delicate effervescent wines, both white and red, which form around a quarter of Portugal's wine production.

Food Shops

As with London's Italian food stores, the older Spanish food shops began as corner shops, selling everyday ingredients to their community. Brindisa, the pioneering importer of top-notch Spanish foodstuffs, has done a huge amount to raise the profile of Spanish cuisine in the UK but through its imports and its Borough Market food shop at Borough Market and its tapas bars.

Central

Brindisa Shop

🏠 Stoney Street, Borough Market, SE1 9AF
☎ 020 7407 1036
🚌 London Bridge LU
🖱 www.brindisa.com
🕐 Tues-Thurs 10am-5.30pm,
Fri 10am-6pm, Sat 8.30am-5pm

Importers Brindisa have been one of the pioneers of Iberian cuisine in London. Their airy shop is one of the highlights of a visit to Borough Market, where you can source their trademark, top-quality Serrano and Iberico (pata negra) ham, expertly hand-carved to order, top-notch chorizo and other carefully selected Spanish foodstuffs, from cheeses to jarred pulses.

Caleya Iberica

🏠 195 Great Portland St, W1W 5PS
☎ 020 7636 8650
🚌 Great Portland Street LU
🖱 www.ibericalondon.co.uk
🕐 Mon-Sat 11am-6pm

This smart delicatessen, housed under the same roof as a flourishing tapas bar and Spanish restaurant, is the retail arm of an experienced Spanish exporters, specialising in gourmet foods. As one might expect, therefore, the emphasis is on both quality and breadth, from mouthwatering Serrano and Iberico hams on the bone to the cheese room, which houses an impressive range of cheeses. The extensive stock includes some interesting Spanish wines.

Delicias de Portugal

🏠 43 Warwick Way, SW1V 1QS
☎ 020 7630 5597
🚌 Pimlico LU, Victoria LU/Rail
🕐 Mon-Sat 8am-8pm, Sun 9am-2pm

This pretty delicatessen caters to hungry office workers, offering pasteis de bacalhau and a selection of Portuguese cakes and pastries as well as sandwiches. There is a large range of deli goods, including huge slabs of bacalhau (cut on demand), packets of 'flan' and a choice of goat's cheeses.

Madeira Delicatessen

- 46C Albert Embankment, SE1 7TL
- 020 7820 1117
- www.madeiralondon.co.uk
- Vauxhall LU/Rail
- Daily 6am-9pm

Under the railway arches at Vauxhall, Madeira Delicatessen is a cavernous, down-to-earth shop. It offers an impressive range of Portuguese foodstuffs, from everyday basics to treats including Portuguese pastries and a large selection of wines.

North

Delicias de Portugal

- 1008 Harrow Road, NW10 5NS
- 020 8960 7933
- Kensal Green LU
- Mon-Sat 8.30am-7.30pm, Sun 9am-2pm

A well-stocked Portuguese food shop.

Ferreira

- 40 Delancey Street, NW1 7RY
- 020 7485 2351
- Camden Town LU
- Mon-Sat 8am-9pm, Sun 8am-8pm

A friendly Portuguese corner store-cum-café offering a selection of foodstuffs as well as wines and beers.

Lisboa Patisserie

- 4 Plender Street, NW1 0JP
- 020 7387 1782
- Camden Town LU
- Tues-Fri 9.30am-6.30pm, Sat 9am-7pm, Sun 10am-2pm

A branch of the established Portuguese delicatessen, serving up its trademark pasteis de nata and bacalhau croquettes.

Villa Franca

- 3 Plender Street, NW1 0JT
- 020 7387 8236
- Camden Town LU
- Mon-Sat 7am-8pm, Sun 9am-7pm

A small down-to-earth shop and café selling a mixture of Portuguese and English patisserie plus a range of foodstuffs including bacalhau (stored beneath the counter), cured meats, soft drinks and cheeses. Downstairs is a smoking room from which blares the sound of Portuguese satellite TV.

The Wine Cellar

☐ 193 Kentish Town Road, NW5 2JU
☎ 020 7267 9501
🚌 Kentish Town LU/Rail
🕐 Mon-Fri 8am-8pm, Sat 9am-8pm

Nuno Lobo's narrow, homely Portuguese food shop and café stocks basic foodstuffs including cheeses, pancetta, chourico as well as tinned seafood, pulses and packets of 'pudim'. Downstairs, the reason for the shop's name becomes clear: the entire basement is stocked with a wide variety of Portuguese wines plus port and Madeira.

West

Garcia R. & Sons

☐ 248 Portobello Road, W11 1LL
☎ 020 7221 6119
🚌 Ladbroke Road LU, Notting Hill Gate LU
🕐 Daily 9am-6pm

Founded in 1957, this large food shop is still run by the Garcia family. There is an extensive range of groceries and store-cupboard basics, from pimenton and saffron to pulses, paella rice and a huge range of tinned seafood. The deli counter does a roaring trade in anchovy-stuffed olives, chorizo sausages and costly Jamon Iberico (from acorn-fed black-footed pigs). Turrons are kept throughout the year, with the range expanding at Christmas time.

La Plaza Deli

☐ 288 Portobello Road, W10 5TE
☎ 020 8968 0900
🚌 Westbourne Park LU
🕐 Mon-Sat 9am-7pm, Sun 9am-5.45pm

This small friendly shop, owned by La Plaza Tapas bar, carries an excellent range of Spanish foodstuffs and does a roaring lunchtime trade in sandwiches.

Lisboa

☐ 6 World's End Place, SW10 0DR
☎ 020 7376 3639
🚌 Fulham Broadway LU
🕐 Mon-Sat 8am-6pm

A branch of the well-established Golborne Road emporium.

Lisboa Delicatessen

☐ 54 Golborne Road, W10 5NR
☎ 020 8969 1052
🚌 Westbourne Park LU
🕐 Daily 8am-7.30pm

When Carlos Gomes opened this shop it was the first Portuguese delicatessen in London and he and his partners 'imported' their own stock in suitcases from Portugal. All the ingredients for Portuguese cooking can be found here: pungent bacalhau, pulses, sausages and pickled and salted pig's trotters, snouts, tails and ears. A back room contains offers Portuguese wines and spirits.

Lisboa Patisserie

- 57 Golborne Road, W10 5NR
- ☎ 020 8968 5242
- 🚇 Westbourne Park LU
- 🕐 Daily 8am-8pm

Across the road from the delicatessen, this small, down-to-earth popular patisserie, a pioneer of Portuguese baking in the capital, supplies a constant stream of customers with delicious, freshly baked Portuguese pastries and tasty bacalhau croquettes and sandwiches. Queues quickly build up for Lisboa's trademark pasteis de nata (custard tarts) and competition for the handful of tables is fierce.

South-West

A & C Continental Grocers

- 3 Atlantic Road, SW9
- ☎ 020 7733 3766
- 🚇 Brixton LU/Rail
- 🕐 Mon-Sat 8am-8pm

Under the arches, Jose and Bella's friendly neighbourhood shop has an excellent range of both Spanish and Portuguese ingredients, from fresh fruit, vegetables and herbs outside, to loaves of bread inside. Portuguese chourico, morcela (black pudding) and cheeses can be found at the deli counter. Pasties de nata and baccalau rissoles are delivered daily.

Delicias de Portugal

- 280 Wandsworth Road, SW8 2JR
- ☎ 020 7622 9811
- 🚇 Wandsworth Road Rail
- 🕐 Mon-Fri 8am-8pm, Sat 9am-7pm, Sun 9am-4pm

A down-to-earth, friendly food shop, filled with a good selection of Portuguese staples.

Sintra Delicatessen

- 146-48 Stockwell Road, SW9 9TQ
- ☎ 020 7733 9402
- ✎ www.sintradeli.co.uk
- 🚇 Stockwell LU
- 🕐 Daily 9am-8pm

The scent of bacalhau and the hum of conversation evoke Portugal as you enter this homely shop, which is attached to a down-to-earth café and restaurant. There is a good selection of foodstuffs including chourico, presunto and morcela as well as Portuguese cakes and bread. The shelves are lined with all kinds of Portuguese groceries including cereals, olive oil and Portuguese wines.

Eating Places

Recent years have seen a heightened awareness in Britain of the quality of Spanish foodstuffs. With tapas fitting perfectly into the current dining trend for small dishes and 'grazing' menus. London's Spanish dining out scene has experienced a 'tapas boom' and now features a number of outstanding tapas bars and Spanish restaurants. London's Portuguese eateries range from simple cafés in which to enjoy bacalhau fritters, pastries and coffee to restaurants offering hearty dishes such as caldereida or caldo verde.

Central

Barrafina £££-££££

⬛ *54 Frith Street, W1D 4SL*
☎ *020 7440 1463*
✉ *www.barrafina.co.uk*
🚇 *Tottenham Court Road LU*

This sleek restaurant, part of the Fino stable, in which diners perch at the central bar and sample dishes, has made a name for itself with its outstanding tapas made from prime ingredients. A no-booking policy together with this tapas bar's popularity means that finding a seat can be an issue, so come prepared to queue.

Casa Brindisa £££

⬛ *7-9 Exhibition Road, SW7 2HE*
☎ *020 7590 0008*
✉ *www.casabrindisa.com*
🚇 *South Kensington LU*

This attractive tapas bar from noted Spanish food importers Brindisa offers an appetising showcase for their fine Spanish foods. Diners tuck into dishes including good-quality Spanish charcuterie from the Jamoneria, a fine range of Spanish cheeses and prawns with chilli and garlic.

Dehesa £££

⬛ *25 Ganton Street, W1F 9BP*
☎ *020 7494 4170*
✉ *www.dehesa.co.uk*
🚇 *Oxford Circus LU*

A convivial tapas bar, part of the Salt Yard group, offering Spanish and Italian-inspired sharing plates, from plates of pata negra ham to goat's cheese-stuffed courgette flowers, drizzled with honey.

Fino £££-££££

⬛ *33 Charlotte Street, W1*
☎ *020 7813 8010*
✉ *www.finorestaurant.com*
🚇 *Goodge Street/Tottenham Court Rd LU*

A stylish Fitzrovia basement eatery, noted for its creative, contemporary tapas, plus an excellent range of sherries and wines.

Iberica Marylebone £££

- 195 Great Portland Street, W1W 5PS
- 020 7636 8650
- www.ibericalondon.com
- Great Portland Street LU

This spacious Spanish establishment combines a handsome, airy tapas bar and delicatessen area. Tapas dishes to look out for include gloriously flavourful black rice with cuttlefish, prawns and alioli and the exemplary ham croquetes Casa Marcial. An extensive Spanish wine list ranges from refreshing whites to elegant reds.

Moro £££-££££

- 34-36 Exmouth Market, EC1R 4QE
- 020 7833 8336
- www.moro.co.uk
- Farringdon LU/Rail

Run by culinary husband-and-wife team Sam and Samantha Clark, this is a relaxed, convivial restaurant, drawing on Spanish and North African cuisines to create a simple yet richly flavourful menu. The selection of Spanish wines and sherries is another draw.

Navarros £££

- 67 Charlotte Street, W1T 4PH
- 020 7637 7713
- www.navarros.co.uk
- Goodge Street LU

A prettily decorated, traditional tapas bar, with a loyal following. It serves consistently tasty classic tapas, from simple tortilla to prawns in garlic.

Opera Tavern £££

- 23 Catherine Street, WC2B 5JS
- 020 7836 3680
- www.operatavern.co.uk
- Covent Garden LU

In the heart of theatreland, this appealing tapas bar (part of the Salt Yard stable) is deservedly popular for its creative 'small dishes', showcasing carefully-sourced, seasonal, good-quality ingredients.

Salt Yard £££

- 54 Goodge Street, W1T 4NA
- 020 7637 0657
- www.saltyard.co.uk
- Goodge Street LU

This popular, relaxed tapas bar draws its inspiration from both Spanish and Italian cuisines. It offers classic Italian charcuterie such as Prosciutto di Parma alongside Jamon Serrano and wines from both countries. Dishes range from stylish bar snacks such as quails' eggs with paprika salt to salt cod fritters with orange alioli or Old Spot pork belly confit.

Spanish & Portuguese Eating Places

Tapas Brindisa £££

⌂ *Borough Market*
8-20 Southwark Street, SE1 1TJ
☎ *020 7357 8880*
✐ *www.brindisa.com*
🚌 *London Bridge LU/Rail*

On the corner of Borough Market, this pleasantly informal, contemporary tapas bar, bustling with diners, was set up by Brindisa, the noted Spanish food importers and showcases their quality ingredients including their famous Joselito hams. Tapas range from old favourites such as potato tortilla or croquetas to more modish offerings, such as deep-fried Monte enebro goat's cheese with fragrant honey. All the tapas can be washed down with a glass of fine sherry, cava or good Spanish wine.

Tapas Brindisa £££

⌂ *46 Broadwick Street, W1F 7AF*
☎ *020 7534 1690*
✐ *www.brindisa.com*
🚌 *Oxford Circus LU*

A relaxed Soho tapas bar, part of the Spanish food importers Brindisa's group, offering regional dishes, such as grilled baby squid and Iberian pork.

Tramontana Brindisa ££-£££

⌂ *152 Curtain Road, London EC2A 3AT*
☎ *020 7749 9961*
✐ *www.brindisa.com*
🚌 *Old Street LU*

This latest offering from the respected Brindisa group specialises in the cuisine of the Spanish Mediterranean, offering dishes with a seafood flavour such as mojama (dry-cured tuna) and fideua al sepia (noodles with cuttlefish).

North

La Bota £££

⌂ *31 Broadway Parade*
Tottenham Lane, N8
☎ *020 8340 3082*
🚌 *Finsbury Park LU/Rail, then the W7 bus*

A modest, traditional tapas bar which has a loyal local following.

El Parador £££

⌂ *245 Eversholt Street, NW1*
☎ *020 7387 3789*
🚌 *Camden Town LU*

This well-established tapas bar comes into its own in the summer, when you can sit in the garden at the back and sample a variety of tapas accompanied with Spanish wines and beers.

West

Café Garcia £-££

🏠 *246 Portobello Road, W11*
☎ *020 7221 6119*
🚌 *Ladbroke Road LU, Notting Hill Gate LU*

Owned by the Spanish food shop next door, this contemporary café serves up 'proper' Spanish hot chocolate with churros, own-made horchata (the almond-flavoured drink made from tigers nuts), and assorted tapas.

Café Oporto £

🏠 *62A Golborne Road, W10*
☎ *020 8968 8839*
🚌 *Ladbroke Grove LU*

Small, friendly Portuguese café in which to enjoy savoury croquettes, sandwiches or delicious, freshly made, coffee.

Galicia £££

🏠 *323 Portobello Road, SW10*
☎ *020 8969 3539*
🚌 *Ladbroke Grove LU*
   Notting Hill Gate LU

This atmospheric tapas bar and restaurant, is popular with the local Spanish community. It specialises in food from Galicia, hence the large number of fish and seafood dishes.

Lisboa Patisserie £

🏠 *57 Golborne Road, W10*
☎ *020 8968 5242*
🚌 *Ladbroke Grove / Notting Hill Gate LU*

This delightful Portuguese patisserie, with its excellent cakes (including delectable pasteis de nata custard tarts), is usually full of regulars sampling coffee and pastries.

South-East

Bar Tozino ££-£££

🏠 *Lassco Ropewalk*
☎ *Maltby Street, SE1 3PA*
🖥 *www.bartozino.com*
🚌 *London Bridge LU/Rail*

Atmospherically housed under the railway arches, this mellow jamoneria is a relaxed place in which to enjoy a glass of sherry and a plate of hand-carved Spanish ham.

Jose £££

🏠 *104 Bermondsey Street, SE1 3UB*
☎ *020 7403 4902*
🖥 *www.josepizarro.com*
🚌 *London Bridge LU/Rail*

Chef Jose Pizarro's small, characterful tapas bar serves a range of classic tapas plus daily market specials (recommended). Customers perch at the bar, sipping a glass of palo cortado sherry and watching the chefs grilling seafood. A real taste of Spain.

Spanish & Portuguese Eating Places

Pizarro £££

- 194 Bermondsey Street, SE1 3TQ
- ☎ 020 7403 4902
- ✍ www.josepizarro.com
- 🚌 London Bridge LU/Rail

On the same road as his popular tapas bar, chef-patron Jose Pizarro, a charming and hospitable host, also has an equally popular Spanish restaurant, seemingly forever bustling with diners enjoying Jose's dishes such as duck livers with capers and fino or seared Iberico pork fillet. Bear in mind that the no-booking policy and Pizarro's reputation make it likely that you'll have to wait to get a table.

South-West

Cambio de Tercio £££-££££

- 163 Old Brompton Road, SW5
- ☎ 020 7244 8970
- ✍ www.cambiodetercio.co.uk
- 🚌 Gloucester Road/South Kensington LU

High-calibre tapas, both traditional and 'signature', excellent service and an attractive décor on offer here at this smart, contemporary Spanish restaurant.

Funchal Bakery £

- 141-143 Stockwell Road, SW9 8EG
- ☎ 020 7733 3134
- 🚌 Stockwell LU

In addition to the bakery and deli, Funchal offers a relaxed café area in which to enjoy delicious Portuguese cakes and pastries. The pasteis de nata and coffee are both to be recommended.

Lisboa Grill ££-£££

- 256A Brixton Hill, SW2
- ☎ 020 8671 8311
- 🚌 Brixton LU

Excellent value, seriously tasty portions of grilled chickens and meat are the speciality at this restaurant.

Lola Rojo £££-££££

- 78 Northcote Road, SW11
- ☎ 020 7350 2262
- ✍ www.lolarojo.net
- 🚌 Clapham Junction Rail

This diminutive tapas bar restaurant is perpetually buzzing with contented diners and drinkers enjoying a delicious selection of classy tapas and quality wines.

Rebatos £££-££££

- 169 South Lambeth Road, SW8 1XW
- ☎ 020 7735 6388
- 🚌 Stockwell LU
- ✍ www.rebatos.com

A veteran of London's tapas bar scene, Rebatos is run with jovial professionalism and remains hugely popular. The front bar area is the place in which to enjoy tapas, while the roomy, tiled restaurant at the back offers an extensive a la carte Spanish menu, with fish and seafood a speciality.

East

Eyre Brothers ££££

⊞ 70 Leonard Street, EC2A 4QX
☎ 020 7613 5346
✎ www.eyrebrothers.co.uk
🚌 Old Street LU

Accomplished, flavourful Iberian food, including signature dishes such as grilled Iberico pork fillet or tiger prawns with piri piri, pull in a loyal regular following at this well-established, discreetly smart restaurant.

Iberica Canary Wharf £££-££££

⊞ 12 Cabot Square, E14 4QQ
☎ 020 7636 8650
✎ www.ibericalondon.com
🚌 Canary Wharf DLR/LU

This Canary Wharf restaurant from Spanish importers Iberica is a spacious, airy and glamorously stylish affair, spread over two levels. The cooking offers Iberica's characteristic offering of tapas with a twist, while an extensive drinks menu takes in sherries, cocktails, fine wines and cavas.

Cookbooks

My personal recommendations of cookbooks for this cuisine, including new books and out-of-print classics:

Moro: the Cookbook
Sam & Sam Clark
A classic cookbook from the chef-owners of Moro restaurant, filled with delicious Spanish and Arabic recipes.

Seasonal Spanish Food
Jose Pizarro
From the acclaimed Spanish chef and restaurateur, an accessible collection of recipes and anecdotes.

The Food of Spain
Claudia Roden
A wonderfully knowledgeable and evocative exploration of Spain's food culture, combining recipes and history.

Rick Stein's Spain
Rick Stein
An engaging journey through Spanish regional food by the British TV chef.

The Taste of Portugal
Edite Vieira
An appetising cookbook, offering a useful insight into Portuguese cuisine.

Scandinavian Kitchen

Afghan

Afghan Kitchen £-££
🏠 35 Islington Green, N1
☎ 020 7359 8019
🚌 Angel LU

This tiny, restaurant offers simple, tasty home-style Afghani food at very reasonable prices and with friendly service.

Masa £-£££
🏠 24-26 Headstone Drive, HA3
☎ 020 8861 6213
🚌 Harrow & Wealdstone LU

This smart restaurant has a loyal following among London's Afghan community. Dishes include kebabs and mantoo (filled pasta).

American

American Food Store
🏠 2 Ladbroke Grove, W11 3BG
☎ 020 7221 4563
🚌 Holland Park LU
🖱 www.usafoodstore.co.uk
🕐 Mon-Sat 6.30am-6.30pm, Sun 7am-3pm

An American food store, serving the expat community. Despite the shop's small size, it carries an extensive range of American foodstuffs. Bestsellers include A & W Root Beer and Nerds candy.

Hummingbird Bakery
🏠 133 Portobello Road, W11 2DY
☎ 020 7229 6446
🖱 www.hummingbirdbakery.com
🚌 Notting Hill Gate LU
🕐 Mon-Fri 10am-6pm,
   Sat 9am-6.30pm, Sun 11am-5pm

This small American-style bakery, the first of what is now a chain, played a key part in creating Britain's cupcake obsession. Best-known for its eye-catching, brightly frosted cupcakes it offers other American-style treats such as whoopie pies, muffins and layer cakes.

Outsider Tart
🏠 83 Chiswick High Road, W4 2EF
☎ 020 7096 1609
🖱 www.outsidertart.com
🚌 Turnham Green LU/Rail
🕐 Mon-Wed, Fri-Sun 8am-6pm,
   Thurs 9am-10pm

In addition to its mouth-watering range of American-inspired baked goods, from coffee cakes to cookies, this friendly shop and café has a wall of American groceries, such as kosher salt, American cereals and condiments. There is now also an informal café next door, Blue Plate, offering a chance to sit down and enjoy both the sweet baking and savoury dishes.

Panzer's

- 13-19 Circus Road, NW8 6PB
- ☎ 020 7722 8596
- ⌨ www.panzers.co.uk
- 🚌 St John's Wood LU
- 🕐 Mon-Fri 8am-7pm
  Sat 8am-6pm, Sun 8am-2pm

St John's Wood's affluent American expat community is shrewdly catered for by this large Jewish delicatessen. Panzer's makes a point of stocking American favourites.

Partridges

- 2-5 Duke of York Square
- 🚌 King's Road, SW3 4LY
- ☎ 020 7730 0651
- ⌨ www.partridges.co.uk
- 🚌 Sloane Square LU
- 🕐 Daily 8am-10pm

This upmarket grocers, proud holders of a Royal Warrant, stocks a range of American foodstuffs.

Partridges

- 17-21 Gloucester Road, SW7 4PL
- ☎ 020 7581 0535
- ⌨ www.partridges.co.uk
- 🚌 Gloucester Road LU
- 🕐 Daily 8am-11pm

A smaller branch of the King's Road establishment, with a particular focus on American foodstuffs.

Violet Cakes

- 47 Wilton Way, E8 3ED
- ☎ 020 7275 8360
- 🚌 Hackney Central Rail
- 🕐 Tues-Fri 8am-6pm,
  Sat 9.30am-6pm, Sun 9.30am-5pm

Founded by baker Claire Ptak, who was formerly a pastry chef at California's famous Chez Panisse restaurant, this small, appealing cake shop-cum-café is famous for its dainty American-style cupcakes and whoopie pies.

Argentinian

Buen Ayre £££-££££

- 50 Broadway Market, E8 4QJ
- ☎ 020 7275 9900
- ⌨ www.buenayre.co.uk
- 🚌 London Fields LU

This friendly, intimate restaurant does a roaring trade in Argentinian beef dishes, including grill-cooked meat selections.

Freggo £

- 27-29 Swallow Street, W1B 4QR
- ☎ 020 7287 9506
- ⌨ www.freggo.co.uk
- 🚌 Piccadilly Circus LU
- 🕐 Mon-Thurs 8am-11pm, Fri 8am-2am,
  Sat 10am-2am, Sun 10am-11pm

An off-shoot of the Gaucho restaurant chain, specialising in Argentinian cuisine, this smart ice cream parlour offers luxurious ice cream – in flavours including Malbec and Berries and Dulce de Leche.

Gaucho Piccadilly   £££-££££

⌨ *25 Swallow Street, W1B 4QR*
☎ *020 7734 4040*
✍ *www.gauchorestaurants.co.uk*
🚌 *Piccadilly Circus LU*

This smart restaurant is famous for its prime Argentinian beef steaks and also offers dishes such as empanadas and assorted ceviches.

Austrian

Delicat

⌨ *124 Northcote Road, SW11 6QU*
☎ *020 7924 3566*
✍ *www.bistrodelicat.com*
🚌 *Clapham Junction Rail*

Recommended by Austrian friends, this casually stylish and pleasantly informal Austrian bistro serves up brunch, lunch and dinner dishes to an appreciative local crowd.

Kipferl   £-££

⌨ *20 Camden Passage, N1 8ED*
☎ *020 7704 1555*
✍ *www.kipferl.co.uk*
🚌 *Farringdon Rail /St Paul's LU*

A delicious taste of Austria is on offer here at Christian Malnig's café-cum-restaurant. Customers can enjoy a Melange (Viennese coffee) and slice of Sacher torte or Apfelstrudel in the café or tuck into more substantial fare such as Wiener Schnitzel or beef goulash. Also on offer to buy are a small selection of carefully sourced selection of Austrian foodstuffs.

Kipferl Park Café   £

⌨ *Gordon Square Kiosk,*
🚌 *Gordon Square, WC1H 0PD*
✍ *www.kipferl.co.uk*
Euston Square or Russell Square LU

Bringing a touch of Vienna to Bloomsbury, this small kiosk serves up Viennese coffee, cakes and light lunches.

Speck Mobile   £

✍ *www.speckmobile.com*

A joint venture between two Austrians, chef Franz Schinagl and food importer Marco Reiner, which sees them serving tasty Austrian dishes from their mobile van in various locations around the city.

Brazilian

Harlesden in north-west London is home to a number of Brazilian food shops, from butchers specialising in the sausages and meat cuts beloved of Brazilians, to grocery shops.

Acougue do Gaucho

- 24 Station Road, NW10 4UE
- ☎ 020 8961 2600
- 🚌 Harlesden LU
- 🕐 Daily 9am-9.30pm

This bustling Brazilian food shop comes complete with popular butcher's counter and a range of grocery stock.

Casa de Carnes

- 1096 Harrow Road, NW10 5NL
- ☎ 020 8964 3034
- 🚌 Kensal Green LU
- 🕐 Daily 8am-7pm

A Brazilian butcher, recommended by Brazilian friends for its specialist barbecue cuts of beef and own-made sausages.

Katavento £-££

- Unit 4, The Long Shop,
  Merton Abbey Mills,
  Watermill Way SW19 2RD
- ☎ 020 8540 8386

Warmly recommended by Brazilian friends, this relaxed, family-run restaurant is known for its pastel (stuffed pastries), tasty feijoada and picanha, pulling in a loyal clientele of Brazilian expats enjoying a taste of home.

Mineiro Café

- 63 Station Road, NW10 4UX
- ☎ 020 8965 2050
- 🚌 Willesden Junction LU/Rail

A small, relaxed café offering both Brazilian snacks such as pastel and bolinha de queijo and substantial dishes including feijoada.

Mercearia Brasil

- 733 Harrow Road, NW10 5PA
- ☎ 020 8962 0252
- 🚌 Kensal Green LU
- 🕐 Daily 9am-9pm

A well-stocked Brazilian food shop, complete with butchers counter selling all own-made sausages, ingredients for feijoada and a range of groceries.

Bulgarian

Bulgarian Food Shop

- 369 Uxbridge Road, W3 9RH
- ☎ 078 5212 5275
- 🖉 www.bulgarianfood.co.uk
- 🚌 Ealing Common LU
- 🕐 Daily 8am-10pm

A large West London Bulgarian food specialist.

Burmese

Mandalay ££-£££
- 🖃 *444 Edgware Road, W2 1EG*
- ☎ *020 7258 3696*
- 🖎 *www.mandalayway.com*
- 🚌 *Edgware Road LU*

This relaxed, friendly restaurant offers a rare chance to sample Burmese cuisine. A fascinating blend of Asian, Chinese and Thai ingredients and cooking techniques. The owners are happy to offer menu advice.

Colombian

Brixton Market
- 🖃 *Brixton Station Rd, Pope's Rd, Atlantic Rd, Electric Rd & Electric Av, SW9 8JX*
- 🚌 *Brixton LU/Rail*
- 🕓 *Mon, Tues & Thurs-Sat 8am-5.30pm, Wed 8am-1pm*

Brixton Market houses a number of Colombian businesses, ranging from cafés and bars to food shops, including butchers.

Czech

Czechoslovak Restaurant
- 🖃 *74 West End Lane. NW6 2LX*
- ☎ *020 7372 1193*
- 🖎 *www.czechoslovak-restaurant.co.uk*

Housed in Czechoslovak National House, this old-fashioned restaurant serves up large portions of classic Czech-Slovak dishes such as halusky, brawn, roast goose and goulash. Desserts – such as apricot dumplings – are similarly substantial.

Georgian

Tbilisi ££
- 🖃 *91 Holloway Road, N7 3BT*
- ☎ *020 7607 2536*
- 🚌 *Highbury & Islington LU*

A hospitably-run restaurant offering a chance to sample Georgian cuisine, from soups to hearty stews as well as some fine Georgian wines.

German

Backhaus

- 175 Ashburnham Road, TW10 7NR
- 020 8048 6040
- www.backhaus.co.uk
- Richmond LU/Rail, then bus 371
- Mon-Fri 7.30am-5pm, Sat 7.30am-4pm

This neatly arranged delicatessen stocks a wide range of products imported from Germany, including frozen ready-meals and a huge choice of hams and sausages, such as bratwurst and leberwurst. Just down the road is the shop's bakery which produces an impressive array of German baked goods, including rye breads, pretzel and caraway sticks. At Christmas, lovingly prepared stollen, made in September and matured for eight weeks, is available.

German Deli

- 3 Park Street, SE1 9AB
- 020 7378 0000
- www.germandeli.co.uk
- London Bridge LU/Rail
- Mon-Fri 9am-7pm, Sat 9am-5pm

This small orderly shop sells an extensive range of German foodstuffs and has a predominantly German clientele. Customers can choose from sausages and cured meats, the shop's own-baked sourdough breads and fresh pretzel rolls. They also stock an array of tinned, jarred and packaged goods, including addictive salty liquorice. Christmas sees the stock increase to include seasonal treats such as lebkuchen, stollen and marzipan.

Herman ze German £

19 Villiers Street, WC2N 6NE

- 020 7930 4827
- www.herman-ze-german-co.uk
- Charing Cross LU/Rail
  or Embankment LU

Humorously named, this cheery establishment specialises in German sausages (such as bratwurst and bockwurst) – gluten-free, grilled not fried, served in rolls with crispy fried onion and lashings of mustard and optional sauerkraut.

Hungarian

The Gay Hussar £££-££££

- 2 Greek Street, W1D 4NB
- 020 7437 0973
- www.gayhussar.co.uk
- Leicester Square / Tottenham Ct Rd LU

A venerable Soho restaurant, noted for its literary and political clientele as well as its generous portions of authentic Hungarian food. Renowned dishes include Transylvanian stuffed cabbage.

Louis Patisserie £

⌨ *32 Heath Street, NW3*
☏ *020 7435 9908*
🚌 *Hampstead LU*
🕐 *Daily 9.30am-6pm*

Set up by Mr Louis in 1963, this charmingly old-fashioned, gently courteous patisserie and tearoom sells Hungarian cakes and pastries such as dobos (caramel cake) and makos (poppyseed slice).

Korean

Asadal ££-£££

⌨ *227 High Holborn, WC1V 7DA*
☏ *020 7430 9006*
✎ *www.asadal.co.uk*
🚌 *High Holborn LU*

A discreet doorway, leading to a roomy basement, is the only street-level sign of this Korean barbecue restaurant. Dishes include flavourful hotpots, barbecue dishes, rice and noodles and good-value lunch box offerings.

Centre Point Food Store

⌨ *20-21 St Giles High Street, WC2H 8LN*
☏ *020 7836 9860*
✎ *www.cpfs.co.uk*
🚌 *Tottenham Court Road LU*
🕐 *Mon-Sat 10am-11pm,
    Sun 12noon-11pm*

In the shadow of Centre Point's looming tower, the Centre Point Food Store is a large, well-stocked food shop, usefully open late into the night. Around half the shop is given over to a comprehensive selection of Korean foodstuffs.

Duri

⌨ *10 Station Parade, W3 3LD*
☏ *020 8752 1766*
🚌 *Ealing Common LU*
🕐 *Tues-Fri 10am-8pm,
    Sat 9am-8pm. Sun 11am-7pm*

A neatly-arranged Korean food shop, offering a range of Korean store-cupboard, chilled and frozen foodstuffs as well as Korean dishes to take away.

Korea Foods

⌨ *Unit 5, Wyvern Industrial Estate
Beverley Way, KT3 4PH*
☏ *020 8949 2238*
✎ *www.koreafoods.co.uk*
🚌 *New Malden Rail*
🕐 *Mon-Sat 9am-9pm, Sun 12noon-6pm*

Opened in 2005 and serving the local Korean community, this spacious Korean supermarket sells the largest range of Korean foodstuffs in the UK, many of them directly imported, with the fresh fish counter a particular highlight.

Nippon & Korea Centre

⌨ *9 Wardour Street, W1D 6PF*

☎ *020 7434 1777*

🚌 *Leicester Square, Piccadilly Circus, LU*

🕐 *Daily 10am-7pm*

In the heart of Soho, this shop offers a range of Korean and Japanese foodstuffs.

O'Food

⌨ *24-25 Denman Street, W1D 7HU*

☎ *020 7494 9660*

🚌 *Piccadilly Circus LU*

🕐 *Daily 10am-11pm*

In the heart of Soho, this small shop offers a range of Korean and Japanese foodstuffs, including frozen dumplings and seafood.

Song's Supermarket

⌨ *76-78 Burlington Road,*
New Malden, Surrey, KT3 4NU

☎ *020 8942 8471*

🚌 *New Malden Rail*

🕐 *Daily 9am-8.30pm*

Song's is next to Jie's Café, an informal Korean café from where the most appetising, savoury aromas waft. Neatly arranged, Song's has an impressive range of stock: fresh meat and fish counters, fresh fruit, vegetables and herbs and assorted groceries. Particularly tempting is the extensive range of chilled, ready-made dishes such as spinach with garlic and chilli.

Mauritian

Chez Liline ££-££

⌨ *101 Stroud Green Road, N4 3PX*

☎ *020 7263 6550*

✎ *www.chezliline.co.uk*

🚌 *Finsbury Park LU/Rail*

This family-run Mauritian restaurant is a Finsbury Park institution, a pleasantly hospitable place in which to enjoy large portions of Mauritian seafood, combining both tropical and French flavours.

Mexican

Casa Morito ££

⌨ *9 Market Row, Brixton Market, SW9 8LB*

☎ *020 8127 5107*

Nestling in a Brixton Market shopping arcade, this charming, intimate Mexican restaurant, prettily decorated with fairy lights and Mexican tin ornaments nailed to the walls, serves up tasty Mexican dishes including quesadillas, tacos and tostadas.

Cool Chile

✎ *www.coolchile.co.uk*

Founded by Dodie Miller in 1993, Cool Chile have been promoting authentic Mexican food in the UK long before it became fashionable. Visitors to the website can stock up with an awesome range of Mexican chilles as well as ingredients such as fresh tomatillos, mole poblano paste and Mexican drinking chocolate. These are also on offer at Cool Chile's restaurant, Taqueria, and their stall at Borough Market.

Mestizo ££

103 Hampstead Road, NW1 3EL
020 7387 4064
www.mestizomx.com

A firm favourite of Mexican friends, this roomy, informal Mexican restaurant offers substantial portions of tasty Mexican food, with the molcajete especially recommended.

Taqueria ££-£££

139-143 Westbourne Grove, W11 2RS
020 7229 4734
www.taqueria.co.uk

A relaxed Mexican restaurant from the Cool Chile company, specialising in tacos made from fresh corn tortillas, made on the premises. Fillings and toppings range from grilled jalapeno peppers to shredded slow-cooked pork.

Wahaca ££-£££

66 Chandos Place, WC2
020 7240 1883
www.wahaca.co.uk

Founded by Masterchef winner Thomasina Miers and inspired by her love of Mexican market food, this cheery basement restaurant, the first in what is now a chain, is a lively affair, buzzing with customers. The wide-ranging, seasonally-varying menu offers a chance to sample Mexican dishes such as huitlacoche quesadilla and chicken pibil burrito.

Peruvian

Ceviche £££

17 Frith Street, W1D 4RG
020 7292 2040
www.cevicheuk.com

Martin Morales's appealing Peruvian restaurant and pisco bar brings a taste of Peru to London. Ceviche, as one might expect, is a highlight of the menu here, as are its pisco sours.

Tierra Peru £££

164 Essex Road, N1 8LY
020 7354 5586
www.tierraperu.co.uk

A pleasantly stylish taste of Peru is on offer here at this attractive restaurant, with a menu showcasing classic Peruvian dishes, from ceviche to carapulcra.

Russian

Café Samovar £

Queensway Market, Unit A1-A2
23-25 Queensway W2 4QP

☎ 020 7243 6125

A tucked away Russian café, set up by Kalinka down the road, offering a bargain-priced taste of Russia with dishes such as borsch, golubsi and pancakes.

Kalinka

35 Queensway, W2 4QJ

☎ 020 7243 6125

www.kalinkafood.co.uk

Bayswater LU, Queensway LU

Mon-Sat 11am-8pm,
Sun 12noon-6.30pm

Behind its window proudly decorated with a Moscow scene, this long narrow shop is well-stocked with Russian and Ukranian foodstuffs, catering to the nearby Russian and Ukranian embassies. Food ranges from basics such as savoury salted fish and sausages to condiments, biscuits, cakes and a colourful display of confectionery.

Scandinavian

Hansen & Lydersen

www.hansen-lydersen.com

Norwegian Ole Hansen lovingly smokes fresh salmon over juniper and beech wood in his Stoke Newington smokery. The flavourful smoked salmon has acquired a loyal following and can be found in shops, such as La Fromagerie, and at various markets, including Broadway.

Harcourt Arms

32 Harcourt Street, W1H 4HX

☎ 020 7723 6634

Edgware Road LU, Marylebone LU

Known to London's Swedish community as 'the Swedish pub', this pub pulls in an expat Swedish crowd who meet to socialise and watch Swedish sport on TV.

Madsen ££-£££

20 Old Brompton Road, SW7 3DL

☎ 020 7225 2772

www.madsenrestaurant.com

South Kensington LU

Charlotte Madsen's light, contemporary restaurant offers a taste of modern Scandinavian cuisine. Lunchtime dishes include Danish open sandwiches or herring platters, while dinner sees more substantial dishes such as Frikadeller (meatballs).

Scandinavian Kitchen

🏠 *61 Great Titchfield Street, W1W 7PP*

📞 *020 7580 7161*

🖥 *www.scandikitchen.co.uk*

🚌 *Oxford Circus LU*

🕐 *Mon-Fri 8am-7pm,*
   Sat 10am-6pm, Sun 10am-4pm

Husband-and-wife team Jonas Aurell (Swedish), and Bronte Aurell (Danish), run this bright and cheery café-cum-deli with genuine hospitality and it comes warmly recommended by food writer Signe Johansen. The grocery and deli section here stocks a carefully selected range of foodstuffs from Denmark, Norway, Sweden and Finland, from sweets and condiments to crispbreads and tinned seafood. For a truly extensive range of Scandinavian foodstuffs, however, visit their impressive online shop at www. scandikitchen.co.uk. On offer in the café area at Scandinavian Kitchen are an appealing array of smorrebrod (open sandwiches), freshly made each morning in the downstairs kitchen, and own-baked sweet treats, including Bronte's addictive kladdkaka (sticky chocolate cake), cinnamon buns and, for Lent, exquisite cardamom-flavoured semla.

During the run-up to Christmas look out for Christmas fairs and bazaars at the following Scandinavian churches and also at the Danish YWCA which offer a chance to buy and sample a host of Danish, Finnish, Norwegian and Swedish seasonal treats.

Danish YWCA

🏠 *43 Maresfield Gardens, NW3 5TF*

The Danish Church

🏠 *4 St Katherine's Precinct*
   Regent's Park, NW1 4HH

🖥 *www.danskekirke.org*

The Finnish Church in London

🏠 *33 Albion Sreet, SE16 7JG*

🖥 *www.finnishchurch.org.uk*

St Olav's (the Norwegian church)

🏠 *1 St Olav's Square, SE16 7JB*

🖥 *www.sjomannskirken.no/london*

Ulrika Eleonora Church (the Swedish church)

🏠 *6-11 Harcourt Street, W1H 4AG*

🖥 *www.swedishchurch.com*

Scandilicious

◢ www.signejohansen.com

Signe Johansen, the author of *Scandilicious* and *Scandilicious Baking*, two appetising and appealing Scandinavian cookbooks, also runs a popular series of Scandi Brunch and Supper Club events, featuring treats such as hot cardamom doughnuts, home-cured gravadlax and meatballs.

Totally Swedish

▣ *32 Crawford Street, W1H 1LS*

☎ *020 7224 9300*

🚌 *Baker Street LU*

🕐 *Mon-Wed 10am-6pm,*
  Thurs 10am-7.30pm,
  Fri-Sat 10am-6pm, Sun 12noon-4pm

Patriotically painted in yellow and blue this pretty shop carries a whole range of Swedish edibles, from pickled herrings to treats such as liquorice sweets and aquavit.
Branch: 66 Barnes High Street, SW13 9LD

Swiss

KäseSwiss

▣ *104 Druid Street, SE1 2HQ*

◢ www.kaseswiss.com

Saturday mornings between 9am and 2pm offer a chance to buy quality Swiss cheeses, from the delectable Fleurette to wonderful gruyeres, from this discriminating importer and wholesaler.

Taiwanese

Leong's Legends £-££

▣ *4 Macclesfield Street, W1D 6AX*

☎ *020 7287 0288*

🚌 *Leicester Square LU*

In the heart of Chinatown, this restaurant offers authentic Taiwanese cuisine and is noted for its soup dumplings.

Venezuelan

Sabor Venezelano

▣ *Covent Garden Real Food Market*

◢ www.caracascornhouse.co.uk

Offering a rare chance to sample Venezuelan cuisine in London, this friendly stall sells cachapas (corn 'pancakes') and arepas (corn 'bread') to go, as well as a few ingredients.

Central

David Mellor

📖 *4 Sloane Square, SW1W 8EE*
☎ *020 7730 4259*
🖱 *www.davidmellordesign.com*
🚌 *Sloane Square LU*
🕐 *Mon-Sat 9.30am-6pm, Sun 11am-5pm*

Since its opening in 1969, this elegant shop has consistently championed good design. It stocks a carefully selected range of quality kitchenware and tableware that both looks great and works well. Stock here ranges from iconic David Mellor cutlery, designed both by David Mellor and Corin Mellor, to hand-turned wooden salad bowls, horn serving spoons, ceramic mugs and elegant wine glasses. A shop in which to find both gifts and genuinely useful kitchenware staples.

Denny's

📖 *55A Dean Street. W1D 6AG*
☎ *020 7494 2745*
🖱 *www.dennys.co.uk*
🚌 *Leicester Square, Piccadilly Circus LU*
🕐 *Mon-Fri 9.30am-6pm, Sat 10.30am-4.30pm*

A Soho institution, run with down-to-earth, knowledgeable expertise. Denny's has supplied generations of chefs with their kitchen kit, including uniform jackets, footwear and a range of professional knives. Because this is a shop for professionals, all prices are quoted without VAT

David Mellor

Cookware

Tableware

Cookery School

DIVERTIMENTI
*The ultimate
cookware destination*

227-229 Brompton Road
London SW3 2EP
020 7581 8065

33-34 Marylebone High St
London W1U 4PT
020 7935 0689

View our culinary collection
and cookery school
classes at
www.divertimenti.co.uk

celebrating 50 years
of culinary genius
www.divertimentififty.co.uk

Divertimenti

⊡ *227-229 Brompton Road, SW3 2EP*
☎ *020 7581 8065*
⌲ *www.divertimenti.co.uk*
🚌 *Knightsbridge, South Kensington LU*
🕐 *Mon-Tues, Thurs-Fri 9.30am-6pm*
  Wed 9.30am-7pm, Sun 12noon-5.30pm

This smart, spacious shop – a sister shop to
Marylebone's Divertimenti – offers the same
tempting mixture of attractive tableware and
good quality kitchen equipment, as well as an
AGA and La Cornue showroom and cookery
theatre.

Divertimenti

⊡ *33-34 Marylebone High Street, W1U 4PT*
☎ *020 7935 0689*
⌲ *www.divertimenti.co.uk*
🚌 *Baker Street LU*
🕐 *Mon-Wed & Fri 10am-6.30pm,*
  Thurs 10am-7.30pm, Sat 10am-6pm,
  Sun 11am-5pm

This is an attractive, airy kitchenware store,
complete with AGA showroom. It offers a
discerning mixture of ceramic tableware
– from classic white French porcelain to
colourful rustic ware – alongside pots, pans
and Magimix and Kitchen Aid gadgets. The
downstairs Cookery Theatre hosts a range of
cookery classes by well-known food writers
and chefs.

Nisbets

⌑ 121 Shaftesbury Avenue, WC2H 8AD
☎ 0845 140 5555
✎ www.nisbets.co.uk
🚌 Covent Garden or Leicester Square LU
🕐 Mon-Fri 9am-6pm, Sat 9.30am-6pm

This central London outlet for Nisbets, a major UK catering supplier, offers a useful range of professional equipment, from crockery and cutlery to utensils, gadgets and gizmos, while their website stocks over 18,000 products. Service is efficient and knowledgeable.

North

Gill Wing Cookshop

⌑ 190 Upper Street, N1
☎ 020 7226 5392
✎ www.gillwing.co.uk
🚌 Highbury & Islington LU/Rail
🕐 Mon-Sat 9.30am-6pm, Sun 10am-6pm

An Upper Street institution, this friendly, well-stocked kitchen shop offers a comprehensive range of kitchenware, ranging from stainless steel saucepans to decorative tableware and baking utensils for home bakers.

James Nicholas

⌑ 45 Park Road, N8 8TE
☎ 020 8348 3451
✎ www.james-nicholas.com
🚌 Finsbury Park LU, then bus W7
🕐 Mon-Sat 9.30am-6pm, Sun 11am-5pm

A friendly and helpful Crouch End-based kitchen shop, stocking a useful range of kitchenware, from cookie cutters and colanders to baking trays, pots and pans.

Richard Dare

⌑ 93 Regent's Park Road, NW1 8UR
☎ 020 7722 9428
🚌 Chalk Farm LU
🕐 Mon-Fri 9.30am-6pm, Sat 10am-6pm

This long-established, attractive Primrose Hill shop offers a tempting mix of stock, including cookware, ceramic tableware, wine glasses and knives.

The Scullery

⌑ 123 Muswell Hill Broadway, N10 3RS
☎ 020 8444 5236
🚌 Highgate LU, then bus 134
🕐 Mon-Sat 9am-6pm, Sun 11am-5pm

A neatly-arranged, cheery shop with a wide range of kitchen utensils and cookware.

North-West

James Nicholas

⌨ *166 West End Lane, NW6 1SD*
☎ *020 7794 4055*
🖱 *www.james-nicholas.com*
🚌 *West Hampstead Rail*
🕐 *Mon-Sat 9.30am-8pm, Sun 11am-5pm*

One of a mini-chain of kitchenware shops, offering an appealing range of cookware.

Popat Stores

⌨ *138 & 156-158 Ealing Road, HA0 4PY*
☎ *020 8902 2543 / 020 8903 6397*
🚌 *Alperton/Wembley Central LU*
🕐 *Mon-Sat 10am-6.30pm,*
   Sun 11am-6.30pm

Mr Popat opened his first shop at No 138 in the early 1970s. There are now tow shops specialising in Indian kitchenware and household goods, the extensive stock ranges from spice tins to pestles and mortars.

West

Whisk

⌨ *2 The Green, High Street, Ealing, W5 5DA*
☎ *020 8579 3444*
🖱 *www.whiskcooking.co.uk*
🚌 *Ealing Broadway LU / Rail*
🕐 *Mon-Fri 9.30am-5.30pm,*
   Sat 9.30am-6pm, Sun 10.30am-5pm

This bright, airy shop offers a good range of cookware and kitchenware, from Le Creuset pans to tagine dishes and barbecues. Home-bakers are well catered for with a range including cookie cutters and cup-cake cases. *Branch: 1a Devonshire Road, Chiswick, W4 (020 8995 8900)*

South-West

Dentons

⌨ *2-4 Clapham High Street, SW4 7UT*
☎ *020 7450 0466*
🖱 *www.dentonscatering.com*
🚌 *Clapham Common LU*
🕐 *Mon-Fri 8.30am-5.30pm,*
   Sat 8.45am-1pm

This established family-run firm offers an extensive range of catering equipment. Stock is neatly displayed in this roomy showroom and there is plenty of knowledgeable staff at hand if you need any help or advice.

James Nicholas

⌨ *99 Balham High Road, SW12 9AP*
☎ *020 8673 7067*
🖱 *www.james-nicholas.com*
🚌 *Balham LU*
🕐 *Mon-Sat 9.30am-6pm, Sun 11am-5pm*

A friendly, helpful kitchenware shop, offering a nicely chosen range of cookware and tableware.

Kooks Unlimited

2-4 and 12C Eton Street, TW9 1EE
☎ *020 8332 3030*
✎ *www.kooksunlimited.com*
🚌 *Richmond LU/Rail*
🕐 *Mon-Sat 9.30am-6pm, Sun 11am-5pm*

This friendly shop is crammed to the gills with stock, ranging from reputable cookware to gastro-gizmos. Down the road at 12C Eton Street, is their Bakeware Studio.

La Cuisiniere

81-83 Northcote Road, SW11
☎ *020 7223 4487*
✎ *www.la-cuisiniere.co.uk*
🚌 *Clapham Junction Rail*
🕐 *Mon-Sat 9am-6pm, Sun 11am-5pm*

La Cuisiniere has two shops on the same road. Pots, pans, knives and kitchen gadgets are stocked at this shop. Bakeware, barware and glassware can be found at *La Cuisiniere Too,* down the street at *91 Northcote Road, SW11 (020 7223 4409).*

East

Denny's

47 Cannon Street, EC4M 5SH
☎ *020 7489 8189*
✎ *www.dennys.co.uk*
🚌 *Mansion House LU*
🕐 *Mon-Fri 9am-5pm*

A smart City branch of the established Soho business, specialising in chefwear and footwear.

Mail Order

Lakeland Ltd

Alexandra Buildings, Windermere, Cumbria LA 23 1BQ
☎ *05394 88100*
✎ *www.lakeland.co.uk*

This well-established, efficient Cumbria-based mail order kitchenware company inspires a loyal following across the UK. The range of stock is impressive, from essentials such as baking tins, quality cookware and kitchen knives to specialised gadgets.

Squires Kitchens

Squires House, 3 Waverley Lane Farnham, Surrey, GU9 8BB
☎ *0845 225567*
✎ *www.squires-shop.com*

Squires Kitchens specialise in manufacturing and retailing cake decorating and sugarcraft products. Their website offers over 6,000 products, from frivolous cup-cake cases to professional food colourings.

Thanks to the Internet, it is now possible to track down and order many specialist foodstuffs, from great meat and organic vegetables to chillies and spices.

Argan oil

www.myarganic.co.uk

Dana Elemara's mail order business offers own-imported fine quality, organic, cold-pressed Moroccan argan oil, one of the world's rarest oil, prized for its distinctive nutty flavour.

Bacon & Ham

Emmett's Stores

Peasenhall, Saxmundham, Suffolk, IP17 2HJ

01728 660 250

www.emmettsham.co.uk

This remarkable village store is noted for its superb, own-made, traditional Suffolk cured bacon and ham, including its famous 'black' bacon and ham, cured using molasses and black porter.

British Foods

Forman & Field

30a Marshgate Lane, London, E15 2NH

020 8525 2352

www.formanandfield.com

Top quality British foods are on offer from this mail order business – established by Forman's, famous producers of smoked salmon. The emphasis is on fine and artisanal foods such as rare breed meat or farmhouse as well as seasonal treats.

Cakes

Bettys by Post

1 Parliament Street, Harrogate, North Yorkshire, HG1 2QU

0845 345 3636

www.bettysbypost.co.uk

Established in 1919 by Swiss baker Frederick Belmont, Bettys Tea Room has become a much-loved Yorkshire institution. Bettys' mail order service offers a chance to try their own-baked cakes and specialities including Yorkshire fat rascals, Simnel cakes and parkin.

Chillies

Cool Chile Company

⌕ *P.O. Box 5702*
London, W11 2GS
☎ *0870 902 1145*
✎ *www.coolchile.co.uk*

A must for chilli connoisseurs, Dodie Miller's mail order company sells an extensive range of dried Central American chillies from mild guajillo to intensely hot habaneros, in both whole and powdered form. Cool Chile also offers difficult to find Mexican ingredients such as blue Masa Harina.

Peppers by Post

⌕ *Sea Spring Farm,*
West Bexington, Dorchester,
Dorset, DT2 9DD
☎ *01308 897 892*
✎ *www.peppersbypost.biz*

Chilli-experts Michael and Joy Michaud run a mail order service selling fresh chillies and tomatillos grown on their own Dorset farm. On offer are a carefully selected range of chillies, including the Michauds' famous Dorset Naga, available seasonally and posted out on the day they are picked, as well as chilli seeds and chilli plants.

Fresh Food & Groceries

HubBub

✎ *www.hubbub.co.uk 020 7354 5511*

An enterprising, London-based food shopping service, sourcing foodstuffs from local independent shops and delivering them to your doorstep.

Natoora

✎ *www.natoora.co.uk*
☎ *020 7627 1600*

Top-notch, seasonal fresh produce and fine ingredients, from Italian peaches to O' Shea's beef, from a noted restaurant supplier

Geese

Goodman's Geese

⌕ *Walsgrove Farm, Great Witley*
Worcestershire, WR6 6JJ
☎ *01299 896 272*
✎ *www.goodmansgeese.co.uk*

Judy Goodman's free-range geese are traditionally reared on the Goodman's farm and have won many awards. They are particularly busy in the run-up to Christmas when their quality geese are sought after for festive feasting.

Seldom Seen Farm

⌨ *Billesdon, Leicestershire, LE7 9FA*
☎ *0116 259 6742*
✍ *www.seldomseenfarm.co.uk*

Claire and Robert Symington specialise in free-range geese, carefully reared on their own Leicestershire farm. The geese are slaughtered humanely, dry-plucked and hung for at least 10 days. A seasonal treat, the geese are available in November and December.

Italian Ingredients

Fratelli Camisa

☎ *01992 763 076*
✍ *www.camisa.co.uk*

An on-line Italian delicatessen established by Fratelli Camisa, which started life as an Italian delicatessen in Soho. They offer a great range of Italian foods to your door, from charcuterie to pasta.

Valvona & Crolla

☎ *0131 556 6066*
✍ *www.valvonacrolla.co.uk*

An on-line shop from Edinburgh's famous Italian delicatessen, run with flair and dedication by the Contini family.

Machiavelli Foods

✍ *www.machiavellifoods.co.uk*
☎ *020 7498 0880*

Machiavelli Foods are a well-established importers of Italian foodstuffs. Their mail order shop offers high-quality, artisanal, D.O.P. foods.

Japanese Ingredients

Mount Fuji

✍ *www.mountfuji.co.uk*

A useful website offering an extensive range of Japanese ingredients, from noodles to sushi seasoning.

Meat and Game

Chestnut Meats

⌨ *Radmore Green Farm*
   Radmore Green, Spurstow,
   Tarporly, Cheshire, CW6 9RL
☎ *01829 260 437*
✍ *www.chestnutmeats.co.uk*

Own-reared kid and goat meat is Chestnut Meats's speciality, with cuts ranging from fillets and shanks to an adult goat, butchered into various cuts.

Fletchers of Auchtermuchty

⌂ *Reediehill Farm, Auchtermuchty,*
  Fife, Scotland, KY14 7HS
☎ *01337 828 369*
✎ *www.seriousgoodvenison.co.uk*

Nichola and John Fletcher sell prime Scottish venison from deer raised on their own farm in Fife. Their mail order business offers numerous cuts of venison from medallions and carpaccio to osso buco or boned and rolled haunch of venison. If you're uncertain how to cook venison, Nichola is happy to share her expertise in game cookery.

Graig Farm Organics

⌂ *Dolau, Llandrindod Wells,*
  Powys, LD1 5TL
☎ *01597 851 655*
✎ *www.graigfarm.co.uk*

This enterprising organic meat company is noted for the quality of its meat and offers a large range of organic meat and poultry.

Heal Farm

⌂ *Kings Nympton,*
  Devon, EX37 9TB
☎ *01769 574 341*
✎ *www.healfarm.co.uk*

Anne Petch's passionate commitment to creating a market for rare breeds has created a flourishing mail order business offering beef, lamb, pork and poultry.

Mediterranean Foods

Belazu

⌂ *The Fresh Olive Company Ltd*
  74 Long Drive, Greenford,
  Middlesex UB6 8LZ
✎ *www.mybelazu.com*

A discriminatingly chosen, high quality range of Mediterranean specialities, including rose harissa, good olives and fine olive oils.

Middle Eastern

www.ottolenghi.co.uk

From Yotam Ottolenghi, the chef and food writer, comes an elegant mail-order website offering both Ottolenghi's own products and a range of carefully selected ingredients.

Organic Produce

Riverford Organic Vegetables

⌂ *Wash Barn, Devon, TQ11 0JU*
☎ *01803 762 059*
✎ *www.riverford.co.uk*

Founded by Guy Watson in Devon, Riverford offers an exemplary organic box scheme supplying homes around the country with weekly boxes of organic vegetables, fruit and meat. The foodstuffs come from both Riverford and other organic farms.

Abel & Cole

⌨ *www.abelandcole.co.uk*

☎ *020 8944 3780*

Founded in 1988, Abel & Cole have a large following for their well-organised organic veg box delivery service. They offer an extensive range of organic produce and foodstuffs and a fast and efficient order and delivery system.

Smoked Fish

L. Robson & Son

⌨ *Craster,*
Northumberland, NE66 3TR

☎ *01665 576 223*

✑ *www.kipper.co.uk*

Craster kippers have a distinctive, rich smoky flavour and are the speciality of this Northumbrian smokery. You can order this unique product directly from Robson over the phone or via the website.

Alex Spink & Sons

⌨ *24 Seagate, Arbroath*
Scotland, DD11 1BJ

☎ *01241 879 056*

✑ *www.abroathsmokiesonline.co.uk*

Traditionally-produced, tasty Arboath smokies (smoked small haddock) are on offer from Spink & Sons.

Brown and Forrest

⌨ Bowden Farm Smokery
Hambridge, Somerset, TA10 0BP

☎ 01458 250 875

✑ www.smokedeel.co.uk

This family-run smokery, which offers smoked fish and meats, are particularly noted for their succulent smoked eel.

Specialist Ingredients

Sous Chef

✑ *www.souschef.co.uk*

Founded by Nicola Lando out of frustration at being unable to track down specialist ingredients used by chefs, this offers an interesting and unusual range of ingredients from salts to flours.

Thai

Thai Food

✑ *www.thai-food-online.co.uk*

A web-based business offering an extensive range of Thai ingredients, including fresh herbs and vegetables, curry pastes and noodles.

Bibliography

The books used for my research include the cookbooks recommended in each section of the book. The books below are additional sources.

Across Seven Seas *Caroline Adams*
(Tharp Books 1987)
The British Museum Cookbook
Michelle Berriedale-Johnson
(British Museum Publications 1987)
Just Like It Was *Harry Blacker*
(Vallentine, Mitchell & Co 1974)
Fruits and Vegetables of the Caribbean
M.J. Bourne, G.W Lennox, S.A. Seddon
(Macmillan 1988)
The Club *Stephen Brook* (Constable 1989)
Polish Cookbook *Zofia Czerny*
(Panstowowe Wydawnictwo Ekonomiczne 1975)
The Oxford Companion to Food
Alan Davidson (Oxford University Press 1999)
Galing Galing *Nora and Mariles Daza*
(Daza 1974)
The Fine Art of Japanese Cooking
Hideo Dekura (Bay Books n.d.)
Inside Soho *Mark Edmonds*
(Robert Nicholson 1988)
The Streets of East London *William Fishman*
(Duckworth 1979)
Staying Power *Peter Fryer* (Pluto Press 1984)
Jewish Cookbook *Florence Greenberg*
(Hamlyn 1980)
Jane Grigson's Vegetable Book
Jane Grigson (Penguin 1980)

Exotic Fruits & Vegetables *Jane Grigson and Charlotte Knox* (Jonathan Cape 1986)
Singapore Food *Wendy Hutton*
(Times Books International 1989)
Filipino Cooking Here and Abroad
Eleanor Laquian and Irene Sobrevinas
(National Book Store Inc 1977)
Old Polish Traditions in the Kitchen and at the Table *Maria Lemni and Henryk Vitry*
(Interpress Publishers n.d.)
East End Story *A.B. Levy*
(Vallentine, Mitchell & Co. 1950)
Guide to Ethnic London *Ian McAuley*
(Michael Haag 1987)
The Peopling of London *Nick Merriman*
(Museum of London 1993)
Flavours of Korea *Marc and Kim Millon*
(Andre Deutsch 1991)
A Popular Guide to Chinese Vegetables
Karen Phillips and Martha Dahlen
(Frederick Muller 1983)
Fruits of South-East Asia *Jacqueline M Piper*
(Oxford University Press 1989)
The Oxford Companion to Italian Food
Gillian Riley (Oxford University Press 2007)
Living London *George Sims* (Cassell 1904-06)
The Best of Singapore Cooking *Mrs Leong Yee Soo* (Times Books International 1988)
Penang Nonya Cooking *Cecilia Tan*
(Times Books International 1983)
Sushi Made Easy *Nobuko Tsuda*
(John Weatherhill Inc 1982)
The London Encyclopaedia *Ben Weinreb and Christtopher Hibbert* (Papermac 1987)
Cooking the Polish-Jewish Way
Eugeniusz Wirkowski (Interpress Publishers 1988)
Jewish London *Linda Zoff* (Piatkus 1986)

Index

About us:

Metro is a small independent publishing company with a reputation for producing well-researched and beautifully-designed guides on many aspects of London life. In fields of interest as diverse as shopping, bargain hunting, architecture, the arts, and food, our guide books contain special tips you won't find anywhere else.

Pocket London Series

LONDON'S CEMETERIES
SPEND THE DAY WITH KARL MARX, ENID BLYTON, KEITH MOON AND MANY MORE

LONDON'S HIDDEN WALKS
EXPLORE LONDON AND DISCOVER HOW 2000 YEARS OF HISTORY HAVE SHAPED THIS CITY
Volume 2

LONDON'S HIDDEN WALKS
THE LONDON WE KNOW IS JUST THE SURFACE!
Volume 1

LONDON'S MONUMENTS
FROM BOUDICCA AND BYRON TO GUY THE GORILLA

LONDON'S HOUSES
FROM WORKHOUSE TO ROYAL PALACE, COME IN, CLOSE THE DOOR AND STEP BACK IN TIME...

LONDON'S CITY CHURCHES
SEE THE SCORCH MARKS OF THE GREAT FIRE, OR VISIT AN ALTAR BY HENRY MOORE

LONDON'S PARKS AND GARDENS
COVER MORE THAN TWENTY-FIVE PERCENT OF THE CAPITAL – THAT'S A LOT MORE GRASS BETWEEN TOES THAN ANY OTHER CITY IN EUROPE

www.metropublications.com

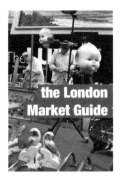

Acknowledgements

First of all, my thanks to Metro Publications – Andrew and Susi and Lesley – for all their work on Food Lovers' London. Rosie Kindersley at Books For Cooks was the person who, many years ago, suggested that I contact Metro Publications regarding a new edition of Food Lovers' London. This is now the seventh edition published with Metro Publications – so many thanks, Rosie.

Food Lovers' London simply wouldn't be the book it is without Chris Windsor's great photographs. He deserves special thanks for putting so much time and energy into travelling around London with me on the quest for photos for the book. Many thanks to my mother Lydia Linford for her meticulous proof-reading and editing. As ever, her loving support is much appreciated.

Over the years, many people have spared time to talk to me and offer advice, suggestions and recommendations and my grateful thanks go to the following: Fernando Albuquerque, Yasmin Alibhai-Brown, everyone I spoke to at the BBC World Service (especially Nina Dekhan), Penny Beauchamp, Jonas Aurell and Bronte Blomhoj, Monique Borst, Jon Cannon, Antonio Carluccio, Pek Choo, Anna del Conte, Fuchsia Dunlop, Sarah Edington, Richard Ehrlich, Claire Ferguson, Anna Giacon, Wendy Godfrey, Roopa Gulati, Susan Hackett, Pat Howard, Shehzad Husain, The Jewish Chonicle, Signe Johansen, Naomi Knill, Sav Kyriacou, Rosie Lovell, Michael Michaud, Ray O'Connor, Sri Owen, David Papp, Hedy Parry-Davies, Laki Pattelis, Catherine Phipps, Sudi Pigott, Mary Pininska, Jackie and Mike Robins, Claudia Roden, the late Evelyn Rose, Polly Russell, the late Margaret Shaida, Siyu magazine, Imogen Smith, the late Yan Kit-So, Marlena Spieler, Randal Twisk, the late Kate Whiteman, Jan and Dinah Wieliczko. Finally, my thanks go to the shopkeepers themselves who patiently answered my many questions and from whom I learned so much.